Original illisible
NF Z 43-120-10

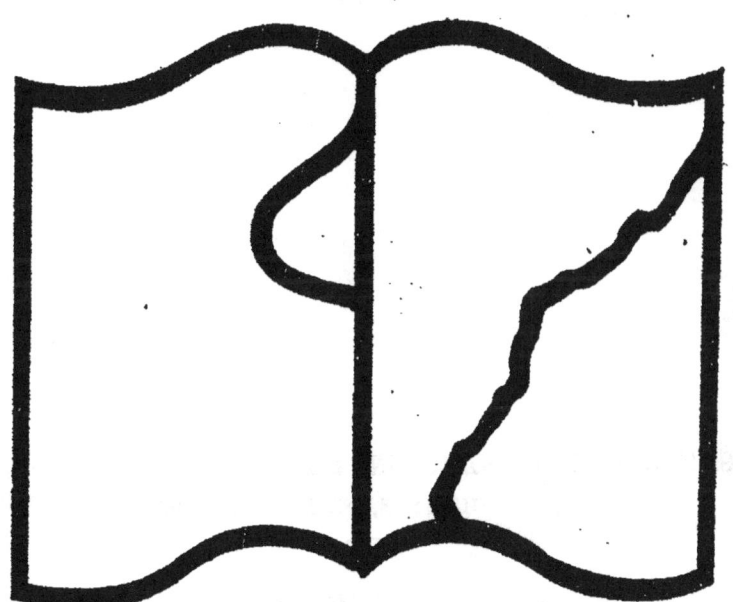

Texte détérioré — reliure défectueuse
NF Z 43-120-11

"VALABLE POUR TOUT OU PARTIE DU DOCUMENT REPRODUIT".

EL MAGHREB:

1200 MILES' RIDE THROUGH MAROCCO.

BY

HUGH E. M. STUTFIELD.

London:
SAMPSON LOW, MARSTON, SEARLE, & RIVINGTON,
CROWN BUILDINGS, 188, FLEET STREET.
1886.

[All rights reserved.]

LONDON:
PRINTED BY GILBERT AND RIVINGTON, LIMITED,
ST. JOHN'S SQUARE.

PREFACE.

THE following pages are an elaboration of the author's diary containing the record of visits to Marocco in each of the years 1882—1885. The journey which forms the principal subject of the volume was taken in 1883. In this journey we do not claim to have entered on any absolutely new ground, though in many places we quitted the ordinary caravan routes to the interior. Dr. Gerhard Rohlfs, who travelled wearing the garb, and professing the faith, of a Mussulman, no doubt preceded us not only at Wazan, but also along the road thence to Fez; to the best of our belief, however, we were the first Europeans to follow in his footsteps along that road.

With reference to the title of the book, it may be mentioned that *El Maghreb* is the short Arabic name for Marocco. Such other English works on

Marocco as have appeared during the last seventy years being confined to descriptions of either the Southern or Northern districts, my aim here is to give a complete and accurate account of nearly the whole of a land which deserves to be better known and more frequently visited. I am sensible that my experience of the country (though greater than that of most modern writers on Marocco) is yet not sufficient to give that complete knowledge of the subject which can only be acquired after prolonged residence among the people. At the same time, freshness of observation and the sense of novelty which must wear off after long familiarity with strange scenes, must be held to count for something in favour of the visitor. They say lookers-on see most of the game, and certainly very strange games are some of those to which the attention of the new-comer in Marocco is directed. Be this as it may, my sojourn in the country was enough to make me return deeply impressed with the melancholy waste of its immense resources, the deplorable condition of its inhabitants, and the strange way in which it is neglected by European States. My book, therefore, is a plea for the civilization of the country and the development of its agriculture, so as to utilize the magnificent properties of the soil for the benefit alike of the natives and the outside world, particularly England. It is to be hoped that the power of Christian States, now active enough for mischief in the country in many respects, may ere long be exerted for the attainment of this good object.

Considerable space has also been devoted to the question of the "Protection" of Moors and Jews by Europeans, and to the subject closely allied thereto, the fraudulent claims preferred, and too often enforced, against natives by Christians and their *protégés*. The subject is an unpleasant one to deal with, and is not unnaturally omitted in the works of other English writers on Marocco. At the same time, in any book pretending to be a complete description of the country, it is impossible to avoid mention of the nefarious system which plays so important a part in its internal economy.

I obtained the skeleton of my map from the French War Map of 1848, which, though inaccurate in many particulars, as was only to be expected in a work compiled in a large measure from native information (Wazan and the adjacent districts had not then been visited by Europeans), remains still the most trustworthy map of the country. The details are from personal observation, with certain additions collated from the works of Dr. Rohlfs, Sir J. Hooker, and others.

The substance of the first chapter appeared in *Blackwood's Magazine,* and is now republished by the kind permission of Messrs Blackwood.

In conclusion, the present is the author's first attempt at book-making. Such as it is, it is the result of much careful observation, and considerable study at leisure moments during the last year or so. If I shall have succeeded in directing in any degree the attention of Englishmen to this fascinating but most unhappy country, with a view to utilizing its riches and bettering the condition of its long-suffering inhabitants, I shall be more than content.

CONTENTS.

CHAPTER I.

First impressions of Tangier—The prison—Court of Justice and its procedure—Sights of Tangier—Ride to Cape Spartel—Snipe-shooting—Pig-sticking and boar-shooting—An accident—Start for Larache—El Khemis—Description of Larache—Ancient legends—A house on fire—Boar-hunt—Boo el Kheir—Moorish tea—Off again—Arzeilah—A ghostly camping-place—Journey to Tetuan—The Spanish war of 1859—The town and its inhabitants—Gunsmiths' shops—An inquiring mind—The unexplored Riff—Fierceness of the Riffians 1

CHAPTER II.

Feast of Mohammed—Lab el baroud—Triple murder—Indifference of the Moors—The Aissauias—Jewish entertainment—We start for the interior—Arab villages—Fertility of El Gharb—Alcazar—Its exceeding filth—Leo Africanus—Moorish decay—

On the road to Wazan—Sabab—Our "warriors"—
Curiosity of natives—Wazan—Its aspect and view
therefrom—Our house—The Shereef—Now a French
subject—Results of the step 32

CHAPTER III.

The Bascha objects to our company—His ultimate fate—
Courteous kaid—Wad Wergha—Native distress—
Ouber Mohammed—*Mona*—Our qualms at accepting
it—*Matamors*—Wad Seboo—Arab school—Approach
to Fez—Magnificent view—Entry into Fez—First
impressions of the city—The Bascha gives us a house
—Official dislike of strangers—Its cause . . 58

CHAPTER IV.

History of Fez—Description of the town—Guilds of craftsmen—Moorish shopmen—Moorish lunacy laws—
Prisons — Justice and punishments—Tortures—
Mosques—Old library—Decay of learning—The
Kessaria—Jews in Fez—Native fanaticism—Moorish
bread—Our last evening in Fez 76

CHAPTER V.

Moorish vet.—Visit to the Bascha—Cruelty to animals
—Shelluh village and noisy "warriors"—Berbers
of Marocco—Their origin and characteristics—Conflicting theories—Semites or Hamites—Review of
evidence 102

CHAPTER VI.

Arrival at Mequinez—Immense vaults—Sultan Moulai
Ismael—Ruins of Mequinez—Eno—Second visit to

ruins — Vast wall — Magnificent gate — Jews of Marocco — Their malpractices and unpopularity — Protected Jews — Hebrew women — Debasement of the Jews and their excuse 123

CHAPTER VII.

Gorgeous escort — Moorish saddlery — Saraoun — Volubilis — Moulai Idrees — Saint-worship in Marocco — Its inconsistency with the true creed of Islam — Probable causes of saint-worship 144

CHAPTER VIII.

Sects of Islam — Its practice — The Hadj — Fasts — Prayer — Status of women in Marocco — Faith of Islam — Beliefs concerning the next world — Superstitions — Parallelism with popular Catholicism — Spread of Islam in Marocco — Causes of its decay — Hopelessness of reform 152

CHAPTER IX.

Obeisance to our escort — Moorish mendacity — Blood-tax — Irregular proceedings of the Sultan's cavalry — High-handed oppression — Iniquities of native rule — Mirage — Beni Hassen — Dangerous neighbours — Hadj Absalam's ablutions — Distress of the people — A kaid in irons — Sallee — Idiotic ferry over the Boo-ragrag — Rabat — Moorish sepulture — Shellah — Tower of Hassen — Mosque 171

CHAPTER X.

N'zalla of Boo Z'neka — Moorish melody — A bad camping-place — Casablanca — Trade of Marocco — War indem-

nity—Women-flogging—Off again—Ben Rajit—
Terrible scenes of starvation—Moorish appetites—
Z'ttatt—Sharp frost—Hospitable kaid—Extortion by
a Jew 193

CHAPTER XI.

Fraudulent claims—Facilities for extortion by foreigners—
Oppression of the natives—" Protection " in Marocco
—Its abuses—Protected Jews—Malpractices in the
interior—Madrid Conference of 1880—Its provisions
inoperative—Proposed remedies 207

CHAPTER XII.

First view of the Atlas—Kasbah Boo-siri—A little learning is a dangerous thing—Ornithology of Marocco
—Entertainment at Beni Miskeen—Tadla—Wad
Oom R'bea—A dangerous ford—Ambassadors' mona
—The Atlas—Beauty in distress—Alcala—Terrible
misery—Tamilelt 218

CHAPTER XIII.

Palm-groves—Marocco—Entry into the city—Description
and history of the place—El Kutubia—Soko and
auction—The Sultan's army—Lynch law—Tame
sparrows—El Kantra—Lepers' Town—Moulai Hassan and his Grand Vizier—Power of the Sultan—
The palace and its appurtenances—Sunset in Marocco
—The City by night 242

CHAPTER XIV.

En route for the coast—Numerous guard—Ain el Baida
—Onkh el Jimmel—A thaleb out of work—Argan

forest—Sok el Tletta—Mogador—Highly scented Mellah—Sus and Wadnoon—Independent Jews—Soudan trade—Slave trade in Sus—Flooding the Sahara 268

CHAPTER XV.

In the plain of Akermout—Journey to Saffi—Fat women—Status of the sex in Marocco—The barb—Dukala—Lovely flowers—Numerous ruins—Zaouias—Marketing in Azamoor—An upright Bascha—Rabat again—Excursion up the Boo-ragrag—The Zair tribe—Moorish yarns—Mehediah—Journey up the coast—A would-be embezzler—Larache and El Khemis again—We meet an old friend—Boar-hunting extraordinary—Back at Tangier—Our impressions of Marocco and the Moors 281

CHAPTER XVI.

General description of Marocco—Its climate and resources—Historical sketch—Government and laws—Trade—Political affairs—British interests in Marocco—Gibraltar *v.* Ceuta—Marocco a possible basis of our food-supply—Sir John D. Hay and his critics—Suggested embassy at Fez—The chief reforms needed in Marocco—Probable results of the introduction of civilization—Desirability of a speedy settlement of the Marocco question 310

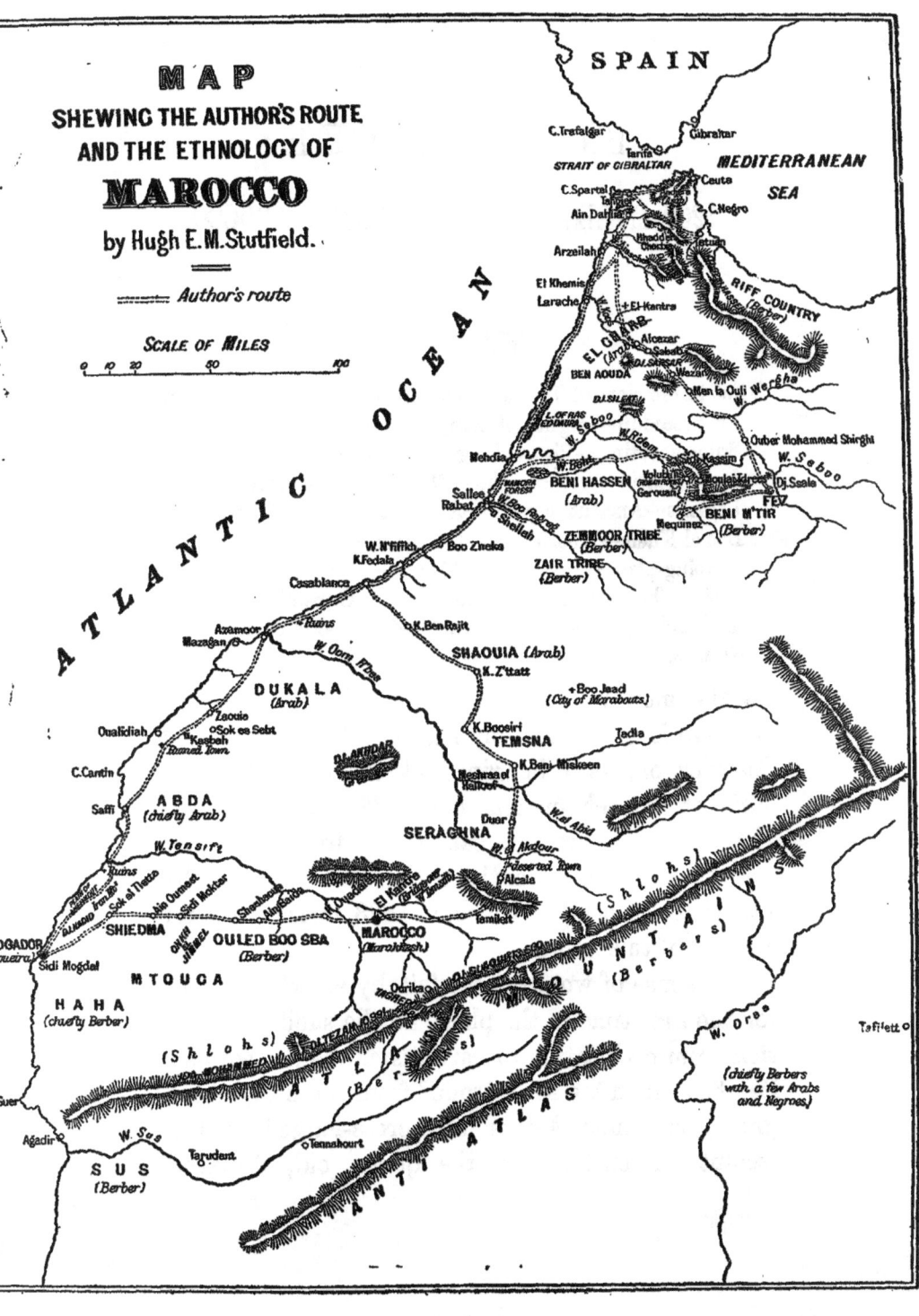

EL MAGHREB:

1200 MILES' RIDE THROUGH MAROCCO.

CHAPTER I.

First impressions of Tangier—The prison—Court of justice and its procedure—Sights of Tangier—Ride to Cape Spartel—Snipe-shooting—Pig-sticking and boar-shooting—An accident—Start for Larache—El Khemis—Description of Larache—Ancient legends—A house on fire—Boar-hunt—Boo el Kheir—Moorish tea—Off again—Arzeilah—A ghostly camping-place—Journey to Tetuan—The Spanish war of 1859—The town and its inhabitants—Gunsmiths' shops—An inquiring mind—The unexplored Rif—Fierceness of the Riffians.

In the month of November, 1881, being compelled to leave England for my health, I found myself at Tangier, on, as I imagined at the time, a flying visit of a week or ten days. The fascinations of the country, however, caused me to extend that visit to over four months, and it was succeeded by others, the second of which, in 1883, forms the chief subject of this volume.

The sense of wonderment felt by all who set foot for the first time in the place, at the sudden transition from civilization to barbarism, was not without its effect upon me as I strolled from the port, where grave, turbaned Moors sat cross-legged at the receipt of custom, up the queer, old, ill-paved street, thronged with white-robed Arabs, Jews, negroes, mulattoes, and Europeans; the motley crowd, with its strange variety of types, shades of complexion and costume, that composes the population of Tangier. The impression is deepened as one passes out through the principal gate into the open *Soko* or market-place, filled with camels, mules, donkeys, and an excited crowd of natives jabbering over their bargains with that intense ardour of gesture and expression peculiar to the Arab; or else lying idly about—men in their *jelabs* (white woollen cloaks), muffled women, and prettily-clad children arranged in picturesque groups. The scene is familiar to all who have travelled in the East, but nowhere else is the change so rapid and complete as in Tangier, which, more Eastern than the East itself, and seemingly more remote, is yet within three hours' sail of Europe, and westwards of Piccadilly. The short passage of the straits carries you back, as it were, some thousands of years; or, as an American put it more forcibly, makes you feel as though you had been "taken up by the scruff of the neck and sot down in the Old Testament." Here one is living not merely among relics of the past, but in the past itself, only with good hotels and modern comforts about you as well; and the Old-World, patriarchal life around one has a charm of its own, arising from a sense of tranquillity and repose, which few other health-resorts possess. The hoof of the British tourist has not yet succeeded in effacing this impression, though the growing presence of the European is evidenced by the numerous gorgeous bazaars, villas, and hotels which are springing up all over the place. Mr. Cook has now annexed Tangier to his domains, and the sad spectacle of a telephone-wire stretched across the Soko and the antique walls and battlements of the town, brought home to me, on my last visit, the fact of the resistless inroads of civilization.

Guided, perhaps, by the natural instincts of a man of law, I found myself, in my first walk through the town, making the tour of the *Kasbah* or citadel, wherein are the prisons, the palace of the Bascha, and his court of justice. The prison, though a sufficiently loathsome place, seems to have improved of late years, and in spite of its darkness and stench, and the famine-stricken faces of its inmates, it was always a luxurious abode compared with those of the interior. The court of justice and the proceedings therein do not recall to mind the Old Bailey, any more than its presiding genius does Mr. Justice Hawkins. The judge, who is the Bascha or Mayor of Tangier, reclines at length on a couch, listening to the evidence which is given with much energy and volubility, with flashing eyes and excited gestures. There is a confused hubbub of chattering and recriminations on all sides. The prosecutor calls the accused a *kilb ben el kilb* (dog and son of a dog), and the prisoner replies with similar aspersions on the moral character of the other's parents and grandparents; the judge roars like a bull of Basan at them both, and there is general confusion. Sometimes, in the middle of it all, the prisoner will jump up and exclaim that he can get another witness on his behalf. He then runs out of court, unguarded, and presently, without fail, returns with his man. Meanwhile, the next case is called and proceeded with in similar fashion.

It is not my intention to describe so well described a place as Tangier. The best thing my readers can do is to go and see it for themselves, and I think I can promise them they will not be bored. There is always something of interest to be seen, whether it is an Arab funeral, with its long train of mourners chanting their plaintive dirge; or the still quainter wedding processions, where the bride is borne in triumph, cooped up in an ornamented box on a mule's back, attended by her kinsmen, all decked out in holiday attire, with pipes and tom-toms, and dancing and firing of guns. Very different, but no less comical, is a Jewish wedding, which, however, is an entirely indoor performance. There the bride sits, gorgeously arrayed, on a raised daïs or throne, with her eyes shut, speechless and motionless as a statue, in a room full of her relations and friends, who are got up quite regardless of expense. The proceedings are said to last a fortnight, during which there is much feasting and merry-making, but the unfortunate bride takes no part in the festivities, further than as described above.

The weekly markets and festivals, too, with their

buzzing crowds and picturesque surroundings, the peasant folk passing to and fro, and the caravans of camels bringing merchandise from the interior—all visible from the windows of M. Bruzeaud's hotel—are a never-ending source of entertainment. Besides this, there are walks and rides in abundance along the pleasant bridle-paths. Roads, be it observed, do not exist in Marocco; hardly a pair of wheels to be found in the country; and only half a dozen bridges, so that if you do not ride, you must go on your own legs. A very favourite ride is that to the Roman ruins of Old Tangier, along the shore of the bay, where the sands, at low water, are a splendid place for a gallop, and charming views the whole way.

For a longer and still more charming excursion, the visitor should go to the lighthouse at Cape Spartel. The road at first leads past a Roman aqueduct fairly preserved, up the wooded slopes of the Djebel Kebir, through narrow lanes between the gardens of the pretty villas which now dot the sides of the mountain; then over hills covered with heath, broom, convolvulus, gum-cistus, and other flowering shrubs. Further on the track approaches the sea and winds along the side of the mountain, whose slopes, descending precipitously to the water's edge, recall to mind parts of the coast of North Devon. The ride should be taken, if possible, in spring, when the bushes, bursting into bloom, cause the hill-sides to be ablaze with colour. And then what lovely views are there, over the blue waters of the straits, teeming with ships of all shapes and sizes, like some huge marine canal, to the yellow sands of the bay where Trafalgar was fought, and the little town of Tarifa, backed by the purple hills of Spain. Eastwards, the prospect is bounded on the right by the lofty crest of the Beni Hassan range, still flecked with snow, and standing out in clear relief against the bright blue African sky. To their left, the Mediterranean stretches away between the opposing cliffs of Gibraltar and Djebel Moossa, the old Pillars of Hercules, twin guardians of the outlet to the western world, which frown at each other across the passage. The lighthouse itself, a magnificent structure with a large Moorish court attached, stands immediately below the summit of the Djebel Kebir, which here rises straight from the sea to a height of nearly 1000 feet. The scenery is worthy of the great cape which forms the north-west corner of the African continent, and on the summit of the shattered cliffs one is tempted to linger and gaze over the vast Atlantic, and listen to its rollers booming on the iron-bound shore below.

The excursion is generally prolonged to the grindstone caves, the old Caves of Hercules, three miles down the Atlantic coast—vast, waterworn caverns, into which the waves dash with a roar as of thunder. In their recesses, a number of wild-looking, half-naked creatures, like gnomes, are usually to be seen at work cutting out the mill-stones, by which the caves have been hollowed out to their present dimensions.

During my first stay at Tangier, excellent snipe-shooting was to be had at the lakes of Sharf-al-Akab, some fifteen miles from the town, to which myself and a friend were not slow in paying a visit. In two and a half days' shooting, we got eighty-two and a half couple of snipe, with a few extras. There are also partridges, hares, rabbits, duck, &c., to be got, but the number of sportsmen, professional and otherwise, has increased to such an extent that the game is rapidly getting exterminated within a radius of about twelve miles.

The sport *par excellence*, however, of the place is pig-sticking, for which expeditions are periodically organized by Sir John Drummond Hay, our Minister to the Court of Marocco. I enjoyed few things more than these hunting trips: the pretty encampment on the hill at Awara, the excitement of the day's sport, the pleasant company and chat round the big camp-fire at night, are among my pleasantest memories of the country.

The other method of boar-hunting is by the *battue* system, the guns being posted in front, and the game driven up to them. This, if not equal to pig-sticking, is likewise excellent fun,—the shrieking and uproar of the beaters, accompanied by the barking of dogs, the braying of horns, and the discharge of guns, rendering it very exciting. The curses and imprecations, mingled with the most biting sarcasms, that are showered on the unfortunate animals, are enough to oust the most stubborn boar from his lair. An Arab oath is a very elaborate affair, being sustained through a number of parentheses and subordinate phrases to an indefinite length. "May Allah burn the ashes of your great-grandfather, who was the miserable offspring of a brother and sister," &c., &c., may serve as an example. They imagine the unclean animal to be the abode of *jins*, or evil spirits, and maintain sometimes a running conversation with him, every word of which he is supposed to understand. There is a curious ceremony connected with the sport, to which all successful novices are subjected. After killing my first pig, the chief hunter came up and took away my gun, and a ring being formed, the piece was put up to auction. After it has been bidden for a while, you have to buy it in yourself at a certain price—say, four or five dollars. It is a way of paying the beaters, who otherwise contribute their services for nothing. The sheikh of the village called next morning for the money, and I was told my health would be duly drunk in cups of green tea at an Arab kettledrum. I thought the least they could do would be to send me a card of invitation, but they didn't.

Boar-hunting has its disadvantages, for it is unquestionably a dangerous amusement. There are perils of the pig, which, if wounded, will turn and rend you; perils of the gentleman who *will* ride with his lance in rest, instead of carrying the point in the air, or of the no less objectionable individual who shifts from his post and fires wildly down the line; of the ambushed Moor, who shoots impartially in any direction; while, unless you are well mounted, you have a very tolerable chance of breaking your neck. One accident occurred as follows. While posted one day, waiting for boar, we heard a more than usual commotion among the beaters, which lasted for some time, till at length a huge grey old tusker broke cover, and came across the intervening space up to my left-hand neighbour. He fired and wounded the beast, which immediately charged; and whether he fell or was knocked over, I never could make out, but the next thing I saw was my friend sprawling on the ground, and the boar jumping clean over him. Several people rushed up to the rescue, and blazed away promiscuously, so that, though no one was injured by the pig, I was more shocked than surprised to find that one gentleman had received a slug in the arm. Fourteen shots were fired at poor piggy, who made off notwithstanding, and was seen crossing a river by one of the Moors, who, in their familiar language of hyperbole, described him as descending the hill, "quarrelling with himself, and with a large tree on each tusk!" He added, that though his gun was loaded, the charge had been there since a very uncertain date, and it contained what he called a "running bullet," so that he thought it prudent not to fire.

During the first two months of my stay at Tangier, I did not extend my excursions to any distance into the country, with the exception of a week's camping in the hilly district of Andjrâ, which lies to the east of Tangier, in the direction of Ceuta.

In January, however, four of us arranged an expedition to Larache, a seaport town, some seventy miles to the south-west, where we were told that game, especially partridges, in fabulous quantities was to be found.

After a few busy days, spent in hiring servants, animals, tents, and other equipments, we effected a start early one morning in January along the broad and well-defined track which constitutes the highway to Fez. The road for the first few hours lay through undulating country, cultivated for the most part, and giving promise of a good crop. Farmers were at work tilling the ground with ploughs of patriarchal shape and construction, drawn by queer, mixed teams, such as a donkey and a goat, or a cow and a horse. The Arab husbandman makes a mere scratch of a furrow, throws in the seed, and lets it lie. He never uses a harrow, for it would be an unwarrantable interference with the workings of nature, not to leave the seed in the ground to shift for itself, and anything approaching scientific farming would be accounted little short of impious. "Allah will provide." If the elements are propitious, and there is a bounteous harvest—well. If, on the contrary, the crop should fail, and famine ensue, he will not complain, but bear his sufferings with the characteristic patience of his race. Why it should be in accordance with the laws of Kismet to use a plough, but not a harrow, it boots not to inquire, for fatalism seldom concerns itself with logic.

Marocco is now nearly destitute of trees. It was once densely wooded, but the forests have been almost entirely cut down for fuel, or else because they afforded refuge to robbers and wild beasts. Here and there a grove of olives, remaining untouched, marked the tomb of a saint, where religious scruple preserved the trees from destruction. A tidal river, the Wad el Kharrub, was forded, and then a steep hill clothed with bushes and palm-scrub, called the Akhbar el Hamra (Red Mountain), had to be climbed by a terribly rough and stony path. We camped at a village called Hhadd el Gharbia, the site of an important market, five-and-twenty or thirty miles from Tangier, where we had our first experience of haggling with the natives over the price of provisions and corn, they evidently thinking that they ought to make the most out of such rare birds of passage. The next morning saw us early on the road, so as to reach our destination before sundown. The country became more hilly and variegated as we advanced, and in many bushy glens, amid steep and rocky hills, we saw traces of the wild boar, who had rooted up the ground in all directions. Passing through some woods of mingled cork and olive trees, with a rich and tangled undergrowth of mosses, ferns, and flowering creepers, we reached a good-sized village of mud-huts, enclosed by fences of cactus and prickly pear, which they told us was to be our head-quarters for shooting. It was called El Khemis, or place of the Thursday market, a common way they have of naming places after the day on which the weekly market is held there. Our camp was pitched some six miles from Larache on a breezy common, near the edge of a high plateau, which descended, precipitously at first, then in a gradual slope for three miles, to the shore of the Atlantic.

The partridges were not in such multitudes as to darken the air with their wings, in the way Arab hyperbole had led us to expect, but there were enough, with a few snipe and teal, hares, rabbits, &c., to give us very fair sport. The Barbary partridge is a species of red-leg, similar to, but not identical with, the obnoxious "Frenchman" of our islands. One peculiarity he has, is that of perching in trees, and the whirr of wings, as a covey gets out of a thick bush close to your head, is very startling at first, and apt to lead to a miss. Singularly enough, they are to be found on the Rock of Gibraltar, but not on the mainland of Spain, where the ordinary red-leg alone exists. Like the Barbary apes, which are supposed to pass to and fro from Ape's Hill by means of a subterranean passage beneath the straits, they seem to regard the Rock as belonging by rights to the other continent, to which, no doubt, it was joined in bygone ages.

Next Sunday we rode into Larache. The town lies at the mouth of a big river, the Wad el Koos, on rising ground, but surrounded by extensive marshes. The Wad Koos is the Lixus of the Romans, but not that of the Periplus of Hanno, which must have been some river further to the south.[1] Larache, according to some ancient authors, was the site of the Garden of the Hesperides, so that the magnificent orange-groves in the vicinity of our encampment doubtless bore the golden apples guarded by the terrible monster which Hercules overcame and slew. Pliny explains the fable of the dragon as having its origin in the serpentine windings of the Koos, which forms a figure of 8 as it winds away to the east. Here also was the palace of the giant Antæus, and the scene of the hero's combat with him. He was buried near Tangier, where they say a large mound was till late years pointed out as his tomb. The story further goes that some sacrilegious persons once ventured to open the grave, but horror-struck at the spectacle of the vast skeleton, sixty cubits in length, they hurriedly closed it again in alarm. His wife, Tinge, is said to have given her name to the town which formed her husband's burial-place.

To pass from these airy regions of romance to the domain of sober fact, little is known of the early history of Larache. It may very well have been founded by the Phœnicians, and remains of the old Punic town of Lys exist some four miles up the Koos, where the traveller may make a pleasant excursion of combined duck-shooting and antiquarianism. In later times Larache has suffered many sieges and bombardments, and has often changed owners. In the sixteenth and seventeenth centuries it was alternately in the hands of the

---

[1] See Hooker's "Marocco," p. 372.

Portuguese, Spaniards, and Moors, till in 1689, after a protracted siege, the Sultan Moulai Ismael finally wrested it from the Spaniards. In 1830 it was bombarded by the Austrian fleet, which destroyed the last remnant of the once-dreaded navy of Marocco; the skeletons of one or two ships are yet to be seen at low water at the mouth of the river. The Spaniards again assaulted it from the sea in 1860.

We left our horses on the river-bank, and were ferried across into the town, which looks very picturesque on its eminence overlooking the harbour-bar. The principal Soko is inside the walls, a long enclosure surrounded by pillared arcades, evidently not the work of Moorish hands. In fact, Larache seems to show more signs of Christian occupation in past times than almost any other town in Marocco. The fortifications are Portuguese, and are said to be built in imitation of the side of a line-of-battle ship, though it is rather hard to trace the resemblance. There is not much of interest to see in the place, which is of no great size, containing a population of about eight thousand, including several European families.

After making some necessary purchases, we rode back to the tents. During dinner the same evening we heard a great commotion in the village, and on looking out saw one of the adjoining Moorish houses on fire, every one standing round and screeching, but not a soul making the slightest effort at extinguishing the flames. We all ran out and assisted in the rescue of effects (consisting chiefly of a few old pots and stools) from the burning mansion. It was warm work; and while endeavouring to drag out a lot of bamboo canes which they were anxious to save, we noticed that all the thatch-roof over our heads was in a blaze. We just had time to bolt out, when the whole affair fell in with a crash, giving us a rather narrow escape. The owner bore his loss with characteristic equanimity, accepting it as the decree of fate—that strange fatalism of theirs, which is the fatal bar to all progress, teaching them, by way of compensation, at least to endure misfortune.

A few weeks later I was present at a big fire in Tangier, when the helplessness of the Moors in cases of emergency was exemplified. A sort of extemporized fire-brigade of blacks and Moors was formed, but their method of extinguishing the flames would have astonished Captain Shaw. It consisted in sending niggers by twos and threes down to the beach, some quarter of a mile distant, each with one small basket on his head, which he filled with sand, then trotting back, poured it on the fire, and returned for more. If jabbering and gesticulating could have put out the flames, little damage would have been done; as it was, the house was completely gutted.

A few days after, we joined in a boar-hunt, which had been organized in some adjoining hills. It was the day of the Aissaouia festival, and we heard a great din of music and gun-firing at three o'clock in the morning. It had been settled that the sheikh of the village should be ready for us with the hunters and dogs at 9 a.m.,—a rather futile kind of arrangement in a country where time is not regulated by clock or watch. After waiting an hour and a half we sent up to inquire when they were likely to put in an appearance. The messenger returned to say that the sheikh was engaged at his devotions, but that he had nearly done, and then, after he had had his breakfast, he would be very much at our service. You never can surprise a Moor in his house, but he will tell you he is saying his prayers or engaged in other religious exercises. They are true Pharisees, and like to gain a reputation for external piety. There was nothing for it but to wait; and at length, some hours after the appointed time, we made a start. The first few beats were in a wild, hilly country, covered with dense bushes. As the day wore on, we were joined by numbers of hunters from the villages round about, all armed with their long guns, the consequence being that, while waiting for the boar, we were surrounded by these fellows, all standing with their guns "at the ready," in attitudes of the most intense expectation. If the boar appeared at a safe distance, they blazed away at him anywhere, and for a while we seemed to carry our lives in our hands; only, if he came their way, they all fled in the direst terror, without firing a shot. They never touched the pig by any chance, but simply jeopardized their neighbours; so that next time we stipulated that no native sportsmen should be allowed, or at least, that they should be kept under proper control. The best of it was, that when we came to the payment of the beaters, the uninvited gentlemen with the guns claimed their share of remuneration for their kindness in having endangered our lives and spoilt our sport. Needless to say, they did not get much.

After we had been encamped nearly a week, we were fortunate in making the acquaintance of a Moor in the village, named Boo el Kheir, who supplied us with all necessaries. He was a most charming old fellow, quite one of nature's gentlemen, and was reported to be extremely rich. His mode of life did not indicate great wealth, but in Marocco any such display would be the height of imprudence. The rapacious governors have a keen scent for such prey, and directly any one is suspected of hoarding riches, they are not long in finding an excuse for relieving him of them.

One afternoon he asked us to his domain in the village, where, after spending an hour in a superb orange-grove, he invited us to take tea with him at his house. Arriving at the porch, he bade us welcome in the set phrases used by the Moors on such occasions, and bade us be seated. Tea was served in the usual Moorish fashion; the teapot is almost filled with sugar, and then a small quantity of green tea being added, the water is poured in. They next add a strong infusion of mint and verbena, the result being a pale syrupy compound, in which the flavour of tea is hardly perceptible. However, we managed to swallow it, and a brasier of incense was then passed round till the room was filled with its sickly fumes. We became great friends after this visit, and he used to sit for half an hour in our tent every evening when he brought us our supplies. He never asked for payment at the time, but let us keep the accounts, naïvely remarking that "we had eaten bread in his house, and he was sure we should not swindle him." Talking of accounts, it became a rather serious matter keeping them in the copper coin of the country, which is of so little value and so cumbersome, that three pennyworth will fill your pockets to bursting, while if a man gives you change for half-a-crown, you have to hire a donkey to carry it away.

We had capital sport on the whole during our stay, bagging between 500 and 600 head in a little over a fortnight. There was some difficulty in disposing of the game after it was shot, and in the end we had to send mule-loads of partridges into Tangier. The natives are so fanatical that they will not eat game killed by Christians. The Mohammedans regard the slaughter of any animal as a sacrifice to Allah, and if this sacrifice is performed by an infidel, the flesh is necessarily unclean. At first we tried cutting the throats of the partridges ourselves, but the stricter among our servants were not satisfied with this, and insisted on having the operation performed by a Moor. They did not mind borrowing my knife for the purpose, however, and finished by stealing it.

Towards the end of our stay, the game naturally began to show signs of decreasing, and as we were getting tired of the *toujours perdrix* fare to which we were subjected, and beginning to sigh after the flesh-pots of Tangier, it was decided to make a move. We managed to get some very sorry baggage animals, and started off by a new road, which led by the town of Arzeilah and the coast. Our old friend accompanied us a short distance from the village, where we bade him a fond farewell. Half the morning had been wasted in the usual squabbling and jabbering over trifles, and our beasts of burden required a great deal of repose, which they secured by tumbling or lying down, at intervals of half an hour throughout the day, so that it was nightfall before we neared the town. Here one mule came hopelessly to grief in a gloomy lane between high banks topped with trees, and very boggy at the bottom. The Moors all began to swear and weep, and almost struck work. After much trouble we got the brute unloaded, and putting half the cargo on the backs of the men, at last arrived under the walls of Arzeilah—an old Portuguese fortress, whose half-ruined battlements stood out in picturesque relief against the star-lit sky. The gates were locked, and not a soul stirring, and though we thundered away at them with big stones, and fired guns, we could not get them opened. We therefore ordered our servants, sorely against their will, to move on to what looked a tolerably open spot, and there pitch the tents. At this, they all broke out afresh, cursing each other and ourselves, and gibbering like madmen, and for a while nothing could be done. When they had quieted down a little, we discovered the cause of all this commotion. The place was a Mohammedan graveyard, and we were desecrating the tombs of the dead. However, there was no help for it, as it was nearly pitch-dark, the grass reeking with dew, and one of our party seriously unwell; so by dint of great exertions, and doing half the work ourselves, we got the tents fixed for the night. There was a tombstone under my bed, but no ghost disturbed my slumbers. The Mohammedans say that the souls of the departed are disturbed if a Christian walks over their graves, and one should be careful to avoid doing so. What dire commotion there must have been among the souls of the defunct faithful, with four infidels sleeping above their last resting-place, I hardly like to imagine.

Next morning we strolled through the quaint little town, whose numerous ruins evidenced the antiquity it boasts. In the days of the Romans, it was called Zilis, and, strangely enough, was exempt from subjection to the kings of Mauritania, being included in the Spanish province of Bœtica. There is a story to the effect that Arzeilah belonged to the English in the tenth century, and that they destroyed and abandoned it, the Khalif of Cordova, Abder Rhaman, rebuilding it some years later. The

Portuguese occupied it many years, and its general history is similar to that of Larache and the other coast towns.

Our lazy muleteers wanted a great deal of pressing to make them start, but a deep tidal river, the Wad el Ayascha, had to be crossed, and it was necessary to take it at low water. We arrived at Tangier without mishap the same evening.

My next trip was to Tetuan. I was unwilling to quit Marocco without visiting this interesting place, and the result proved it to be well worth the trouble. My friends having left for Italy, I procured the services of an escort—a fine-looking barbarian—and a baggage-mule, and started off alone. The distance is about forty-five miles, which we accomplished in eleven hours, including the customary halt for an hour at midday. We passed several heaps of stones, or murder-cairns, by the wayside, marking the spot where some poor wretch had been sent to his last account; and pious wayfarers should never omit to add their stone to the pile.

Our stopping-place was at the *fondak* or caravanserai, a square stone building, erected for the accommodation of travellers near the top of a wild mountain-pass. Here we regaled ourselves with Moorish coffee and such provisions as we had brought with us. From the summit of the pass there is a grand view of Tetuan, with its white-roofed houses glistening in the sun, and the blue Mediterranean beyond. The town is magnificently situated in a valley, watered by the Wad Martin, which, unlike the generality of Marocco rivers, always has some water in its channel. To the east, a plain some five miles wide extends to the sea-shore; while in front, the hills of the wild Riff country rise to a height of 3000 feet, backed by the loftier spurs of the Beni Hassan range. The lower slopes of the hills are dotted with numerous white Moorish villas, and covered with luxuriant orange-groves, interspersed with olive, fig, peach, and other fruit trees.

In view of its picturesque situation and charming surroundings, Tetuan is certainly one of the most beautiful places in Marocco. The town itself is Tangier over again in its general aspect—only more so. It is perhaps a more typically eastern city, and remaining in a more fossilized condition. The streets are dirtier and worse paved, while the comparative absence of the European element in the population lends it a more barbarous air. Many houses are still in ruins from the war of 1859, when the Spaniards, under Marshal O'Donnell, captured the town. The battle which decided the campaign was fought in the plain to the north-east, when the Moors, badly armed, and worse led, displayed desperate valour, and caused the issue of the day for some time to hang in doubt. The Spaniards, delighted at the humiliation they had inflicted on their ancient enemy, plumed and prided themselves on their victory in true hidalgic style, and fancied that the days of the Cid had returned once more. The political results of the campaign, however, were *nil*, beyond the imposition of a war indemnity of 4,000,000*l*., which has only just been paid off.

Of the early history of Tetuan little is known. Leo Africanus says vaguely, that it was built by the ancient Africans. Its old name was Tetteguin, which signifies an eye. The story goes, that when the Vandals gained possession of the town, they bestowed the government of it on a woman, with one eye, hence the name. It has suffered, even more than most Moorish towns, the horrors of native warfare, as, chiefly owing to the turbulence and piratic habits of its inhabitants, it has been several times destroyed. It has never recovered the damage done to it in the Spanish war, when some thousands of houses were laid in ruins, and the population has now dwindled down from some 40,000 to 25,000.

I had two very fair days' shooting, getting about thirty couple of snipe and duck, and devoted the rest of the time to sight-seeing. I was lodged in the Mellah or Jewry, which, as elsewhere in Marocco, is a separate quarter of the town, remarkable for its squalor and filth, and the miserable appearance of its denizens. My host, Mr. Isaac Nahon, is the English consular agent, and he was most obliging in showing me through the town. I was struck with the number of mosques, many of which are large and fine, but no infidel dare set foot within a Moorish mosque, not even in semi-civilized Tangier.

There are no less than three *sokos* inside the walls, the first of which was filled with countrywomen selling embroidery and richly worked vestments; the others contained the usual mob of marketers, and the same accessories that I had seen elsewhere. What a clatter of barbarous and quarrelsome tongues, mingled Riffian and Maghrebbin, and what throats of brass these people must have, to utter such unmelodious sounds! If I try and speak their language myself, half a sentence blisters my tongue, and the gutturals make me cough and sneeze. And then the frightful amount of muscular energy they expend, even in ordinary conversation. The traveller, new to the country, thinks his interlocutor is threatening to cut his throat, when, as likely as not, he is merely wishing him good morning, or saying that it is a fine day. As Leo wrote three hundred years ago: " abounding exceedingly with choler, they speake alwaies with an angrie and lowd voice. Neither shall you walke in any of their streetes in the daytime, but you shall see two or three of them by the eares." In this, as in other respects, they have changed little since his day.

The shops in the town were very curious, the two chief trades being in leather-work and Moorish guns. The manufacturers of the latter occupy a large section of the town, and here these antique weapons are turned out by hundreds, half of Marocco being supplied from Tetuan. It was a most interesting process to watch: rude handwork, unassisted by machinery of any kind, with the single exception of a large wheel, which, turned by hand, served to roll the barrel into shape. One set of workmen made the barrels, another the hammers and locks, and a third the woodwork. A plain gun will fetch about five dollars, but some of them are beautifully worked in ebony and ivory, and sell for a much higher price. From the gunsmiths' shops we walked down to the ancient palace of Tetuan, once the residence of the Court, but now for the most part in an uninhabitable condition. There was a fine Moorish court in the centre, with some fine wood-carving, and a stalactite roof in places; the walls were in the well-known Arabesque stucco-work of delicate patterns, but daubed over and disfigured with whitewash, as were the walls of the Alhambra before the work of restoration was begun. It is probable that this white-washing was done at an epoch when a wave of Puritanism passed over Islam, similar to that which wrought such havoc among our church architecture in England.

Returning through the streets, we met a noisy procession of men and boys with music and singing, going to pray for rain, which was sorely needed, at the tomb of a patron saint. One man directed the proceedings, walking backwards and halloing, just like a Salvation Army major; his function seemed to be to keep every one in their proper place, occasionally administering sound knocks to sundry youths whose movements were unduly erratic. The thing was for all the world exactly like the processions of "the Army" one sees in England, only less rowdy and demonstrative. It is customary to place dishes of *kus-kussoo* (the national dish of Marocco) upon the tomb in the evening. The next morning the grave is revisited, and if, as in famine time is not unlikely to happen, the food has disappeared, it is considered a favourable sign that the saint will incline his ear to their prayers. We next made our way up the *kasbah*, and thence through a large Arab cemetery, where, it being Friday (the Mohammedan Sabbath), white-robed women were flitting about like ghosts, weeping and praying at the tombs of departed relatives.

On the way down I saw a black slave following his master like a sheep, being hawked through the town for sale. There is much work for the Anti-Slavery Society in Marocco, with the slave-trade in full swing so close to our doors, and the traffic in human flesh being carried on actually at Tangier.

Through the courtesy of the owner, I was permitted to visit the house of a rich Moor of Tetuan, and at two in the afternoon presented myself at the door. I was received in a very cordial manner by my host, and conducted through a court richly decorated with mosaics and tile work, and a fountain in the centre, into an inner room. Here he pointed to a luxurious divan, and seating himself opposite me, proceeded to pump me quite dry on a most astonishing variety of subjects. He was an elderly man—of a grave and intelligent cast of countenance, and with that air of well-bred dignity which seems habitual with Orientals. He had travelled a great deal for a Moor, and spoke French with tolerable fluency. He was anxious to know if the French were still in Tunis, and expressed his dislike and contempt for them in no measured terms —saying they were good enough to fight against half-armed Arabs, but that the Germans could beat them any time they liked. He felt certain, moreover, that they had designs upon Marocco, and inquired if there was any truth in the rumours of a recent engagement on the frontier. He was much interested in England, and said he had been in London, where he had seen the queen, and wanted to know her Majesty's mode of life and all about her, till it became necessary to explain that, not being an intimate at Court, I was hardly qualified to answer.

At this point my host's brother came in and followed the conversation with evident interest—suggesting questions for his relation to put to me, my replies being translated to him in Arabic. A wonderful string of interrogatories here followed: "Was there not much sugar and corn in London?" (two great necessaries of Moorish existence). What was the extent of the British empire? and how many subjects had wé in India? When I replied that her Majesty ruled over 200,000,000 natives, with 40,000,000 Mohammedans, they opened their eyes; and I think it was only native politeness that prevented them expressing incredulity at the statement. What was my age and profession? Was I a Protestant or a Roman Catholic? and what was the difference between them? Did the Protestants believe in Jesus Christ? and was He the Author of the Bible? On my replying in the negative, a slight pause ensued, after which he wanted to know how old the world was according to the Bible. I said that by strictly following the Bible narrative we made the world out to be 6000 years old. He was greatly pleased at this, and said that coincided with the Koran. "But," he went on, "can you tell me how it is that, while the Koran and the Bible both agree in saying that the world is 6000 years old, the Chinese Book, on the contrary, declares it to be 33,000?" This was rather a stumper; so I replied cautiously, that I really could not say, but that many wise and learned men in Europe thought that the world was a great deal older even than that. At this they both relapsed into silence, and became awhile absorbed in reflection.

The celibacy of the clergy was also a question that interested him, and he appeared quite relieved when I told him that our priests might marry like other people. After some further conversation we adjourned upstairs into a little room on the second storey, commanding a beautiful view eastwards over the plain. The whole house was richly furnished; and he showed me an American "Champion Regulator" clock with especial pride, though he did not say by what means he regulated the time. I was afterwards informed, on excellent authority, that my friend's name was Kteeb, and that he was of very ancient lineage—being, in fact, a direct descendant of Boabdil. His uncle still keeps the keys of the gate in the Alhambra by which that monarch sallied forth to meet Ferdinand at the final conquest and surrender of Granada, and which the latter granted him at his special request. It is said that several of the Moors in Tetuan still retain the keys of their ancestors' houses, and the title-deeds to their estates in Granada—that earthly paradise to which, every Friday, they devoutly pray they may one day be restored.

I would have given a good deal to be able to make an expedition into that terrible unknown Riff country, which extends eastwards of Tetuan to the Algerian frontier. Such a proceeding, however, would, in the present state of affairs, be little short of suicidal, and no Moor could be found to accompany the traveller, whose life would not be safe beyond ten miles from the town. It is an extraordinary thing, and one which, beyond all others, points to the barbarism and practical remoteness of Marocco, that within sixty miles of Gibraltar, and in full sight of Europe, there is a large, unexplored country; where no Christian can venture, or has ventured for centuries. The Sultan is powerless to deal with these turbulent hillmen, and the Moors themselves dare not trust themselves in their midst.

These Riffians, who are almost identical with the

Kabyles of Algeria, are a branch of the great Berber or aboriginal stock of North Africa, the Shlohs of the South being the other chief representatives of the race in Marocco. So fierce and fanatical as to be unapproachable even in these late days, in history they have ever been known as robbers and brigands and blood-thirsty pirates, whose audacity and the barbarities they inflicted on their captives, rather than their actual power, caused them to be a terror to all mariners, and who extended their depredations to every corner of the Mediterranean, and even as far as the English Channel.

Numbers of them are to be seen in the streets of Tetuan and in Tangier during the great feasts and markets. They are wiry, athletic-looking fellows, often with fair hair and blue eyes, which is probably the result of an infusion of Northern blood at the time of the Vandal occupation. They are recognizable by their wild appearance and garb, their different language, and the shaven crown, whence grows the scalp-lock by which Azrael, the Angel of Death, is to pull them up to heaven on the Last Day. This appendage is cultivated with the care its importance demands, for on its reliability rests the Riffian's hope of a blessed immortality. I once gave a small pot of hair restorer to a stalwart young fellow whom nature had adorned with so scanty a tuft as to be quite unequal to his weight. He thought at first it was meant to eat, but on being explained its use, accepted the present with profound gratitude. I trust it may be the means of his securing a happy hereafter. This was the only missionary work I attempted during my stay in Marocco.

I had one more good turn at my friends the snipe, and then rode back with "the escort" to Tangier. Two weeks later, I quitted the shores of Africa, not without regret, and a firm resolve to return to this delightful country at no distant date. I finished my tour with a ride to Ronda, and a month's travel in glorious Andalusia, before returning to England. The traveller who winters in Marocco, the last relic of dominion surviving to the Moor, amid the shreds and tatters of his former splendour, should not fail to visit the land where he once reigned supreme, and which contains the grandest monuments of his vanished genius and greatness.

CHAPTER II.

Feast of Mohammed—Lab el baroud—Triple murder—Indifference of the Moors—The Aissauias—Jewish entertainment—We start for the interior—Arab villages—Fertility of El Gharb—Alcazar—Its exceeding filth—Leo Africanus—Moorish decay—On the road to Wazan—Sabab—Our "warriors"—Curiosity of natives—Wazan—Its aspect and view therefrom—Our house—The Shereef—Now a French subject—Results of the step.

In January, 1883, I found myself once more in Tangier. The very pleasing impressions of the country left by my previous visit had induced me to return, with the idea this time of extending my travels further afield.

I had to wait a fortnight for my friend and future companion in travel, Mr. Sidney Hoare, and spent the time in making the necessary arrangements for the trip. I was fortunate to be just in time for two great Moorish festivals. The first of these was that of Sidi Mohammed, the tutelary Saint of the City, which is likewise, as its name implies, the "Protected of the Lord." His large white *kubbah*, or dome-shaped tomb, is a conspicuous object from the city walls, as it peeps out from its encirling grove of trees. The feast was held on a Sunday, and the whole Soko was filled with crowds of holiday-makers, who had come in from far and near to take part in, or to witness the proceedings; in fact, the whole thing—the aspect of the mob especially, and their *al fresco* amusements—suggested the idea of a sort of Moorish Derby Day. Jugglers, tumblers, musicians, mountebanks, and such like caterers for the popular entertainment were there; water-carriers, with their goat-skins and bells, calling out, "El ma, el ma" (*Anglicé*, "Who'll have a cooler?"); vendors of cakes and *Moulai Idrees* (sweetmeats called after the patron saint of such things), all drove a brisk trade with the crowd.

The ceremony of circumcision, which the Moors put off till the child is ten or twelve years old, is performed at the feast of Mohammed, and numbers of children were there, clad in their bright-hued holiday attire, ready for the "christening." Here and there may be seen an infant son of a Shereef or some other great gun of Islam, with vestments of gold and sea-green (the colour of the Prophet), and mounted on gorgeously caparisoned horses.

Processions of devotees are formed, which file down the roadway leading to the saint-house, each with a heifer led along by a cord, which is duly sacrificed with prayer at the tomb, the carcase being, as a rule, cut up and distributed among the poor. This ceremony over, the procession re-forms, and goes slowly back amid an incessant din of tom-toms and gun-firing. The warriors execute a curious sort of warlike dance, with figures like a quadrille, accompanied by wild shouts and the discharge of guns and feats of jugglery, in which the leaders vie with one another, spinning their long guns round their heads with astonishing rapidity. Now and again a gun will burst, and some one is maimed for life, owing to the reckless way in which they shovel huge charges down the barrel. Interspersed with the mob were detachments of foot and horse soldiery, knots of Riffians in their wild attire, with their red cloth gun-covers twisted as turbans round their heads, contrasting well with the lighter kit of the men of Sus, a very smart lot, who showed themselves pre-eminent in various feats of arms. The chief feature in the scene, however, is the charging of the gorgeously apparelled horsemen in the *Lab el baroud*, or powder-play, who fire their guns simultaneously when galloping at full speed. Groups of shrouded women, scattered about, encourage their lords with shrill cries; every one is tremendously in earnest, and even among the spectators the sea of upturned faces and eyes, glistening with excitement, betoken the interest taken in the performance.

Often the harmony of the proceedings is broken by more tragic events. Human life is held cheap in Marocco, and the vendetta, or blood-feud system, is in full force. These annual gatherings afford the avenger of blood an opportunity of meeting his intended victim, and the last feast at which I was present (Christmas, 1884) was marked by one of these deeds of blood. Two Riffians, who some time back had had a relation killed by a man, and whose death they were bound by their unwritten but inexorable law to avenge, had marked out the slayer sitting among the crowd in the Soko. They forthwith fired at him, but missed, shooting a poor woman instead through the brain. Two more shots were fired with similar result, an inoffensive male spectator this time receiving one ball in the calf of his leg and another in the face. A fourth shot was better aimed, and, striking the right man in the body, he fell dead instantly. One of the murderers was likewise badly wounded in the fray. The second victim was conveyed to a house, where he died in two hours. The head of the woman was wrapped up in some coarse sacking, and the body carried past us on a bier; the other corpse I saw lying in a small inclosure, covered with a jelab drenched in blood. A hole was dug in the Soko, and both were interred in the most casual fashion imaginable. Nobody appeared at all disconcerted, the horsemen charged, the powder-play and dancing went on, just as if nothing had happened, within ten yards of the place of burial. Other similar cases occurred while I was at Tangier, and the victims either got off scot free or had to pay a few pounds blood-money to the relations of the slain. *Chacun à son tour*, however, and visitors to Tangier next year may be in time to see the tables turned on the murderers by the above-mentioned relations; only they must be careful not to be in the line of fire, as these Moors are shocking bad shots, and one would almost prefer that they would shoot at you rather than at any one who happened to be near you at the time.

The day after the feast arrived the "Jesuits" of Marocco, the Aissauias, or Society of the Order of Aissa (Jesus), a sect of fanatics deriving their origin from Mequinez, but which afterwards spread over many parts of the East. Gerhard Rohlfs says [1] that they recognize the prophet Jesus as their spiritual chief, and claim to work miracles in his name, "quoting that passage of the Koran in which Mohammed says, 'he had not the gift of working miracles, but that God had bestowed it upon Jesus.'" It is very probable, however, that the idea of Jesus being their founder is a late invention, arising from the name of the real originator of the sect, one Sidi Mohammed Ben Aissa, a celebrated Moorish saint of the seventeenth century, concerning whom various marvellous legends are circulated. They profess to be able to swallow broken glass and sharp stones, to touch venomous snakes, and to bruise and gash themselves, and to commit other more repulsive acts—all in the name of Aissa. They resemble somewhat the dancing dervishes of Turkey, and may be described as the Salvation Army of Marocco, their antics bearing about the same relation to the civilization existent there as do those of our dervishes to contemporary enlightenment in England.

They began quite close to the hotel; half a dozen lunatics with shaven crowns and black wavy hair

[1] "Adventures in Marocco."

streaming down their shoulders, formed a circle, and commenced a sort of dance, bobbing up and down, and wagging their heads in unison with monotonous howlings, till they worked themselves up into a frenzy. Behind came the inevitable tom-toms and three large banners. Other devotees soon joined the band, and as their numbers swelled, their frenzy increased proportionately. So they went slowly forwards, throwing themselves about in grotesque contortions, but always keeping up the regular beat of the dance, and emitting convulsive gulps and groans and sobs, which in the aggregate swelled into a hoarse murmur. One or two, apparently finding it warm work, stopped, and took off every stitch of clothing, except a thin pair of linen drawers, and in this airy costume went to work at the orgie with a will. In the Soko a live sheep was brought them. The whole mob of devotees rushed upon it like a pack of ravening hounds, and tearing the beast limb from limb, tossed the fragments in the air, smearing themselves with blood, and swallowing gobbets of the warm and quivering flesh. A second and a third sheep were thus served, and no doubt a Christian or Jew would have been a still more welcome prey; in fact, the scene recalled to mind the description in the *Bacchæ* of Euripides, of the Mænads rending Pentheus in pieces. At the gate of the town I climbed up on to a wall, and from this safe coign of vantage looked down on the throng as it passed a few feet below. By this time there was a perfect mob of fanatics, all worked up into transports of delirium. Some grovelled on the ground, imitating the cries and actions of wild beasts, foaming at the mouth, and rolling about in contortions, calling loudly upon Allah the while. One fellow had gashed his arm with a knife, and was covered with blood; at another performance I witnessed, a huge negro was to be seen literally gnawing at a woman's arm, from which a stream of blood flowed, she suffering it quietly, and looking as though she rather enjoyed it. Two or three had their hands tied behind their backs, to prevent them doing mischief, for the *mokaddems*, or high priests, have complete power over them, and seem to be able to soothe them, even in their greatest fury. The actions of the women were particularly loathsome as they jumped about and yelled with excitement. Now and again one would embrace another, or sink into the arms of a friend (generally of the "male persuasion," I observed) from sheer exhaustion.

Altogether it was a most beastly spectacle, instructive only as showing to what depths of degradation our common humanity can sink. The whole thing, be it observed, is perfectly *bonâ fide;* there is no suspicion of sending round the hat at the close of the performance, which takes place in the mosque, unseen by Christian eyes. Pretended devotees may perhaps be occasionally detected secreting fragments of sheep in their *jelabs*, with a view to roast mutton at dinner, but imposture is certainly the exception. Our English dervishes, and their "mokaddems" in particular, have a much keener eye to business!

One day, not long after, I was asked to accompany a party to the house of a rich Jew, who had kindly consented to show us his wife's wardrobe. The Marocco Jewesses have most magnificent *trousseaux*, sometimes worth hundreds of dollars, and the dresses we saw were certainly very handsome. All the natives of this country are so dreadfully hospitable, and our entertainer insisted on our tasting some of his wine, which, he assured us, was excellent and quite genuine, as it was made on the premises, he said, by his own mother, who would permit her offspring to touch no other. All I can say is, if that Jew obeyed and drank that stuff—a sort of blend of elder-wine and treacle—he showed a filial affection which the pious Æneas himself could not have rivalled. The next treat in store for us was jam, served round in a pot, with one spoon for six people. On the whole, I fully agreed with an American lady of the party, who "guessed she had the best of it, in getting first go," and my turn coming last but one, I declined with thanks, explaining that I never took sweets.

We had a splendid day's pig-sticking before we left, under the auspices of Sir John Hay, no less than fourteen boar being speared, and then, our preparations being at length complete, we, that is, Hoare and self, effected a start on Friday, the 9th of February. We had two tents and seven animals in all, including two very satisfactory saddle-horses. Mine I had bought from Sir John Hay; he was a first-class pig-sticker, and enjoyed the sport as much as his master.

Our servants were Manuel Correa, a Gibraltarian, cook and head man; two Moors called Mohammed (every one is in this country, nearly), and a soldier. One of the Mohammeds, a magnificent mulatto, was called Santo, by way of distinction. The sponsors of the soldier must have been of an original turn, for they had christened him Absalam, to which he had earned the prefix of Hadj, or pilgrim. He was a personage of some distinction, ranking as kaid or captain in the imperial army, and not a bad fellow in his way, with a very imposing exterior, but the most useless person in camp imaginable. However, in a country where appearances count for so much, a man of such regal port as our escort, Al-kaid Hadj Absalam, was worth his dollar a day, if only for ornament. We did not get off till late, owing to rain in the early morning, and spent our first night in camp at the foot of the Akhbar el Hamra, or Red Mountain, some fifteen miles from Tangier. From here the toilsome climb up the steep hill and its abominable road, then through the wild woods, the chosen home of our friends the boars, led us past the sok or market of Hhadd el Gharbia, our camping-ground of the previous year. A picturesque crowd of country folk were busy marketing, with all the usual accessories of a Moorish fair, jugglers, snake-charmers with their pipes and tom-toms, native doctors, story-tellers, &c. We soon left the Larache road upon our right, and late in the afternoon reached our camping-place for the night, a village with a name sounding like Kuk-shut, or Cockshot. The inhabitants of "Cockshot," who were of the *Kabyla* or tribe of Oolad Moossa (sons of Moses), were most uncivil, and told us an astonishing number of lies for the short time we were there. Seeing the soldier, they thought it was a case of "mona," i.e. of being compelled to supply provisions gratis, and swore they had neither barley nor food of any sort. It wanted a great deal of bullying from Manuel to make them produce either. Business is conducted on strictly cash principles in these parts, and they like to see the colour of your money before they supply you. Manuel proved of great service to us by his extraordinary command of strong language. If a man refused to sell us barley, he would shower such horrible imprecations on his flocks and corn that the vendor soon trotted it out, to avert a pestilence. When they knew they would be paid, they were always glad enough to sell. The saying that "hard words break no bones" does not hold good in Marocco. The belief in the efficacy of a good round curse is universal, and I have known it shared even by Europeans resident in the country. The sheikh of the village was said to be at Larache, but he managed to appear early the next morning, to demand "guard-money," which is a means of extorting backsheesh under cover of the fiction that he has been protecting your lives and property during the night. We turned in early, so as to be up betimes in the morning, but sleep in the midst of an Arab village is not easy to get, till you are accustomed to it. There is a perpetual concert of various noises all through the night—the jabber of Moors, sheep and goats bleating, jackasses braying, camels bubbling and gurgling, cocks crowing, dogs barking, baying, and howling, in every conceivable tone. These dogs are a great nuisance. Being, like most things in this country, always hungry, they are ready to eat anything, and prowl continually round the tents in search of it. We were disturbed at midnight by a lean hound trying to make a surreptitious meal off the sheep-skin on which Hoare slept. He was driven out, but promptly returned, and commenced gnawing at mine.

We were up at six the next morning, in time to see the sun rise over the grand Riff mountains to the east. The sky was dark and threatening, but the lofty range of the Beni Hassan rose clear above the mists, pre-eminent over the lower peaks, which loomed dimly through a pale golden haze, that filled the intervening valleys. The brilliancy of the African sky always adds some fresh charm to the landscape, and the evening and morning mists cause a never-ending variety of effects of light and shade.

We were now in the province of El Gharb, the most fertile in Marocco, which extends some hundred and fifty miles inland. The road led through the valley of the Wad el Koos, a tract of magnificent soil many miles in width, and almost entirely under cultivation. The primitive plough of the country was used, but, to do the peasants justice, their method of working was superior to that in many parts of the country. Instead of a donkey and a goat, or a woman yoked to a cow, as may be seen elsewhere, there were sturdy teams of bullocks, or sometimes even horses. The soil is of immense depth, and the fine crops of wheat, barley, and beans showed what it might be capable of under a proper system of cultivation. Only one crop is produced a year, but with good irrigation works, it might well bear two. A traveller of wide experience in the country, forty years ago (Colonel Scott), speaks of it as the richest land in the world. Corn is not allowed to be exported from Marocco, so that there is no inducement to develop the resources of the soil, as even now in good seasons its produce is far in excess of the scanty needs of the population. Vegetables might be grown here in sufficient abundance to supply Covent Garden, but the Moors never think of cultivating such things.

We intended to reach the town of Alcazar, or El Kasr el Kebir, that evening, but the muddy state of the roads delayed us a great deal. Two good-sized rivers had to be forded, the El ma Hassen and the Wad Oumaourour. On the banks of the first of these, close upon our left, was the site of the famous battle of El Kantra on the 4th of August, 1578, in which the Portuguese suffered a crushing defeat at the hands of the Moorish usurper Abd el Malek, surnamed the Mameluke. This defeat was the death-blow to the Portuguese dominion in the country, and takes rank among the decisive battles of the African continent. With Don Sebastian and his knights, perished the last hope of the light of Christianity and civilization being spread over this benighted land, which has ever since been under the uninterrupted dominion of the Moorish sultans.

Alcazar is not an interesting place, either for itself or its surroundings. It lies low, on a heavy, clayey soil, and the air is steamy and unwholesome. Its immediate environs consist of hillocks of manure—at least, they did in the rainy weather during our visit; in fact, this valuable commodity is so abundant everywhere in Marocco, that I think it deserves to rank high among the natural resources of the country. It would pay a man with a little capital to start a depôt for manure here, with perhaps branch offices in all the filthy Mellahs, or Jews' quarters, in the various cities of the empire, if only he could get a permit from the sultan for its exportation. That monarch, however, is so tenacious of his rights and property, that I doubt if he would even consent to the removal of the filth encumbering the dwelling-places of his subjects. He has a rooted aversion to most exports. A short time ago he prohibited the exportation of bones, in which a considerable trade used to be done. His reason was that as bones became an article of commerce, it was found that the graves of the Moors were secretly opened, and the last relics of the faithful deported to be used in the manufacture of sugar for the Nazarenes over the seas.

The morning after our arrival we ventured to explore the town. Moorish towns are nowhere celebrated for their cleanliness, but the filth here in and about the place was inconceivable. The traveller has to wade through liquid muck before he can reach the gates. The Soko is in a like condition, and people bargain and sell their goods, up to their ankles in it. We went up the High Street, an alley some ten feet wide, and then turned down a side lane, about three feet across, till we found ourselves in a sort of *cul de sac*, all exit being barred by a vast muck-heap; after this we concluded not to carry our explorations further. In this den lives a population of some 7000 souls, pale, sore-eyed, fever-stricken, amid misery, squalor, and disease. Rohlf's estimate of 30,000 inhabitants is a long way over the mark. The houses frequently have sloping roofs of thatch, which diversify its appearance, but render it less Eastern-looking. The town is governed by a kaid who is subordinate to the Bascha of Larache, and a very considerable trade passes through it on the road to Fez.

Nobody knows the date of the founding of the town, though Leo Africanus asserts that it was built by the great Sultan Almansor in the twelfth century. As, however, writers of a still earlier period allude to it as existing in their time, the great Moorish historian and geographer must have been wrong for once. I shall have frequent occasion to allude to Leo Africanus, so that a short account of that remarkable man may not be out of place here. By birth a Moor of Granada, he fled from that city to Fez at the time of the expulsion of the Moors from Spain in 1492. Twenty-five years later he was captured by Christian pirates and brought captive to Rome, where he ultimately embraced Christianity. Here he published his great work on African travel and history, which remains to this day the most important and trustworthy book upon the country. He was, in fact, a sort of Murray or Bædeker of the period for Northern Africa, and being a man who had travelled much, and possessed of keen powers of observation, he gives an accurate account of nearly every place of importance in Marocco. His work is chiefly valuable as a means of comparing the state of things prevailing in his day with what exists now, and as throwing light upon the extraordinary decadence and degradation which all things Moorish have undergone. Making every allowance for possible exaggeration in his descriptions of the wealth and magnificence of his time, there can be no doubt but that the three centuries which have passed since the publication of his book have, to the Moorish empire, been fruitful in nought save ruin and decay. Years of sloth, fanaticism, and tyranny have done their work, and this vast territory, " the richest and most beautiful country of Africa," but cursed with the most hopeless of governments, is in a state of stagnation, from which, under the present system, there is no prospect of its recovering. Alcazar itself appeared to be no exception to the general rule of decay, as, judging from the very considerable ruins in the neighbourhood, it must once have been a place of importance. Whether any of these ruins date from the time when the Roman town of Oppidum Novum stood on this site, or are of entirely Moorish origin, it is difficult to say.

One day at Alcazar was enough for us. We could not even get any water fit to drink, but had to buy it from a water-carrier, who poured a pale, clayey liquid out of his goat-skin into our vessels, telling us it was the best in the place. We were provided here, as everywhere else throughout our travels, with guards during the night, unfortunate creatures who had to sit outside our tents in the long grass reeking with dew, unprovided with covering of any sort. Having the soldier with us, we were travelling under government protection, and the sheikh, or chief of every place where we encamped, would be held responsible for any loss or harm which might befall us. On the second morning after our arrival, a messenger arrived to say that the Wad el Koos was still unfordable owing to the heavy rains, and that the ordinary route to Wazan was therefore impracticable. Accordingly, we took another road, in an easterly direction through the hilly country to the left of the Djebel Sarsar, a high conical mountain lying to the south-east of Alcazar. Following the course of a streamlet which led through a narrow defile, we emerged at length into a beautiful plain in the valley of the Koos, shut in on all sides by an amphitheatre of rugged hills. Here we pitched our tents, near a tiny, but prosperous village called Sabab, the solid character of whose buildings showed that its inhabitants had no lack of this world's goods. It would have been strange had it been otherwise with such a soil around them. Our arrival excited the greatest curiosity; the villagers, who had probably never seen a Christian encamped in their midst, trooping out to have a look at the strangers. They were all exceedingly civil and hospitable, and so much were we charmed with the place and its inhabitants, that we resolved to spend a day there. Provisions were abundant, and in the evening the usual guards arrived; a big wood-fire was kindled, at which they warmed their stomachs and made themselves as happy as circumstances permitted. I always felt sorry for these unfortunate guards, or "warriors," as we used to call them, from Manuel's Andalusian pronunciation of the word *guardias*. Imagine two foreigners in England on a journey in a purely private capacity, and respectable citizens being compelled to watch outside their dwellings by night under severe penalties! These "warriors" were also a great nuisance to us, keeping us awake with the noise they made, and we would gladly have dispensed with them.

On emerging from the tent next morning, we found the natives ranged round in rows outside, as if to look on at a show. Women and children sat on the ground to the right and left, but the elders and *élite* occupied *fauteuils d'orchestre,* so to speak, or a dunghill right opposite the tent-door. The way in which they all, men, women, and children, scrutinized us at our ablutions was most embarrassing to persons of our retiring disposition. We told Manuel that if this sort of thing went on, we should have to charge for admission by ticket, ladies double price. Next to a breach-loader, perhaps a tooth-brush caused most astonishment, and when I used mine, and began foaming at the mouth, the audience evidently expected me to fall down in a fit. A pair of top-boots of H.'s, which had met with a sad accident by being roasted on the embers of a charcoal fire, likewise created a profound impression. It was rather late in the season for partridges, but as we were in want of them for the pot, we went out shooting, and had an excellent day's sport. We lunched in a shady olive-grove, and of course were not long in attracting a crowd. Our chief beater took my gun, and commenced a long dissertation on its merits for the benefit of the bystanders—how it had two barrels, and killed birds high in the air on the wing, and, stranger still, was broken in two and mended after each shot, and powder and shot put in at the wrong end. These fellows are the keenest sportsmen imaginable. Their eyes glistened every time a bird fell, and they simply yelled with delight at a right and left. They never objected to our walking through their crops, but even left their ploughs and bullocks in the furrow, to follow and beat for us.

It was pleasant to be among these simple, kindly peasant folk, but time was pressing, and we took our leave the following day. Several of the villagers accompanied us to the Koos, and helped us in fording the wide and rapid stream. It is rather ticklish work, crossing these Marocco rivers when they are swollen, but all the beasts got through with safety. We bade our friends farewell, Manuel graciously saying that we were well pleased with our reception, and would report thereof favourably to their lord and master the Sultan. These people all thought we were "bashadors," or persons of importance, going on affairs of state to the court, but we told Manuel if he humbugged them in this way, we should drop him on the road. At four o'clock we came in sight of Wazan, the sacred city, the "Mecca of Marocco," picturesquely embosomed in dense groves of olives and evergreens on the side of a hill. Half a mile outside the town we passed what still remains of Old Wazan, now little more than a fine collection of ruins, but with a few inhabited houses, a big mosque, and some Marabouts', or saints' tombs. The thatch and tile roofs we had noticed at Alcazar were still more numerous here, flat-topped houses being quite the exception.

It was market-day, and as we rode through the

Soko we were surrounded by crowds of gaping natives, who hardly seemed to know what to make of us. One little nigger boy, who had never seen a Christian before, ran off with shrieks to tell his mother. Wazan is seldom visited by Europeans,[1] as, being a holy city, it is considered by many to be inaccessible, and it is out of the main road to Fez. The tribes round about are also turbulent and fanatical, and travelling is unsafe there at some seasons. The streets of the town are narrow, and tremendously steep, and it was no light work riding up over the slippery stones till we stopped in a small, open space close to the great mosque of the city, the Djemma Moulai Abdallah Shereef built by the founder of Wazan, whose remains rest within.

Wazan, or Dar el Demena (the House of Confidence), is the place whence the Great Shereef, the chief spiritual potentate of Marocco and Pope of Western Islam, derives his title. I shall give an account of him presently. His son represents him in Wazan, the father having adopted a European mode of life at Tangier, to the increase of his personal comfort, no doubt, but greatly in derogation of his spiritual authority. To the Shereef's son, therefore, we despatched our soldier to acquaint him of our arrival. Moors are never in a hurry, and we had to wait nearly an hour in a very dirty

[1] The first to visit it was Rohlfs, in 1861, after which it remained nearly twenty years unprofaned by Christian feet, till Mr. Watson, and later ourselves, arrived there.

street before Al-kaid returned, giving us lots of time to admire the view. Wazan is certainly a most beautiful place. Behind us the hill rose to a considerable height, its sides shrouded in dusky olive-woods. To the east the rugged Riff mountains rose range after range, with the snowy crest of the Beni Hassan in the centre. All around are rich plains and lovely gardens, vineyards, and well-watered orange-groves. The environs are studded with the white cupolas of marabouts' tombs, as might be expected in a holy city like Wazan, where "saints are many—" I will not finish the quotation and say, "and where sins are few," for the town is notorious for the riotous living and debauchery of its inhabitants.

At last the soldier returned to say the Shereef (junior) was at home, and would be glad to receive us, so we descended the hill to one of his father's many mansions outside the town. We had no letters of introduction to him, but nothing could have been greater than his kindness and hospitality. He even placed the house at our disposal, and sent us presents of provisions—fowls, candles, eggs, tea, sugar, and other luxuries. The house, which was built on the regular Eastern pattern, as seen in the Alhambra, was in an unfinished state. The room we selected to sleep in was not exactly richly furnished, but with the addition of a few tables and chairs, with perhaps a ceiling and a floor, and a door or window or two, it might have had the makings of a very fine apartment. Immediately outside was a large bath, so that one could tumble out of bed and have a plunge—only that there was no water in it. Beyond were beautiful flower-gardens and acres and acres of orange-groves, where we could wander at will. The thing was amusing to us from its novelty, but I must confess to preferring the cosy, if humble, seclusion of our tent to the somewhat bald magnificence of the Shereef's mansion.

The Shereef of Wazan, as already mentioned, is in a sense the head of the Mohammedan Church in Marocco. As the most direct descendant of the Prophet and of Moulai Idrees, the famous founder of Fez, his influence among the semi-independent tribes is greater than that of the sultan itself, and extends far beyond the borders of Marocco. His name is held in reverence by millions of African Mohammedans, from Tripoli to Tunis in the east to the dusky hordes of fanatics in the Sahara and Timbuctoo. In the Riff, and the districts about the Algerian frontier, his authority is immense, and the wild tribesmen from the interior bring him frequent presents, to secure his favour and blessing. The town is always crowded with pilgrims anxious to touch the hem of his garment, or to obtain some memento of their visit, which will cure their ailments or bring good luck. These favours are not bestowed gratis, and any trifling relic, such as a piece of his old *jelab*, will fetch money. The goodwill of a large saint's business, such as the Shereef's, must be immensely valuable. According to Rohlfs, his near relations, who are also Shereefs (i.e. descendants of Mohammed), are sent forth to proclaim his greatness abroad, and he has agents everywhere, who collect Peter's pence for him once a year. Besides these indirect sources of income, he is possessed of immense property in mines, lands, houses, &c. His marriage with an Englishwoman is too well known to need further mention. The Charifa is likewise credited with miraculous powers of healing, and she does much good by vaccinating and physicking the poor, and making them live in a more decent fashion. The Shereef is, of course, very much married elsewhere; in fact, his perseverance at matrimony is quite remarkable. He lives almost entirely at Tangier in European fashion, which, together with his Christian marriage, has detracted much from his authority. He eats at table like a European, and, in truth, it must be added, drinks like one, too. He is, however, such a very holy man that, according to the Moors, he cannot sin, i.e. his sanctity will turn his very trespasses to merits. For instance, wine is forbidden to Moslems, but His Holiness is addicted to champagne. The Arabs, therefore, say that the liquor turns to milk directly it enters his sanctified stomach. Should he get exceedingly drunk (such a thing has been known to occur), it is a trance. The way in which these saints of the East manage to combine business with pleasure, and the maintenance of religious authority and a reputation for sanctity with the most mundane pursuits, is really astonishing; punctual and regular performance of the ritual is all that is required.

A short while ago all Marocco was thunderstruck at a strange piece of intelligence. Like most Eastern saints, the Shereef was known to be quite ready to place his sanctity at the disposal of any one who made him a good bid for its use, but no one ever dreamed of his denationalizing himself and becoming a citizen of the republic of France! Such, however, is the case, and now his whole influence will be at the beck and call of our aggressive neighbours. Before, his authority was often of great service to the sultan in suppressing the revolts of turbulent semi-independent tribes. Now the French can use it in the opposite direction, as a means of fomenting discord and of paving the way for their own future interference.

No better indication of the degradation and approaching collapse of Moorish power can be found than the fact that this great prince and priest of the faithful, the adored of all pious Moslems, has actually stooped to seeking the protection and citizenship of the infidel. Finding, no doubt, his influence decreasing, and that the saint business is less remunerative than in former days, he has cast in his lot with that power to which the march of events seems to point as the arbiter of the future destinies of Marocco. Self-interest is a pretty sure guide, and the action of the Shereef is an index of the course Moorish affairs are taking, and bids us be on our guard.

The son of the Shereef, our entertainer, has followed his father's example, and an account of some remarkable events in connection with this transaction appeared in a letter to the *Standard* of June 3rd, 1884. I was grieved, but not particularly surprised, to read there that our urbane friend had been guilty of flogging a man in a horrible manner, and pouring boiling water upon his wounds till he died. It is always the way in this country. Your courteous host, who has received you with smiles and lavish hospitality, and appears a model of kindness and amiability, may have just come from torturing some one in a fiendish manner, but you will never be able to guess it. Brutality in Marocco has become too much a matter of habit to upset any Moor's suavity of demeanour. Like the Turk, "he is such a gentleman," and his "form" is always of the best, whatever may be thought of his moral qualities.

The Shereef himself is a stout, powerfully-built mulatto, over fifty years of age, with a face full of resolution and power, and a carriage and mien worthy of so exalted a personage. I made his acquaintance at a boar-hunt, where I remember that, a pig happening to pass between us, he did me the honour of covering me with his rifle. This alarmed me considerably, as the Moors are all the most careless people in the world with fire-arms, and I did not want an express bullet in the leg even from a lineal descendant of the Prophet. The negro blood which runs in his veins is far from being considered a disgrace in Marocco. The Imperial family are themselves mulattos, and a town Moor would consider himself much more degraded by a union with a countrywoman than with a negress.

Of the actual town of Wazan, I have little more to say. It has no particular claims to antiquity; in fact, two hundred years ago it was little more than a collection of huts, when Moulai Abdallah Shereef, a descendant of Moulai Idrees, and the founder of the present house of Wazan, improved and beautified it. Leo Africanus makes no mention of it, which may be taken as proof positive that it was a place of no importance in his time. Rohlfs puts the population at 10,000, but it fluctuates greatly with the streams of pilgrims to the shrine of the Shereef.

The Mellah, or Ghetto, is not very large, though the Jews are less bullied here than in most cities. They are, of course, confined to their own quarter after sundown, and have to wear a distinctive dress and go about bare-footed, but otherwise they have a fairly good time, and struck us as presenting a less miserable and dejected appearance than elsewhere.

Of the Jews and their treatment in Marocco, I shall have more to say hereafter.

CHAPTER III.

The Bascha objects to our company—His ultimate fate—Courteous kaid—Wad Wergha—Native distress—Ouber Mohammed—*Mona*—Our qualms at accepting it—*Matamors*—Wad Seboo—Arab school—Approach to Fez—Magnificent view—Entry into Fez—First impressions of the city—The Bascha gives us a house—Official dislike of strangers—Its cause.

BEFORE setting forth on our journey to the capital, we sent Manuel and the soldier to express our thanks to the Shereef for his kindness. We always left to Manuel the composition of the fine speeches which are considered necessary on these occasions. These fellows like it laid on with a trowel, and we felt our best compliments would taste thin and watery to their palates, whereas Manuel managed it excellently. The Shereef sent back word that he was sorry we had to leave so soon, as he had hoped we would join him in some coursing and jackal-hunts he was organizing, but said he would send on a courier to a neighbouring village to tell them to be in readiness to receive us. This done, we sallied forth by the upper gate of the town, and wound round the eastern shoulder of the hill by a very bad road. Big, loose blocks of stone lay concealed in deep, liquid mud, and gave great trouble to our beasts. Every turn of the road disclosed some fresh view over the plains and distant mountain ranges. Arriving at the village named by the Shereef's son, we found an encampment of Moors already on the spot. They were the tents of the Bascha of Wazan, who, on our proposing to encamp, gave us to understand he did not want his sanctified presence contaminated by Christian dogs. This rebuff astonished us rather after the Shereef's recommendation, but there had long been ill blood between the two persons in authority. The Bascha has since got involved in the French troubles, and, I believe, is now in durance vile for his hostility to the "Frenchified Shereef." It is always gratifying to one's vanity when travelling in these countries to know that the poorest and meanest native regards you as so much dirt, as "insects," in fact, to quote one of the numerous polite epithets applied to us from time to time. We were, of course, cursed heartily from morn to eve throughout our journey, while the perpetual "burning" of our poor grandparents was enough to make them turn in their graves.

Not choosing to stay and argue the point, we moved on to another village, where a very different reception awaited us. The sheikh of the place, hearing we had been guests of the Shereef, said we were as his brothers, and must consider his house as our own. As he spoke thus, he touched his head with his hands, which, with the Moors, signifies that the speaker takes all your faults on his head (rather a heavy load sometimes in these parts), and is the highest mark of respect and esteem. The country Moors are far kindlier-natured than the townsmen, and seem to forget their fanaticism in their desire to be hospitable. In the evening a deputation of villagers arrived with "mona," consisting of barley, bread, chickens, milk, and butter. We did not like taking the things, as we had told Correa it was our wish to pay our way through the country, and we feared the people could ill afford them, but it was impossible to refuse to accept their presents, and even the ten "warriors" who guarded our tents declined any reward. We were therefore much disgusted with our servants, the greedy old kaid in particular, on finding that after each had eaten enough for three hungry Christians, they had had the effrontery to send out and ask for more.

We left our cards with the sheikh at his special request, and took down his own name, which I here transcribe in full, to the best of my ability : Mohammed Ben Absalam Men la Ouli. The native names are very hard to catch. They have so many double-barrelled "h's" and unpronounceable gutturals that it is next to impossible to hit the words off exactly. The language of Marocco is a harsh guttural dialect of Arabic, called Maghrebbin. Its chief peculiarity, besides its excessive harshness, is the way in which the words are clipped, and all the vowels omitted, causing them to speak with a sort of sneezing sound. Some of the gutturals are most extraordinary, and I have heard it said that nobody can ever hope to pronounce them aright who has not been brought up within hearing of the grunting of camels, which they resemble more closely than any other sound. I myself spent four months in learning the "gh," and though several times nearly choking, and catching two or three sore throats in the attempt, I never got it properly. I have put down the names of the villages on our route to the best of my ability on my map, but for the above-mentioned reasons, among others, I fear this slight contribution to the geography of Marocco will not be of great value. Of many of the names mentioned in the existing maps no native had ever heard, and a thoroughly reliable map of Marocco has yet to be made. Gerhard Rohlfs is the only traveller I have heard of who traversed our route from Wazan to Fez, but his description is meagre, and he gives no map.

A big river, the Wad Wergha, had to be forded, and the current, flowing like a mill-stream and seventy yards wide, so alarmed Manuel that he refused to take us across, whereupon the soldier with a lordly air said *he* would be responsible for our safety, and walking his horse into the water, called upon the rest to follow. Some natives waded in with us, and urging on the animals with blows and appalling yells, got them all safely across, though the water reached up to our saddle-flaps in the middle. If any of them had stumbled, it would have been all over with him, as he would have been carried off his legs before he could recover. In rainy seasons travellers are sometimes hemmed in between two rivers for days or even weeks, before they become passable. The inhabitants upon the further bank were still suffering from the famine which had been prevailing in the country for some years. The peasantry of Marocco live in a hand-to-mouth fashion at the best of times, and most years theirs is a terrible existence. Large stores of corn are never laid up, as they would be sure to be robbed of it, and they are therefore entirely dependent upon their crops, which are periodically ruined by drought, hailstones, or insect plagues. At this time, five successive bad seasons had exhausted their slender resources, and left a large proportion of the people in a state of utter destitution. Yet the distress in the fertile Gharb province was as nothing compared to what we afterwards saw in the southern districts. Here many of them were living on the roots and grasses of the field, which we saw them digging up, and washing in the river for their evening meal. There is a certain root called Ayerna which, though poisonous when eaten raw, after boiling ten or twelve hours, becomes edible. When thus boiled, it is spread out to dry thoroughly in the sun, then ground in a mill, and a kind of bitter bread made out of the flour. Even then it is highly injurious to the health, and its effects were plainly seen in the pale yellow faces and emaciated bodies of the people. This, with the roots of the palmetto, forms their sole means of subsistence. We encamped at a *duar* or tent village, peculiar to the Arabs, which was governed by a *mokaddem*, or sheikh of a village which contains a Marabout's tomb, an official of a priestly nature. No barley could be got for our horses for love or money, and the *mokaddem* apologized (which was quite unnecessary) for the poor reception he had given us, saying that the whole village was starving, and they had nothing to spare.

If prophecies were to be believed, we were travelling at a most momentous period in the annals of Islām. The year 1300 of the Hijra or Mohammedan era, A.D. 1883, was expected to be one of wars and tumults, and some learned doctors had foretold the end of the world. According to an ancient tradition of the Sunni, or orthodox, the Mahdi ("the Directed"), was to appear with 360 celestial spirits, and to expel the infidel and purify Islām. By the Mahdi I mean the real Messiah, not one of the seven preliminary prophets such as is now making such a stir in Egypt. In Marocco the Mahdi is called "Mool Sāā" (the Coming Man). Here, too, occasional false prophets spring up, asserting themselves to be the true Mahdi, and that no others are genuine, but after attaining more or less success they usually end by having their heads cut off, or being cast into one of the sultan's dungeons. In the present instance the Moorish Dr. Cummings was sadly out, as, owing to the famine, the country was particularly quiet, and we were able to travel in places which in other years are unsafe. Manuel always compared the Moors to beasts which, when underfed, are tame and poor-spirited, but when full of beans, wax wanton and kick. This is the state their beneficent rulers like to keep them in, as then they give less trouble. In civilized countries, on the contrary, riots accompany distress rather than prosperity.

The next day, three and a half hours' march took us to a large village, whose name I find noted in my diary as Ouber Mohammed Ben Shirghi. It was in the midst of a flourishing *kabyla*, where dwelt a kaid who commanded an extensive district. He had one brother, Bascha of Larache, and another, Governor of New Fez, whose acquaintance we afterwards made. On our arrival the great man was occupied (or asleep, more likely), so he sent a deputy to "do the civil" in his stead. This individual saluted us in a courteous but peculiar fashion, seizing the thumb of our right hands with his own, and then kissing his fingers, and pressing his hand to his heart, which last is the customary form of salutation amongst the Moors. Soon after, his superior arrived in person, a stout, dark man, wearing that heavy vacant sensual expression so common amongst his race.

"Mahhaba bic" (you are welcome), "salam alikoom" (peace be with you), were his first words; and other polite speeches, expressive of his extreme gratification at seeing us, followed. A Moor is nothing if not courteous, and whatever his real feelings may be, he will veil them in the softest of words. If he means to cut your throat, he will do it "most politely, most politely," or administer a cup of poison with the profoundest urbanity. The usual presents arrived—piles of *kooskoossoo*, the national dish made of granulated flour and fragments of chopped meat; curious stews served in enormous wicker covers like beehives, with provender for the beasts. Our qualms of conscience at taking these presents, and various suggestions made by Hoare for giving payment in some roundabout way, were a source of great amusement to Manuel, who intimated that if we had lived in the country as long as he had, we should have lost all such little weaknesses long ago. We knew, however, that it was not the kaid who paid for the things, and having regard to the prevailing scarcity in the country, the idea that we were in the smallest degree taking the bread out of the mouths of the poor was not a pleasant one. It would have been pleasanter to believe that the generosity of our entertainers always arose, as no doubt it did sometimes, from that spirit of hospitality which is a traditional characteristic of the Arab race. More often, it was owing to a mistaken notion of our importance, and a desire that we might speak well of our hosts at head-quarters; for if we had said we were travelling for mere pleasure, nobody would have believed us. Our servants, the soldier in particular, secretly encouraged the belief that we were personages of distinction, in order to get food out of the people, while the kaids make use of the advent of travellers such as ourselves for similar purposes, and levy imposts on the plea of being compelled to supply "mona." As it was, we could do nothing. If we had paid, which would have been contrary to all etiquette, the kaid would have simply pocketed the money, and the poor people would have been none the better off.

After paying our respects to our entertainer, the next morning we made our way to the banks of the river Seboo. The country everywhere around was undulating and well cultivated. Here and there we noticed curious holes in the ground, about two feet across the top, ten or twelve feet deep, and about the same width at the bottom. These were the native "matamors," used for storing and concealing corn, which if placed in ordinary granaries would be liable to be stolen—officially or otherwise. Of course the corn rots, and the poor people starve, and so they will continue to do while the present state of things continues. People unacquainted with Marocco draw most unfounded conclusions, from the frequent famines there, that the country is worth nothing, whereas what I have written above shows the real reason of the distress. I repeat, Marocco could grow enough corn for her own population and half England besides. These "matamors" are also of convenience as extemporized prisons, where malefactors or persons who have otherwise offended their rulers may be immured, to rot along with the corn.

The Wad Seboo (the Subur of ancient geographers) is the largest river in Marocco, and we were rather uncertain as to our ability to pass it.

Fortunately, however, the stream had changed its bed recently, so that we could take it at a place where the water was divided into three wide but shallow channels, and it gave far less trouble than either the Wergha or Koos. On the south side we entered on a wilder and hillier country, inhabited apparently by a more fanatical population. They scowled at us as we passed, and even refused to return our servant's salutation of *Salam alikum*, because in the employ of Kaffirs or unbelievers. We were now on the outskirts of the territory of the lawless robber tribes that inhabit the mountains in the neighbourhood of Mequinez and Zaraoun, which doubtless accounted for the more wretched appearance of the numerous *duars* or tent-villages which we passed. As it was thought advisable by Manuel to reach Fez early in the day, in order that our arrival might create the greater stir, we halted at a *kabyla* some ten miles distant from the town, selected, like the last, for its more prosperous condition. We took a great fancy to the kaid, who, besides being very civil, possessed an honest, kindly face. He was a tall, venerable figure, and with his rosary and long russet-brown *jellabia*, or burnoos, looked for all the world like some old Franciscan friar. He was very devout, and we watched him at his prayers, which he performed with great regularity in front of his house, salaaming to the east, and kissing the earth, and telling his beads. Each of these beads corresponds to the name of some holy man of the sect of Malek, which prevails in Barbary, and as he passed each bead along his hand, he murmured the saint's name. The Mohammedan rosary usually has ninety-nine beads to remind them of the ninety-nine attributes of God, and the idea of the rosary in the Catholic Church is said to have been borrowed from the Spanish Moors. Prayer in the East consists entirely of certain formal acts and expressions, and they like to pray in public and upon the housetops, figuratively speaking. Our wicked old soldier was perpetually down on his marrow-bones when a sufficient audience was around, and took care to do his alms that he might be seen of men—that is, he would always give a beggar a *mosouna* (one-tenth of a penny) if in the streets of Fez, but never on the road. Mohammed, on the contrary, the best and smartest of our retinue, was never seen at his devotions.

The kaid gave us of all at his disposal, but the barley had to be fetched from a distance, and he actually wanted to pay a part of its price. He seemed to fear we should go away thinking he had been wanting in hospitality. I could not bring myself to believe that that good old man had ever been guilty of robbing the poor. Perhaps it was well we did not know more about him, but in any case it is pleasant to entertain illusions occasionally.

Tuesday, Feb. 20th.—Woke at 5.30 a.m. by a curious yelping sound as of puppies in a kennel. Found it proceeded from a sort of Arab Board School belonging to the village, saying their lessons.

The education is what we should call strictly de-nominational, consisting entirely of learning passages from the Koran by heart, and repeating them in chorus. The master stands over the boys with a thick stick, and if a pupil makes a mistake, he gets a sharp reminder. As a rule, only Moors of the better class send their children to school, and the mass of the people can neither read nor write. Sometimes elementary (very elementary) arithmetic and geography are taught, but the *tholba* (schoolmasters) are not over-learned themselves, and I am not aware that there has been any outcry against over-pressure, or a too high standard in Marocco. As to geography, one foreign country is pretty much the some as another to a Moor. He knows a few in Europe by name, but without the slightest idea of their relative size or importance; all he is sure of is, that his own is the best, biggest, and most powerful in the world. The schoolmasters receive a small stipend in money or in kind from each of their pupils, who also bring him occasional presents in addition. There seems to be no lack of this education, such as it is, in the country, as nearly every village has a *thaleb* who keeps a school.

A piercing wind driving straight from the snow-mountains to the south-east, made getting up anything but a pleasant operation. We left the village early (by the way, I cannot give its name, as the natives did not know it themselves!), passing among some round-topped hills, partly covered with grass, partly under cultivation. We met a troop of famine-stricken beings shifting their abodes in search of subsistence elsewhere. They looked like so many bundles of rags as they toiled wearily by, with their houses on their backs—a few sticks and bits of matting—one more sign of the poverty and misery everywhere visible in this unhappy country. Several parties of Jews also passed, all wearing the same abject downcast look peculiar to their co-religionists everywhere in Marocco. They all saluted us cordially, and the rare sight of Europeans seemed quite to brighten up these persecuted sons of Israel. A big hill, one of the spurs of the Zaraoun Range, lay in front of us, but a good hour's pull against the collar took us to the top, where a glorious view burst upon us. Fez lay, as it were, at our feet, but almost hidden by an intervening crest. Westwards a vast plain stretched in one unbroken expanse to where the furthest horizon melted away in a purple haze. To the south-east the view was intercepted by the range of Sidi Hassen, culminating in a lofty peak shrouded in a mantle of glittering snow. Southwards a low range of hills bounded the prospect, but now and again, when the atmosphere became particularly clear, the still higher snows of the great Atlas Chain could be dimly discerned. Immediately on our left rose the abrupt crags of the Jebel Ssala, its lower slopes being clothed with olives and other evergreens, while round its base lie vineyards and plantations of orange, fig, pomegranate, and other trees. Descending the hill we passed through numerous vineyards, with labourers hard at work upon them. More vinegar than wine is made from the grapes, but I daresay there is no great difference between those two products. At the same time the soil of Marocco is in parts singularly adapted for vines, being light and friable, and under proper cultivation the manufacture of wine might add much to the resources of the country. Lower down we entered some large and dense groves of olives, wondering the while when we should see Fez. Suddenly turning a corner, we found ourselves within a few hundred yards of the massive walls and battlements which encompass the city, with square turrets at regular intervals, and loftier towers at the angles and salient points. A few minutes afterwards we entered the gate, on the 21st of February, twelve days after our departure from Tangier. The distance by the direct road is about 160 miles, but by our more roundabout way, we made it, roughly speaking, 185 miles, calculating by the pace of the mules.

Our first impressions of the capital were those of surprise at its size and the comparative grandeur of its buildings, which far exceeded our expectations. We had expected to find a repetition, on a larger scale, of the miserable places we had elsewhere seen, whereas Fez is a really fine town, judged by any standard. Inside the gates we rode into a large open space, with a wall on its right some sixty or seventy feet in height, and containing several fine specimens of the Moorish horse-shoe arch. This wall forms part of an immense palace commenced by the Sultan Moulai Yezeed,[1] but never finished. The material used here, as in most Moorish buildings, is *tabia*, a kind of mud concrete, stone being only employed for the arches and to face the angles and corners. From here we passed through several fine gates, and under lofty, crumbling archways, the half-ruined relics of bygone magnificence, and halted in a courtyard. Mr. Horace White, H.B.M.'s consul at Tangier, had kindly furnished us with a letter of introduction to the Bascha of New Fez, so the soldier was despatched to deliver it. The great point to ascertain was what quarters he was going to put us into, and we waited with some anxiety for the answer. Meanwhile we were not long in attracting a crowd, who scrutinized us closely, some of them asking as to our nationality, whether we were from Baris (Paris) or Lundres (London). Presently back came the soldier, to say that his Highness suggested that the filthy Mellah or Jews' quarter should be our dwelling-place, and that we might have a house

---

[1] This Moulai Yezeed was no doubt the same sanguinary lunatic who was the son of Sidi Mohammed's red-haired Irish sultana. He seems to have inherited from his mother a large fund of peculiarly Hibernian humour, which expressed itself in outrages of the most atrocious kind on his subjects. Some he burned alive, or butchered in cold blood: when in want of a little diversion, he would decapitate a couple of his domestics and play at bowls with their heads. Another very Irish trait in this light-hearted monarch was his reckless and impulsive generosity. He would sometimes feast all the poor of a district —at the expense of some rich governor of a province. What was most un-Irish in him was his firm friendship for the English. (See Leared's ".Marocco.")

there. We both declared, however, that we would be hanged if we would go there, and that we should vastly prefer any respectable pig-sty outside the walls, if such a thing were to be found in the country. The soldier was sent back to represent this to the Bascha, and eventually a tolerable house with a garden was found for us, and several soldiers arrived to escort us thither.

Everything in Marocco is strange, but few things more so than the way in which two private travellers like ourselves can, in a measure, dictate to the governor of the biggest town in the empire what quarters they would like to sleep in—as if they had any right to a house at all! Such, however, is the dread of European nations which bitter experience has instilled into the Moor that, sooner than run the slightest risk of offending any of their representatives, he will do pretty much what is asked of him. The ungracious way in which the hospitality is tendered in such cases proves it to arise solely from fear, and not, as some people imagine, out of goodwill towards the stranger.

Our abode was built after the usual Eastern pattern, only rather out of repair, with battlemented walls and towers at the corners. In its palmiest days it was probably, like the rest of such buildings, a model of uncomfortable magnificence, according to European notions. The garden was not extensive, but we found it useful—both as a promenade and as a drying-ground for our clothes. We were given choice of several rooms—three on the ground-floor, damp and evil-smelling; two others in the towers were a little better. We chose one, a fairly roomy apartment, but with bare, white-washed walls, and a rather handsome tesselated floor, which made it exceedingly cold and damp. The light came in (so did the wind) through two square windows without any glass, and barred strongly across, to prevent fractious ladies of the harem from getting out, and perhaps effecting their escape over the roof. Below ran a small stream, the Wad el Fas, on whose opposite bank were the ruins of the palace mentioned above, and a mill which, by means of a large wheel driven by the stream, raised the water which supplied the house. These ingenious water-wheels seem to have existed in Leo Africanus's time, who says, "they were inuented by a Spaniard: and in them there is maruellous cunninge workmanship: for to the conueiance of so huge a quantitie of water each wheele is turned about but fower-and-twentie times onely in a day and a night." The sanitary arrangements were defective, but I was much surprised to see here an attempt at a regular system of drainage, by means of underground ducts furnished with a perpetual supply of water. Bad drainage, however, is worse than none at all, and the sewage of New Fez is all discharged into the river which forms the drinking water for the inhabitants of Old Fez below. Fez is the likeliest place imaginable in which to catch typhoid fever, and travellers should insist upon their drinking water being brought on mule-back from fountains well beyond the risk of contamination by sewage. On the whole, I prefer the primitive system obtaining elsewhere in Marocco, where drains are dispensed with altogether.

We had a large guard of "warriors," appointed by the Bascha to look after us, who commenced operations by removing every stick of furniture (there was not much to start with) out of the place. The authorities were evidently determined: first, that we should steal nothing of theirs; secondly, and chiefly, that no article of ours should be lost, which might furnish us with a claim against the governor. It appeared that some Spaniards, our predecessors here, had lost, or said they had lost (which in this country comes to pretty much the same thing), some trifling articles, and, after the fashion prevailing out here, had sent in a modest demand for some hundreds of dollars, payment of which was ultimately enforced. The reiterated declaration that we were Englishmen, and not Spaniards, had a partially reassuring effect, as we are unquestionably the most popular nation in Marocco. Dr. Rohlfs (a German) asserts that the Moors hate the Spaniards, fear the French, but love the English— a remark which came from the grand vizier himself. They have good reason for this liking, for they are better treated by our countrymen; and Sir John Hay, in particular, will not permit himself to lend the aid of his authority to casual promoters of indefinite claims. It could be wished that as much might be said of all other European functionaries—but of this, more hereafter; at present I must confine myself to a description of the city and its surroundings.

CHAPTER IV.

History of Fez—Description of the town—Guilds of craftsmen —Moorish shopmen—Moorish lunacy laws—Prisons—Justice and punishments—Tortures—Mosques—Old library— Decay of learning—The Kessaria—Jews in Fez—Native fanaticism—Moorish bread—Our last evening in Fez.

Fez, the chief capital of the Sultan's dominions— regarding Marocco City as the second—and the most important town of all Barbary, was founded somewhere about 800 A.D. Authorities differ as to the exact date, but Leo gives it as A.H. 185, which year of the Hijra corresponds with the above-mentioned period of the Christian era. Its founder was Idrees, a son of the celebrated saint, Moulai Idrees, who was a kinsman of Haraoun-al-Raschid and great-grandson of Mohammed. It is a remarkable fact that this Idrees, despite his good ecclesiastical connections, was a heretic against the Mohammedan faith. The Moors, with some reason, regard Fez as a sort of earthly Paradise, and various writers, both Christian and Mohammedan, have hymned its rapturous beauties and magnificence. The few descriptions of it to be found in English works do not give a clear account of its situation or appearance, which, indeed, are not easy to describe. Rohlfs says it is surrounded by mountains on every side except the south; another writer (Captain Colville), that hills are on every side but the west; whereas my recollection rather is that it is environed by *plains* on nearly every side but the north. It is built on the river of the same name, which falls into the Seboo some five miles lower down. Its situation is a most magnificent one. The heights of the Jebel Ssala shelter it completely from the north; to the south and west is a wide expanse of plain extending to the Zaraoun mountains in the latter direction, and in the former towards the Atlas. The soil is very rich, and the approaches to the town lead through beautiful gardens and groves of olives and oranges. The town itself lies chiefly in a slight depression, but upon undulating ground, part of it being built upon the steep sides of the ravine of the Wad el Fas.

The place consists of two distinct towns, Fas el Bāli (Old Fez) and Fez Jedeed (New Fez), each of which is governed by a separate kaid or mayor. By the way, the word "bascha," which, in deference to established custom, I have often used, is entirely of foreign importation—almost every person of authority, whether civil or military, being called kaid indiscriminately. Old Fez is much the larger, and may be described as The City or commercial part, which, as in London, lies to the East. New Fez, where we were located, is the West End, and contains the Sultan's palace and seraglio, the Mellah (Ghetto), and some private residences. The reader will have gathered from my previous description that there was nothing particularly Belgravian about the mansion we occupied; in fact, the finest houses and largest gardens are to be found in Old Fez. New Fez is of later date than the rest of the town, having been built by Yakoob, the first king of the Marin dynasty, to form the chief seat of the court of Marocco. In Leo's time few gentlemen not attendant on the court dwelt here, the residue being "base and mechanicall people;" and he tells us that the courtiers were so hated and despised that no people of good standing would intermarry with them. The Moors, with all their superstitious reverence for their rulers, are a strangely republican people.

The population of the whole place is probably between 100,000 and 150,000 souls, but there are no reliable means of arriving at the exact number. When the Sultan is there (he spends one-half of his time in Marocco), the numbers are swelled by his army and followers, and the increased trade, to about 50,000 more. Jackson's estimate of 380,000, with all due deference to so eminent an authority, must be well over the mark.

The first day after our arrival we naturally spent in exploring the place. Leaving New Fez we passed into an open space that divides the two towns, inclosed, however, by walls of tabia. On our left we were pointed out the imperial barracks, where his Shereefian Majesty's troops are quartered when he is here. The reader must not conjure up visions of the Horse Guards or Knightsbridge.

The barracks consisted of miserable sheds and holes in the crumbling mud walls encircling the town, such as in England would be considered fit habitations for cattle or pigs, and bad ones as such. A few heaps of dust and muck, bones and putrefying carcasses; some miserable beggars covered with sores and rags, loudly demanding backsheesh in the name of Moulai Idrees; a half-naked maniac who cursed us vehemently; an odd donkey or two cropping what scraps of herbage they could find, completed a very sorry picture. Entering Old Fez by a large gate, we soon found ourselves in a big street some fifteen or twenty feet wide, but so blocked with foot passengers and idlers, camels, mules, donkeys, and horses, that it was difficult to make one's way through. This street, the principal thoroughfare of the town, traverses its whole length. The side-streets are, of course, much narrower, and paved as only streets in a Moorish town can be paved, and often choked with refuse. However, compared with other towns, some of the streets are tolerably clean and well-kept, though the dust in hot weather, and the mud in wet, both form serious drawbacks. They are generally covered in as a protection from the scorching rays of the summer sun; but in keeping out the heat, they exclude the air also, and a strange blend of multifarious smells of spices and filth, leather, cooking-shops, human bodies, and many other things, assails one's nostrils. One result of this, alluded to by various travellers, is the extraordinary pallor of many of the inhabitants, whose skins are as white as an English artisan's. All the houses seem in a fearfully rickety condition, and as nobody takes the trouble to repair them, they often come down on people's heads. No one is astonished or put out by such occurrences, and the owners of such houses are not indicted for endangering the public safety. "Mektoob" (it is written) is the remark of the Moorish fatalist when a palpably ruinous wall tumbles down and crushes a passer-by. Some good specimens of Moorish architecture are still visible in various "prout-bits" over the town, and one or two gateways and fountains are decidedly fine. The worst of it is that the windows of the houses all look into the courtyard inside, and the decoration being reserved almost entirely for the interior, the prospect from the streets is not improved.

The different quarters of the town are set apart for separate guilds, as in Old London; one street being occupied by tailors, another by smiths, and the bakers, butchers, drapers, &c., in like manner. One alley we passed down was the Street of Old Shoes, and was inhabited entirely by the Worshipful Company of the Menders of Old Shoes. No new shoes were made here, but the botchers and menders had it to themselves. The shops consist of small stalls with folding doors, fastened by lock and key when the owner is away. The latter sits cross-legged, or more often lies at full length on a couch. You look in. Does he rise and bow, or bustle about, showing you the attractions of his shop? Not a bit of it; he remains in just the same position, looking very much as if he thought you a great bore. If you express a decided wish to buy something, he may condescend to rise lazily and fetch it, but he would vastly prefer you should reach it down yourself. When you pay him he slowly pockets the money, and resumes his seat with a sigh; no obsequious smiling and washing of hands, or asking, "What's the next article?" On the contrary, he looks rather pleased when you have gone and leave him in peace to continue his nap.

The Moorish shopman is typical of the rest of the country. Everything and everybody wants shaking and waking up. Half the nation has nothing to do, and does it admirably. The whole place is in one big sleep, from which, as things are now, it will never wake till the crack of doom. Self-interest itself, that great quickener of energy, cannot rouse these torpid creatures, unless the advantages to be derived from the action proposed be of the most immediate and palpable kind. Future or prospective benefits are far beyond a Moor's mental ken, and if you suggest that such and such results will follow from a certain course of action, he will only think you a bore for your pains. "Ift shallah" (God will show), he will say, with his peculiar shrug, and things will remain as they are. In his pig-headed belief in the superiority of himself and his country to everything else, he will neither permit nor countenance any improvement from abroad.

I must admit, however, that though the above applies to Fez and its inhabitants, it does so in a less degree than any other town in Marocco. Trade here, at times, really is brisk; indeed, there is a comparative life and activity about some parts of Fez that is positively refreshing after the dead-alive air that prevails in other places. The Fez merchant is, as a rule, a sensible, business-like person. He does not concern himself much about sectarian differences, and as long as his visitor brings a well-filled purse, he is welcome, be his religion or nationality what it may. The trade of the place is considerable. From the south, caravans from Tafilet and the desert are continually arriving with dates, spices, and other produce. European imports are chiefly guns and other weapons, powder, tea, sugar, drugs, cotton stuffs, and cloths. We noticed bales of Manchester goods on sale, thoughtfully marked with the figures 1300, the year of the Mohammedan era, a truly gratifying mark of regard on the part of the British merchant for the religion of his customers, and doubtless intended as a set-off against the inferior quality of the article. Rohlfs alludes to the remarkable system of credit which obtains, and which is rarely abused. A large manufacture of hardware is carried on, but the chief export is in leather. Visitors to Tangier cannot fail to have noticed the ground in the soko carpeted with salted goatskins spread out to dry, and filling the air with their fragrance. These are used much more in the manufacture of so-called Spanish leather than for " Marocco " book-bindings.

Fez is full of "fondaks," or inns, where man and beast may find accommodation at a trifling rate. From the look of these inns, I should say it would be dear at any price. There is a large courtyard in the middle, with colonnades all round, where men, camels, donkeys, horses, &c., are huddled together in the midst of indescribable filth. Many of these fondaks belong to the Shereef of Wazan, who derives a large income from the profits. He also owns some large salt mines in the vicinity of Fez. There are likewise a number of coffee-houses, where *kif* and *haschisch* (Indian hemp) are smoked and eaten, and native music played; but such places are very unfashionable. There are no public places of entertainment for the "upper ten" in Fez. The Moorish masher, when he wants a diversion, goes for a day in the country, a form of dissipation which might be advantageously followed by some of our golden youth. He always does himself exceedingly well, and looks sleek and well content with life as he finds it. That fatuous look of hopeless boredom which only comes with a very high degree of civilization is never to be seen on the face of a Fezian man-about-town.

The hospitals mentioned by Leo have ceased to exist. Rohlfs speaks of a madhouse in Fez, but on inquiry I could learn nothing about such a thing. The lunacy laws of Marocco are of a most praiseworthy simplicity. If the lunatic is merely silly and harmless, they leave him at large, and revere him as a saint or inspired being. Should he develop dangerous symptoms, they simply clap him in prison, put a steel collar round his neck, and chain him to a pillar. The madmen are mixed up with the ordinary prisoners in those horrible places, the Moorish gaols, the condition of some of which simply beggars description. Gloomy dungeons reeking with foul exhalations that rise from the putrescent muck upon the floor—here the wretched inmates lie huddled together in unutterable filth, half-starved, or wholly so if they have no friends to bring them food; here, a man so heavily manacled that the iron has eaten into the flesh; there, another dragging after him a heavy shot attached to his ankles; in the midst, chained by the neck to a pillar, a raving lunatic, driven mad perhaps by the ill-treatment he has received. In other places may be seen men in good circumstances, whose offence is that they possess a little property, of which they may be squeezed. These make themselves fairly comfortable as a rule, and will be released as soon as they have sufficiently disgorged. At the same time there is no limit to the extent to which it may please their lord and master to bleed them. Manuel told us that Sidi Mohammed, the last Sultan, once demanded 60,000 dollars of a rich Moor. The man denied possessing so much, so he was promptly "run in." After fifteen days' confinement he gave in, and paid up, whereupon his Majesty remarked that as he disgorged so soon, it was a fair inference that he had a good deal more, and so clapped him in prison again till a further remittance was forthcoming.

Political offenders will not get out so easily, and to them imprisonment must be as the sentence of a lingering death, for there can be little hope of their ever being released alive. Their only hope is in the death of the Sultan, or some revolution which may bring their friends into power. I was shown a few such, mingled with the common herd of criminals in a most horrible den, their pitiful and dejected air contrasting strongly with the villainous faces of the rest. As we looked in, some, whose keen eyes seemed ravenous with hunger, rose and jabbered at the aperture; others were sitting and lying about in the muck, seemingly too utterly worn out even to rise and beg. Over them are placed brutal warders, who carry thick whips, which they are not slow to use. How any one can remain long in these awful places and retain their reason is a wonder—and to think that probably many of the victims are entirely innocent of any crime!

"Justice," such as it is, is administered daily, by the kadi or judges, assisted by the notaries and solicitors (adúl), and in civil cases there is an appeal to the Bascha, and then to the Sultan. In former days the courts were much more highly organized. The civil and criminal jurisdiction was better defined, and separate Ecclesiastical and Divorce Courts existed. The "law's delay" is not a great subject of complaint here, and the cause-list is got through in a very short time. The litigant with the longest purse generally wins, as the judges, being practically unpaid by the State, have to make their living as they best can. Despatch is even more the order of the day in the Criminal Courts, and I never heard of a "remand for a week" in Marocco. If there is any doubt about the matter, the prisoner probably gets the benefit of it—and is fined or flogged. The Bascha is the chief criminal judge, and from his sentence there is an appeal to the Sultan or Wizir. Rohlfs says flogging is rarely appealed against: they probably take care to give you your thrashing at once, after which the appeal would not do much good. Men are flogged on the back as a rule, women bastinadoed on the soles of their feet—one more proof of the delicate consideration shown to "the sex" in these parts. The punishment for theft, derived from the old law of "an eye for an eye, and a tooth for a tooth," used to be hacking off the hand or foot.[1]

Manuel gave us a description of a scene of which he had been a witness when in Fez eighteen years ago. It was market-day, and the soko was crowded with people, when into their midst was led out a wretched culprit convicted of robbery, and condemned to lose one foot and his right hand. The executioner

[1] The teachings of the Sonna (traditions), which forbade this punishment, unless the thing stolen was of a certain value, have now been supplemented by representations from the Great Powers which have secured its abolition.

hacked away till the limb came off, whereupon the poor wretch leaped up on the remaining foot with such a yell that Manuel fled horror-struck from the spot. Their surgery is very unskilful, a blunt knife being often used, and to stop the bleeding the stump is plunged in boiling pitch. The dismembered limbs have to be carefully buried, lest they should be missing at the Judgment Day, in which case the malefactor would enter the next world in an incomplete state. What provision is made to prevent the pieces getting mixed and resurgent criminals appearing with misfits in legs or arms, I cannot say.

An appropriate punishment is that for slander, Cayenne pepper being rubbed freely into the lips that spoke the calumny. Women are often punished in this way, and it might be introduced with advantage into England, as an antidote to tea-table scandal. Capital sentences are rare. His Majesty finds it a simpler method to let his victims die of starvation and ill-treatment in the prisons. It is cheaper too, as it saves the butcher's fee. While we were in the country, a man convicted of theft was sentenced to receive some hundreds of lashes every day for a week. He stood it five days, but on the sixth expired before he had received half the apportioned number of stripes. Poison, as elsewhere in the East, is also administered in a judicial fashion by the Sultan, who sends a polite invitation to the intended victim to take tea with him. It is known that the first cup will contain enough arsenic to poison a whole regiment, and the invitation is simply regarded as a death-warrant.

I could easily lengthen the list of tortures by enumerating others like the "jellabia," or cloak, slicing open the hand, &c., but the subject is not a pleasant one. For fiendish cruelty, I take it, the Moors have few rivals. They probably share with the Chinese the distinction of being the most brutal people on the face of the globe. And yet, for my part, I count individual atrocities, however horrible, as of small importance compared with the daily oppression of the poor, their perpetually recurring misery and starvation, which is the outcome of the present system, but which might so easily be remedied. A time perhaps, will come—soon, I trust—when things will be differently ordered—but this is digressing. Before quitting the subject, however, I must allude to one crying evil connected with their administration of justice, that is, the frightful opportunities it affords for bearing false witness. It would be appalling to know the number of innocent men and women who are the victims of trumped-up charges. Malice and revenge are prominent traits in the Moorish character, and the judges, for the most part, are only too ready to listen to any accusation, which may very possibly have no foundation beyond the personal spite of the accuser. In Leo's time the judges were paid by the number of convictions, and though I cannot positively assert such to be the case now, they certainly have no regular salary, and prisoners become a source of profit by the simple process of "squeezing."

Fez contains many mosques, though the seven hundred spoken of by Leo have dwindled down to a fraction of that number. I can give no account of the interiors of these buildings, as nowhere in Marocco, not even in semi-European Tangier, can a Christian enter one. In Fez we were actually stopped while walking down a street that led past the entrance of the Djemma Moulai Idrees—the temple in which are laid the great saint's bones. An iron chain was stretched across this street, whence its name Bab-es-sinssla, or Chain Street. Rohlfs says that in this street, near the portal of Moulai Idrees, the faithful themselves may not smoke or eat haschisch. The penalty of death, with the alternative of embracing Islam, which he says would be the immediate consequence of any Christian setting foot within it, was fortunately not enforced in our case. This mosque is the oldest and holiest in Fez, but in point of size does not compare with the great Djemma el Kairauin (Mosque of the Cherubim), which is close at hand. Passing one of its doors, I stopped a moment in the street to look in, but was requested summarily to "move on." The glimpse, however, showed me that the building was of immense extent. Long rows of whitewashed pillars formed a succession of shadowy aisles stretching away a distance of many hundreds of feet. It possesses a handsome minaret, but otherwise has no pretensions to architectural beauty.

Leo gives a glowing account of its magnificence, and Rohlfs, quoting him, makes out that the roof rests on 900 pillars, and that the building contains thirty-one great doors, and is the largest mosque in North Africa. Now its former splendour has departed, along with the other vanished glories of the once mighty city.

Against the mosque stand the remains of the great library of Fez, which in the twelfth century was one of the finest in the world, but has now dwindled away to a collection of a few mouldy MSS., concerning which nothing is known. When the country is opened up, they will afford fresh food for antiquarians and *savants*. Of the richly endowed schools and universities that existed in those days nothing remains, except that teaching of a kind is carried on in the two great mosques. When a scholar has become moderately proficient in the Koran, he is invested with a kind of degree, which ceremony is made the occasion of great festivity and rejoicing. If he has acquired a certain amount of secular learning, e.g. geography, mathematics, &c., he becomes a *thaleb*, but it may be imagined the standard required is not a high one.

Travelling as we were in this country, now the greatest stronghold of fanaticism, ignorance, and superstition, it seemed hard to believe that in days gone by Fez was a mighty centre of learning and refinement, the resort of historians, physicians, mathematicians, lawyers, and philosophers; the "Athens of Africa," the "cradle of the sciences," and "the chosen home of wisdom and understanding." So degenerate are these people, that not only has learning died out, but the very names of their great fellow-countrymen, to whom the world is so largely indebted, are utterly unknown to the Moors. What is it to the farmer who tills the soil with an implement that would have been out of date in Homer's time that his ancestors were the greatest agriculturists and gardeners of the world? The men who would now visit with condign punishment any liberal discussion of the teachings of the Koran are the unworthy sons of the scholars who proclaimed erudition to be the greatest ornament of man, and of more importance than his religious opinions.[2] A nation that now regards the revolution of the earth round the sun as a heretical doctrine gave birth to Averroes, Abu Othman, Alhazen, Al Abbas, and a host of other astronomers and scientists. Of the teachings of Almaimon, Ben Husa, and other mathematicians who lived in the palmy days of a people that gave us our present numerals, and some of our arithmetical processes, no Maroquin has probably ever heard. The *hakim*, who prescribes charms and amulets indiscriminately for all the ills that flesh is heir to, little dreams that it is in his own particular science that mankind owes the greatest debt of gratitude to the Moors. "Nothing is known," says Rohlfs, " of those great physicians who once lived in Marocco and Spain;

[2] See Draper's "Intellectual Development of Europe," vol. ii. p. 36.

no Moor knows that Albucasis, who invented lithotomy, was a countryman of theirs. Avenzoar . . . who first had the idea of bronchotomy . . ., the great Averroes, who in the reign of the great Sultan Almansor was invited to Marocco, where he died," are all unknown.

Leo attributes the demoralization of the Moorish Government in part to this decay of enlightenment which, he says, set in after a great war in which many possessions were destroyed by which learning was maintained. Ignorance and bad government were soon followed by a diminution of material prosperity. "Nations perish like trees, at the top first." Corruption begins among the rulers and upper classes, then spreads downwards till the whole body politic becomes rotten to the core. History, however, surely affords no parallel instance of a nation, five centuries ago the first in the world, sinking into such rapid, such complete, such hopeless decay.

The revenues of the mosques are very large, and constantly on the increase. They are derived, in the main, from large house property in the towns, and are continually being augmented by bequests of land and money by pious testators. There are no mortmain acts in Marocco; in fact, the Government encourage the leaving of property to pious uses for their own benefit. Church property may be let out on lease, but it is incapable of complete alienation. Indeed, part of the income is yearly set aside and invested in real estate. When a mosque needs repairing, the inhabitants of the street in which it stands are called upon to contribute. The Church funds are administered by a functionary called a Nadel, who also is charged with the distribution of charities. As may be well imagined, this official has a good time of it, and though supposed to render accounts periodically to the Sultan, he manages to feather his own nest pretty well. I should be sorry to be an inmate of a Moorish institution "supported solely by voluntary contributions," or, in fact, to be dependent in any way on their public charity. There are no priests or clergy, in our sense of the word, in Marocco. The Kadis read prayers in the mosques on Fridays, and a sort of sermon follows; also the decrees of the Sultan are given out after the service. Church and State are inseparably connected; in fact, the union of spiritual with temporal functions is too common a thing all over the East to need comment here. It is the outcome of that all-pervading religious sense which forms so prominent a trait in the Semitic character all over the world.

A curious and interesting part of the town is the Kessaria, or Bourse, where the chief business is transacted. It consists of a maze of narrow lanes, covered in, and lined with shops on either side. There being no stocks or shares in Marocco, the trade done is chiefly in manufactured goods and other merchandise; no manufactures are carried on here. A busy crowd throngs the streets; and what an extraordinary scene it is to the traveller fresh from the very different crowd of the streets of London! "Just like a scene from the 'Arabian Nights,'" is one's natural remark, and the simile, though scarcely original, cannot well be bettered. Sleek shopmen, with their flowing haiks and ample jelabs; blind beggars and lunatics, mere bundles of rags and covered with sores; muffled women walking with their shuffling gait; soldiers wearing tall red caps; barefooted Jews, with their cringeing, persecuted mien, but their keen eyes ever on the look-out for a chance of doing business; stalwart negroes and mulattoes of every shade, clad in little besides their own dark skins; fierce mountaineers, whose wiry frames and well-tanned visages contrasted well with the pallid complexions of the townsmen; every variety almost of African type and costume seemed to be represented here. Now a turbaned Moorish dignitary comes by, mounted upon a mule as fat as its owner, with an attendant crying, "Balak, balak" (Make room, make room), and the throng withdraw before him, or hurry forward to do him obeisance. As a rule, however, a strange and almost ghostly silence pervades the throng, in spite of its busy air. Often in some narrow lane a camel with enormous bales meets a heavily burdened mule or a donkey loaded with entrails or other refuse, and the traveller must get out of the way of both, if he can, and avoid at the same time stepping on the feet of the people who are standing, sitting, or lying about all over the place. I must say the natives are wonderfully good-natured as a rule. I have trodden with my heavy boots on the bare toes of a passer-by in such a manner as would make a European yell with anguish, and the victim has done nothing more than regard me with a look as of surprise and pity at my clumsiness. The whole scene was at once perfectly African and Eastern, and we felt we were blots on an otherwise entirely harmonious picture. No wonder the people cursed us audibly as we passed! What business had two travellers, clad in the common-place boots and breeches of the British equestrian, to be seen in this great city, consecrated to the sole use and occupation of the ample-robed followers of the Prophet? I need hardly say that in Fez, or indeed anywhere in the interior, are there to be found any resident Christians, with the occasional exception of some merchant who may settle there for a while for the purposes of his business.

The Sultan's palace was close to our house, but we could not see it without an order, and his Majesty was away in Marocco. Besides, the ladies of the harem were there, and it would not have been proper. The palace is said to be very handsome inside. Hard by is the Jews' quarter, remarkable here, as elsewhere, for its exceeding filth and squalor, and the unhappy appearance of its inhabitants. The Mellah of Fez, however, is far from being the worst in Marocco in this respect. Of the Jews and their behaviour and treatment in Marocco, I shall have more to say hereafter, but I may briefly enumerate the principal disqualifications under which they labour. They are confined strictly to their own quarter after sundown, the gates which lead into it being locked and barred; they cannot at any time go outside except barefoot, and certain streets are forbidden them altogether; they must wear the black cap and a distinctive dress; no synagogues or public places of worship are allowed them; they must address Mohammedans as Sidi (my lord), and pay them other marks of respect; and they cannot ride on either horse or mule. Besides these, a thousand other petty indignities help to make their lives a burden, and they also run the risk at times of more serious ill-treatment. Some few years ago the Fezians got hold of a Hebrew who had made himself particularly obnoxious, and roasted him alive, an event which caused a great sensation, and had the effect of bettering their condition to some extent, owing to pressure on the Government from abroad. My readers will doubtless recall the exclamation of King Alphonso of Spain in the Ingoldsby legends,

"Pooh! pooh! burn a Jew,
Burn two, burn two!"

when that monarch was at a loss for other means to procure an heir to the throne. So in Marocco, if anything goes wrong, the Jews are apt to be made the scapegoats, or, at any rate, to suffer in some way or another. Some of them, however, manage to put themselves beyond the reach of Moorish ill-treatment. We had letters of credit to one such, a rich merchant, who struck us as a very favourable specimen of his race. He enjoyed American protection, which might have freed him from many of the restraints imposed on his countrymen, but, to his credit, he refused to avail himself of his privileges, for fear of exciting the mob against his poorer co-religionists, and walked the dirty, ill-paved streets barefooted like the rest. America, by the way, appears to throw the ægis of the Stars and Stripes over a surprising number of Jews in Marocco. The cause of this gratifying solicitude for their welfare is, no doubt, true republican sympathy for an oppressed nationality, but the system has its disadvantages, as will be seen by the reader who perseveres to the end of this book.

The Moors have a simple but efficacious method of cleansing this part of the town. When the accumulations of filth have become unbearable, even to Maroquin ideas, the water is drawn off from the river and turned on through the streets. It must be a bad time for the denizens of the lower part of the town when these periodical cleansings take place.

We used to walk about the town unguarded, but were severely lectured by Manuel for our imprudence in strolling alone in the environs after dusk one evening. His opinion was that one should have regard to the fanaticism of these people, and not give them any chance of doing mischief with impunity. The following will serve as an example of the spirit which animates the populace against

H

the infidel. Standing by a stall one day, a tall, strapping Brebber woman came up and asked for a long dagger. The shopkeeper asked her what she, being a woman, wanted with such a thing. She replied that she wanted it to kill the Christians with, and that she wished there were a hundred women like herself who would follow her example. Experience, however, has shown the Moors that it is better to control their feelings, and one's great safeguard now is in their fear of the consequences if harm befalls a European. Forty years ago no ordinary Christian was safe unguarded outside the walls of Tangier. Then the French bombarded their ports, and taught them a little reason; the Spanish war of '59 made matters better still, and now one can travel at most seasons along the beaten tracks with tolerable security. The only thing is to avoid making yourself obnoxious in any way, and above all to take care not to get involved in anything like a row in the streets. A single ragamuffin may throw a stone at you, and when one begins, the rest are not slow to follow. A few months before our arrival a Spaniard who happened to be in the place and had exasperated the people, was stoned with such effect that he died of his wounds on the way back to Tangier.

Catering was always a source of amusement to us. The meat on sale in the markets consists chiefly of very poor beef and mutton, chickens, goat, and camel. Goat is not so bad, when nothing else is to be got, but I cannot conscientiously recommend camel. Prices were very high, owing to the famine, but that of bread is fixed by Government—a very salutary regulation. The loaves are of fixed size and quantity, and the punishment for selling short weight is very severe. It was the same in Leo's time, when the baker detected in that offence was beaten with cudgels and led with contempt up and down the streets. No provision, however, is made for insuring its quality, which is as bad as it can be, and we found it a sore trial. The following is the best recipe for making Moorish bread, if any one would like to try it for a change. Take ¾ lb. of damaged flour, knead slightly; then add ¼ lb. of cinders, fine sand, and powdered grindstone, and bake quickly, so as to leave the inside the consistency of dough. They usually add aniseed in such quantities as to make a loaf only fit to be used as a drag, and you want a gizzard like a fowl to manage the sand and grindstone. The corpses of sundry fleas are always to be found mixed with the bread—whether accidentally, or in lieu of caraway seeds, I could not discover.

Our days in Fez passed pleasantly enough strolling about the shops and taking stock of all the curious sights that everywhere met our eyes. The nights were not such a source of enjoyment to me, as my camp-bed had been despatched to a Jew for necessary repairs, and I had to sleep on the ground. The result was that I was nearly devoured by fanatical fleas, who, "smelling the blood of an Englishman" and an infidel, and eager for change of diet, rushed upon me *en masse,* and made short work of me.

Our last evening was spent in a stroll round the environs. These are pretty and well wooded on the north, and studded with the tombs of innumerable saints, all bearing that ruinous appearance which a Moorish building assumes almost *immediately after* construction. On the south-east of the town are the remains of a large castle where the old Sultans kept their *mona,* or provisions. Not far off we were shown two towers where prisoners reserved for torture used to be confined. Drops of water were let fall slowly on their heads till they went mad or died, or else confessed the place where their treasure was buried. In many cases the secret died with the owner, and no doubt much gold lies concealed in the earth throughout Marocco. Woe be, however, to the unfortunate finder of treasure-trove, if the Kaid or Bascha should hear of his keeping his good-luck to himself! Our pious protector, Hadj Absalam, left us here to perform his devotions at a Marabout's tomb, and to pray, as he said, for our safe and prosperous journey, and we seated ourselves on a tombstone to await his return. All around us were large cemeteries, which the good sense of the Moors induces them to make *outside* their towns, a point in which we have only lately begun to follow their example. We gradually became objects of curiosity, and I tried to sketch some natives who had gathered round us. For some time they did not understand the operation, but at last, seeing what was going on, they made off, fearing the influence of the evil eye. This superstition is as common in Marocco as elsewhere in the East. On nearly every house may be seen the hand or other cabalistic mark painted up on the wall, and the same are frequently tattooed on the persons of the natives for the like purpose.

CHAPTER V.

Moorish vet.—Visit to the Bascha—Cruelty to animals—
Shelluh village and noisy " warriors "—Berbers of Marocco—
Their origin and characteristics—Conflicting theories—
Semites or Hamites—Review of evidence.

BEFORE leaving we had a *mallem* (vet.) to see to the animals. This individual, who combined the functions of vet. and blacksmith, initiated us in the art of the Moorish farrier. The hoof is pared with an instrument like a small shovel; the shoe is a complete circle of iron, and in some places has a bar across the centre. A very peculiar instrument, too, is their twitch, which compresses the horse's nose till it resembles that of a tapir. The fellow evidently understood his business, and, I think, only charged a penny for each shoe.

We of course had to call upon the Bascha to express our acknowledgments. In a courtyard outside his house sat a crowd of country people, some bringing taxes and tribute money which they owed, others with petitions to present, and grievances to be redressed. We were promptly button-holed by a bumptious functionary who seemed to act as a sort of Gold-Stick-in-Waiting to his Highness, and he took us completely in tow. He hustled the people out of the way in the most unceremonious fashion, till we both felt inclined to kick him for his officiousness. The Bascha expressed his great regret at our departure (he probably was delighted to be rid of us), and gave us permission to visit Mequinez, which had been unsafe the previous year, owing to tribal feuds, and ordered one of his black soldiers to accompany us there. A heavy shower of compliments followed; I grasped the great man's hand and kissed my finger-tips with effusion; the obsequious Gold-Stick-in-Waiting kicked the people aside once more, for which service he gratefully accepted a dollar at our hands, and we left.

We sallied forth from the gates of Fez on the morning of the 24th of February. After skirting a long white wall which encircles a new tribunal built by the Sultan, the road entered on the wide plain that extends westwards towards Mequinez. The ground dips beyond, so that its clearly defined horizon resembles the sea-shore, giving it a very striking effect. Behind, we had a clear view of the snows of Sidi Hassen, but the town soon passed out of sight. The rich soil was cultivated throughout for a great distance. Several Jews we met saluted us with "Bonjour, monsieur," a fragment of French probably picked up from the Algerian caravans. There is a route from Fez to Oujda, on the frontier of Algeria, which is interesting and seldom travelled. I had an opportunity of accompanying a Russian gentleman who traversed it successfully the previous year, but happened to be engaged on a shooting expedition.¹ Strings of peasants passed, driving their donkeys to market, which were laden as only these people know how to load beasts. Those poor little prettily shaped Barbary donkeys have a sad time of it. Sometimes, when the pile of luggage is already big enough to break down an ordinary ass, the owner will jump on the top and ride as long as the animal will carry him. To save the trouble of walloping their beasts, they bore a small hole in the withers, and to urge them to go faster, stir up the wound with a short stick which is carried for the purpose. I used to protest against this barbarity, but was of course only regarded with that look of wondering contempt which the Moor always assumes when you venture to point out any little faults in his social system. Their method of carrying live poultry is convenient for themselves, if not for the fowls. They tie the legs of a pair of fowls together and suspend them head-downwards from the panniers, and so will journey several hours together. The Koran places beasts in a far higher rank in the scale of creation than does our religion, so they have no sanction for such cruelty.

An amusing incident occurred further on. A well-to-do Moor was riding a mule, with his lady mounted pillion-wise behind. The pair were regarding us with great curiosity when the mule

---

¹ For a lively and amusing account of this route, see Captain Colvile's "Ride in Petticoats and Slippers." Among others, the same route was travelled twice by Colonel Scott in 1843.

stumbled, and both rolled over together on the ground. They rose with as much dignity as the circumstances permitted, and the mule having received a severe reprimand, enforced by the application of a thick stick, they mounted again and resumed their journey. The grave and respectful way in which the Moors address their ill-used beasts is very comical. I have seen a man thrashing unmercifully an overladen donkey stop for a while and say in a tone of most serious reproach, "Éwa, sidi" (Really, my lord), and then begin walloping it again. All beasts, domestic and otherwise, are credited with powers of understanding, and even speech, by the more ignorant natives.

Several famine-stricken creatures passed us on the way. Two or three of these had found the carcass of a camel by the roadside, and had lit a fire of sticks to make a meal off the remains. Nearly all solicited alms, but, curiously enough, seldom showed any signs of gratitude on receiving it. They give the credit not to you, but to their saint (seldom to Allah), or more probably to the two guardian angels (Malik) which watch over every Mohammedan.

We crossed a stream of beautifully clear water by a good bridge, one of the very few specimens of such things in Marocco, and halted at a village some twenty miles distant from Fez. The people here had a bad reputation, and we were told we had better not shoot; but we went out with permission from the Sheikh, and found the natives very friendly.

To show yourself to be a good shot is the best way to secure the respect and good-will of these people, and they cannot withstand the chance of seeing a bird killed on the wing. Luckily, we were both in pretty good form, so that our reputation was secured amongst them. No small part of Sir John Hay's immense influence with the Moors is due to the fact of his being such a thorough sportsman, and the fame of many a hair-breadth escape from the " Father of Tusks " is spread abroad concerning him among the people.

After dinner a single " warrior " arrived on the scene, who, finding himself alone, loudly expressed his dissatisfaction thereat, making such a noise as only an exasperated Arab can. I rather sympathized with that warrior on the whole. However, presently a whole troop of them arrived, and seating themselves in a circle fell to making jokes and talking at the very top of their voices all through the night. One fellow curled up under the lee of our tent was most aggravating. Now and again in the small hours of the morning some excruciating piece of waggery would suggest itself to him, which he shouted out to another guard, named Abd el Kader, lying some fifty yards away, and the whole lot would explode simultaneously. He had a most distressing cough (I never knew a " warrior " that hadn't!) and his jocularity, combined with the damp night air, made it much worse. This " churchyard " cough is universal in the country, and it seems to have been the same when Leo wrote. He states it to have been especially prevalent among "those of a sanguine complexion," and the venerable wag tells us how he had " no small sporte and recreation " in watching the audiences of the Moorish preachers on a Friday. "Now if any one in the sermon-time fall a-neezing, all the whole companie will neeze with him .... so that a man will reape but little knowledge by any of their sermons." He attributes this cough to their habit of sitting so much on the ground. I think the awful language must have something to do with it, as it is very trying to the throat. They all make such dreadful faces, too, when they are talking, which shows it hurts them a great deal. Seriously, some of their words (e.g. Al R'schid, a common name) cannot be pronounced without a sort of sneeze, and the tremendous gutturals, without any intervening vowels, are a great tax on the vocal organs. I always sneeze in Arabic now. But to return to our warriors; what with their coughing and joking, we never got a wink of sleep all night. Our faint expostulations were met with the rejoinder that no warrior could do his duty upon guard if he didn't keep awake, and that they must talk, or they would fall asleep. This was unanswerable, so we had to put up with it. I remember, it was the same in the City of Marocco, where we heard all through the night the discharge of guns by the sentries to show that they were awake, as if it were quite a remarkable thing for a soldier not to go to sleep on his post.

We were here encamped for the first time among

a tribe of Shelluhs, or Shlohs, the most important representatives in Marocco of the great Berber family. The different language was the first indication that we were among people of another race, but they differed also from the Arabs of the neighbourhood in being more lantern-jawed, and of a sallower complexion, and in wearing their long black hair in ringlets, that descended to their shoulders. By the word "Berber," or "Brebber," as the natives pronounce it, the reader is no doubt aware is meant the aboriginal inhabitants of the country before the Mohammedan invasion—possibly not its earliest inhabitants, but the first of whom we have any certain record—the "historical autochthones" of Marocco. The other great divisions of the race in North-West Africa are the Riffians of the mountainous country on the Mediterranean coast, identical with the Kabyles of Algeria, and the Touariks of the Sahara. To these must be added, as modern research has conclusively proved, the Guanches of the Canary Islands. The Berbers largely outnumber the other Moors, and own, says Rohlfs, at least four-fifths of the land. The term "Moors," by the way, is a very misleading one, being applied sometimes to the Arabs, sometimes to the dwellers in the coast towns, and sometimes indiscriminately to all the inhabitants of Marocco. It obviously belongs by right to the Berbers, the ancient "Mauri;" but when the Berbers crossed over into Spain, under the one-eyed chieftain Tarik, who gave his name to the Rock of Gibraltar, and were followed by the Arabs under Moossa, their amalgamated hordes were called "Moros" indiscriminately by the Spaniards. The two races mingled in Spain, and at the time of their final expulsion in 1492 they settled for the most part in the coast towns of Marocco. Hence the distinction drawn by many writers between the Moors, or dwellers in cities, and the Arabs, or country people and agriculturists. The distinction is obviously valueless from an ethnological point of view, but is of some use as drawing attention to a historical fact.

The various races of Marocco offer a splendid field for the researches of the ethnologist, and one that has been comparatively neglected. Besides the Arabs, the Romans and Vandals settled in the country at various periods of the first centuries of the Christian era, and a few dolmens, cromlechs, and other Druidical remains which have been found, point to men of probably Keltic origin having inhabited it in prehistoric ages. None of these, however, have left any perceptible traces of their occupation in the bulk of the people. Speculation is chiefly rife as to the origin of the great Berber race, and the most eminent authorities have come to the conclusion, from a detailed comparison of the Berber and Arabic tongues, that they are not to be included among Semitic peoples. M. Renan [2] is of opinion that the various Berber dialects and the majority of the indigenous tongues of North Africa

[2] "Histoire des Langues Sémitiques," pp. 81, 189.

belong to a large family of languages which are grouped together under the name of Hamitic, and of which Coptic is the chief representative. The word "Hamites" is of course not used here in its Biblical sense as signifying sons of Ham, but merely as a convenient generic term, though it may be mentioned that the old Arab historians speak of their country having been peopled by Phut, the third son of Ham. Coptic and ancient Egyptian being allied, and the relation of the Berber languages with both being established to the satisfaction of philologists, the three races are regarded as kindred branches of the same stock. Whether, as some have thought, the Berbers are the degenerate descendants of a once mighty race of Hamites who, in the early dawn of the world's history, possessed a high civilization when the Aryan and Semitic races were yet in their infancy; who founded the mighty empires of Chaldæa and Assyria, as well as the ancient kingdom of Egypt, and who have left traces of their vanished greatness in the majestic sculptures unearthed by Mr. Layard at Nineveh and Babylon, the colossal temples of Baalbek and Palmyra, and the more familiar remains on the banks of the Nile—all this must be left for future research to elucidate. Some writers, in accordance with the general tendency which exists to label indiscriminately as "Phœnician" things whose origin is remote and uncertain, and partly also making tradition their guide, have asserted the Berbers to be sprung from the people who founded Tyre and Carthage. The fair hair and blue eyes which are found among certain tribes has, for some reason or other, been supposed to lend colour to this theory. There can be no doubt that in any case Punic words found their way into the Numidian or old Berber tongue, and we have the distinct authority of more than one ancient writer that Punic was the language of the ancient Africans at the time of the Mohammedan invasion, though Renan suggests that the authors of this statement mistook Berber for Punic, being ignorant of both.

The great mass of native tradition in Barbary, and the testimony of old historians, point to the Berbers as belonging to the Canaanæan branch of the Semitic family, and therefore at any rate akin to the Phœnicians. Of the legends which circulate on the subject, the following may be cited. The mountaineers of the Atlas relate that their ancestors were driven out from Canaan by the "robber Joshua," and forced to seek refuge in Africa, a legend which is supported by, if it is not derived from, a passage in Procopius[3] mentioning two columns with inscriptions in Phœnician recording the fact. There is said to be a certain tribe in the Riff country which claims to be descended from the inhabitants of Sodom—a rather questionable distinction, one would think, but one of which they are sufficiently proud. Other tribes boast similar ancestry, and go so far as to specify the particular town in Palestine where their

[3] See Gibbon, ch. lxi.

progenitors dwelt. In an interesting letter[1] of the late Abd el Kader, the Algerian patriot, to General Daumas, passages from Arab authors are quoted as showing that the original domicile of the Berbers was in Palestine. According to one account they were expelled thence by a Persian king, and emigrated to Egypt, where the ruling monarch interdicted their remaining, so that they crossed the Nile and spread themselves over the countries to the west, and in certain districts along the banks of the river. Another writer asserts that they all came from Syria, and that they sallied forth under various leaders to conquer North Africa. Goliath of Gath is mentioned as one of these leaders; but one account says that David headed the chief exodus, which took place after the slaying of Goliath. These legends are said by Renan to be derived from old Jewish fables relating to the passage of the Canaanæans into Africa, but there seems no reason to suppose that they are not partly founded on facts. Leo Africanus speaks of a tradition among the "tawnie Moors," or Berbers, that they are descended from the Sabeans, a people of Arabia Felix, whose ancestor, Saba, was the grandson of Chus, the son of Ham, and he asserts that the Berbers and negroes are sprung from the same origin—a theory no doubt derived from the old idea that the negroes are the children of Ham. This idea, as most people will remember, was fostered and encouraged by pious slave-owners in our time, to prove that the negroes

[1] "Revue des Deux Mondes," February, 1854.

ought to be kept in servitude, if only for the due fulfilment of Scripture prophecy. It is curious to note in this connection that the word Mauri meant in late Greek "blacks," whereas many of the modern Berbers are particularly fair.

Amid much rather wild speculation, resting partly on more or less fanciful etymological analogies, partly on physical characteristics, traditions, customs, habits of life, and the like, where the merest straws of evidence are eagerly caught at, one thing may be regarded as tolerably certain, that the Berbers of Marocco are the modern representatives of the various Gætulian tribes mentioned by Pliny and other ancient geographers, as well as of those Numidians who, under Jugurtha and Masinissa and other leaders, offered such a stubborn resistance to the arms of Rome. The contemporary authors who described the then Africans throw little light on the question of their origin. Sallust,[5] whose information was derived from Punic books, the property of King Hiempsal, says that the Numidians are descended from the Persian remnant of the army of Hercules, which after the hero's death crossed over from Spain into Africa, and settled on the Atlantic coast. Finding no building material wherewith to construct themselves dwellings, they turned their ship's keel uppermost to serve as houses, whence is said to be derived the peculiar beehive shape of the reed huts still common in the country, which are supposed to resemble an inverted boat. The newcomers intermarried after a while with the natives,

[5] Jug. xviii.

and adopting their nomad life called themselves Numidians. This description, by the way, as well as that given by Virgil [6] of the nomadic habits of the Gætulians, hardly applies to their descendants the Shlohs, who live, as a rule, in permanent dwellings of mud or stone, while the Arabs dwell in *duars* or tent villages, which can be shifted at will.

If the opinions of M. Rénan and other eminent philologists are to be taken as settling the question of the origin of the Berbers, Marocco is now inhabited by two peoples originally at opposite poles in respect of race and language, and each with an individuality of its own that should render the one widely dissimilar from the other. We should expect to see a divergence in appearance and characteristics at least as great as that which exists between the various members of the Aryan race—that is to say, a Shloh should differ from an Arab as much or more than does an Englishman from a Frenchman or Russian—whereas nothing could be further from the fact. Most writers on the subject have tried to establish fundamental differences, but without success, as it seems to me. One (M. Rozet), for instance, speaks of the Berbers as having rounder heads than the Arabs; but among the Shlohs long, narrow faces are the rule. Others raise trifling distinctions, such as sallow complexions, high cheekbones, fair hair, blue eyes, &c., but these characteristics are local, not universal, and are to be found among undoubted Arabs. Such distinctions are

[6] Georgics iii. 344.

made as a rule by travellers whose observation was confined to the natives of a particular district. A Riffian differs quite as much from a Shloh as does an Arab, and after seeing many different Berber tribes, I failed entirely to note any special characteristics running through them all, which would serve to differentiate them as a race from the Arabs. I observe, too, that Rohlfs, whose keen observation and true traveller's instinct generally led him to the truth, is of the same opinion. He says there is little beyond their language to distinguish them, and points out that Arabs dwelling in hill districts get light complexions just as much as the Berbers. He is, however, surely wrong when he accounts for the fair hair and blue eyes of some of the Berbers by the law of atavism, as proving them to be descended from some light race who inhabited the country in prehistoric times. "Atavism," perhaps; but more likely the peculiarity is the result of an admixture of Vandal blood. Now and again one sees regular "Sandies" among the Moors, with hair as carroty and complexion as ruddy as the veriest Highlander. The Moors call these Zaar, or fair men, and give them a bad character for lying and deceit. It is surely a much simpler and more probable theory to suppose them to be "throwing back" to Gothic parents than to revert to prehistoric times for their ancestry. The Vandal theory has been strenuously denied, but I cannot see for what reason. It is too much to suppose that a race can have settled for more than a hundred years in the country without leaving some trace of their occupation in the surrounding people. Secondly, the fair-haired Berber tribes are confined to the districts near those which the Vandals occupied. I never saw or heard of any such in South Marocco. Further, one never reads of fair Numidians in the works of ancient authors, whose epithets point to their being essentially a dark race, which looks as if the light complexions were of later importation.

Something must be deducted from the argument derived from identity of appearance on the score of inevitable mixture of race, mutual intercourse, similar conditions of life, and other causes tending to make the two peoples approach one another. But intermarriage is very uncommon in the country, and it is a known tendency of the descendants of mixed races to revert to one or other of the original types, while the difficulty of communication causes such differences as exist between different tribes and peoples to be preserved in a quite remarkable way, which makes Marocco such a favourable ground for ethnological studies. Cases are cited of Berbers who have become black after settling in hot climates, as proving that physical characteristics are not necessarily permanent; but there is nothing in the climate of Marocco to cause any striking change.

It is tolerably well established that the different dialects of the many branches of the Berber race are merely varieties of the same language. The generic name for most of the dialects of North-

West Africa is Tamashek, which is spoken in its purest form by the Touariks. They also call it Masigh, or the Noble Language, a title the equivalent of which is supposed to be found in the name[7] of a tribe mentioned by Herodotus. The differences between the dialects are not so great but that a Shloh can understand a Riffian after a little practice. An Arab is totally at sea with either, though both dialects are largely blended with Arabic words, especially in districts where the two races are most in contact, and the Berbers use the Arabic character in writing. The vocabulary of the Berber tongue is certainly wholly different from Arabic, but its grammatical structure and system of inflection, especially in the conjugation of the verb, is said to be not dissimilar, so that writers well qualified to form a judgment are not wanting who rank it among Semitic tongues, though the balance of authority is probably the other way. In view of this discrepancy of opinion, and even admitting language to be the best basis for the classification of races, may it not be asked whether the evidence afforded by philology is sufficiently strong to upset that derived from identity of appearance and habits and modes of life, as well as from tradition and the testimony of ancient writers? Is it not probable that the Berbers were some prior irruption of Semites, such as is alluded to by the Arab historians, and that, while adopting the vocabulary of the natives of the new country,

[7] Μάζυες, vide "Dict. Anc. Geography," sub tit. Mauretania.

they retained their own grammatical forms? In any case, it seems certain that the Hamites must have come at some early period of their existence into contact with the Semites, and the opinion is growing among *savants* that in far-off ages they were one and the same people. It has been suggested, with much probability, that the Hamites themselves were not indigenous to Africa, but that they dispossessed some other nation, perhaps of blacks.

The Berbers of Marocco are to be found for the most part in the mountainous districts. They are not necessarily a hill people, but have been driven from the lowlands by successive invaders of their country, especially by the Arabs. The latter are of course essentially dwellers in the plains, though Leo's remark that "the Arabians without deserts are like fishes without the sea" is an overstatement, as some of the finest specimens of the race are to be found in hill districts—the natives of Andjra, for instance. The territory occupied by the Berbers in North Africa is vastly in excess of the purely Arab regions. Everywhere they are spoken of by travellers as a fine race of men, tall, well shaped, and with the proud, independent bearing that comes from a sense of freedom and manly qualities. That the North African aborigines can fight, our soldiers who engaged with the fierce warriors of Osman Digna's army, which was composed of men of essentially Hamitic,[3] not Arab,

---

[3] See a paper by Professor A. H. Keane in the *Anthropological Journal* for November, 1884.

extraction, can bear ample testimony. Beside the other inhabitants of Marocco the Berbers shine both in intelligence and industry, which is no doubt chiefly the result of their enjoying greater independence and immunity from oppression. They are less bigoted than the Arabs, and far more ready to adopt innovations and the improvements of civilization. In fact, the religious sense is far less strongly developed in them, which is in itself an argument against their being of Semitic origin; but, on the other hand, it has been seen how the Phœnician Semites relapsed into a faith more material, and religious observances far grosser than any practised by the Berbers. The Mohammedanism of the Berbers is, as a rule, little more than a veneer, and their faith is still tinged with Christian ideas and traditional beliefs derived from ancient pagan religions, which the new creed never entirely rooted out. For instance, some of the Kabyles are said to use Sunday as a day of prayer, instead of Friday, and the Riffs call the months by their Christian names, according to Rohlfs; the name of Mary is still invoked by women on certain occasions, and they often give pagan names to their children, which the Arabs never do.

Women occupy a higher social position among the Berbers, and Rohlfs tells us that in some tribes they have the right to reign and occupy religious posts; while that curious custom mentioned by various travellers, of the sister's son inheriting,[2] to

[2] The quaint reason of this custom, as given by the

the exclusion of the male line of descent, prevails here and there in South Marocco. They seldom marry outside their own people, and union with a negress is a disgrace in their eyes, which is far from the case with the Arabs: hence they have retained their individuality much more than the latter. Pure-bred Arabs are not particularly common in Marocco. They may be distinguished from the mixed races by their slighter frames, wiry, rather than muscular; those who possess great physical strength are generally mulattoes. They have particularly well-shaped heads, aquiline noses, and well-cut features; their limbs are well made but small as a rule, and even among the peasantry I have noticed hands of almost feminine delicacy. The Arabs are naturally a quick-witted race, whereas most of their number in Marocco are hopelessly stupid; but the intellectual degradation of the country is, no doubt, largely due to the admixture of negro blood, especially in the ruling class.

The independent Berbers seem to possess a less patriarchal system of government than the Arabs. Each tribe is a sort of small republic, electing its own councillors and rulers, and owning no authority but what themselves have created. So it was in ancient times, when this tribal system and internecine strife, the curse of Africa, kept them split up

Egyptian historian, Ibn Selim, is that by this means the true line of descent is more surely preserved. There can be no doubt as to the identity of the child's mother, but its paternity must always be more or less open to question!

into separate clans, who never attained cohesion except under able and powerful princes like Masinissa and Bocchus, when large tracts were consolidated into kingdoms. This, no doubt, accounts in a great measure for the unimportant part they have played in the world's history. It certainly does seem remarkable that such a people, brave, industrious, and intelligent, possessing many of the elements of a good civilization—a good system of government, permanent and well-built dwellings, and an excellent social order—should have remained in such a state of utter stagnation, and have had so little influence on the destinies of the human race. One writer,[1] at least, has seen in this the fulfilment of Scripture prophecy, "Cursed be Canaan, a servant of servants shall he be," and he considers that the Berbers, in common with their kindred races, are only working out their destiny as the accursed sons of Ham; that as the Phœnicians and other mighty peoples who once led the van in the march of civilization have now disappeared in so mysterious a manner from off the face of the earth, so the Berber race, though still existent, has yet been overwhelmed with the rest in their common doom of political extinction, in accordance with the decrees of Divine Providence. Whatever may be thought of this idea, it is worked out with much skill and fascination of style; the reader's estimate of its probability will depend chiefly on the temper of mind, religious or scientific, in which he

[1] Mr. Dominic McCausland, in "The Builders of Babel."

approaches the subject. The fact remains, that the Berbers, while retaining their old characteristics of pride and independence, and in point of both physical and mental qualities comparing favourably with the Arabs who can boast such a glorious past, have yet remained stationary, and have taken practically no share in any of the great movements and events by which the history of the world has been made.

CHAPTER VI.

Arrival at Mequinez—Immense vaults—Sultan Moulai Ismael—Ruins of Mequinez—Eno—Second visit to ruins—Vast wall—Magnificent gate—Jews of Marocco—Their malpractices and unpopularity—Protected Jews—Hebrew women—Debasement of the Jews and their excuse.

EARLY next morning we left for Mequinez. The plain dropped suddenly in a steep declivity, and the road skirted the top of a great cleft several hundred feet in depth, reminding me somewhat of the Tajos of Ronda and other places in Spain. We passed two or three other wooded gorges on a smaller scale, and at a short distance from the town descended into a deep valley, and crossed a stream by a very tolerable bridge. Parallel with the Fez road, a few miles to the north, runs the fine range of the Zaraoun mountains, of which little is known. The people we passed were chiefly of the Brebber race, and they regarded us with anything but friendly looks, and remarks more forcible than polite were addressed to us from time to time. Mequinez is noted for the fanaticism of its inhabitants, being, like Wazan, a Holy City, and situated amid turbulent and lawless tribes. It is also, as already stated, the headquarters of the Aissauias. The town is somewhat striking from a distance, owing to the multitude of half-ruined castles and fortresses around, which give it a decidedly warlike appearance. Passing through a gap in a low wall of tabbia, we entered a kind of park, thickly planted with olives, part of the demesne of the Sultan's palace. We had dismounted to stretch our legs, and were walking on foot, till Manuel begged us to remount, telling us that it was shocking "bad form" for the two "caballeros" to be seen walking—especially when their servants were riding. The Moors are such tremendous sticklers for etiquette that we were always afraid of doing something that was not *de rigueur* according to their strict code of proprieties.

Inside the town we despatched to the Bascha our Ethiopian soldier from Fez, and after passing through a magnificent gate which is the entrance to the Bascha's Court of Justice, the tents were pitched in a grass-covered space inside the walls. The Bascha offered us a house, but having had enough of Moorish houses at Fez and Wazan, we declined with thanks, and stuck to our tents. It was a strange and melancholy prospect around. On every side were half-ruined towers and walls, crumbling masses of masonry, untenanted, save by the myriads of hawks and storks that had built their nests therein. The whole place resembled a sort of buried city, whose vast remains showed what it must have been in its palmy days. The solemn stillness which reigned among these mouldering relics of bygone grandeur was a great contrast to the stir and bustle of Fez; the whole place seemed wrapped in the sleep of the dead. While driving our tent-pegs into the grass we encountered some hard substance at a depth of a few inches. On examination we found we were encamped on the vaulted roofs of vast subterranean granaries, according to Manuel, though others said they were the old Sultan's armoury, and used of course as prisons when needed. The arches were of brick and immensely solid. Happening to notice a couple of bats flying out of a small hole in the ground, I managed to descend into the vaults. Scrambling down a big pile of rubbish, I stumbled over something soft, which proved to be the slowly decomposing carcass of a donkey (I *have* seen a dead donkey, and a good many too, in my time), and then thought it better to return for a candle. The soldier begged us not to go down, because, he said, the place was tenanted by *djins* and no Moor would ever venture therein. With the aid of the light we could see that the vaults were of immense extent, covering many acres. The arches appeared to be about twenty-five feet in height. A fetid stench rose from the bones and rotting carcasses, and the vaults appeared tenanted by nothing save bats, who flitted about round our heads in a state of great perturbation at the unwonted light. Daylight appeared further on through a small opening half blocked up with rubbish, but we came back with all speed by the same way that we entered. They told us that similar dungeons extended under the palace to an immense distance, and that many prisoners of "our lord" the Sultan were rotting in their gloomy recesses. It is probably in one of these vaults that the great treasure-house of the Sultan is situated. The Moors give fabulous accounts of the wealth that lies in this "Bit el Mel," which is somewhere in the centre of the palace, and is said to be only approachable by an underground passage.

Immediately opposite our tents, and flanked by ruinous buildings, were two handsome *kubbahs* or mausoleums with pointed roofs, surmounted by golden balls, and covered with green tiles—both in an excellent state of preservation. One was the tomb of the Sultan Moulai Abdurrahman, the other, the larger and handsomer of the two, that of Moulai Ismael. This Moulai Ismael reigned from 1672 to 1727, and having been the most bloodthirsty scoundrel on record, and notorious for his tyranny and hideous cruelties, is naturally venerated by the Moors as a saint of the first water, and the pious worship at his shrine. He was one of the most powerful monarchs that ever sat on the throne of Marocco, and was the first to consolidate the three kingdoms of Fez, Marocco, and Tafilet into one united empire. By his brutalities he enforced law and order, and the consequences of revolt were so terrible that few dared to raise a hand against his sceptre. Many European Powers, England included, entered into treaties with him, and even paid him tribute to secure immunity from the raids of his corsairs. At the beginning of the eighteenth century, there were no less than 1100 Christian slaves in Mequinez, three hundred of them English, on whom he is said to have perpetrated the most horrible barbarities. He enlarged and beautified Mequinez, which, till a few years ago, was the chief residence of the Court of Marocco, and most of the vast buildings and palaces to the south of the town date from his reign. I read in an old book on Marocco[1] that he died in torments from a "mortification in the lower part of the belly," and his end seems to have resembled that of another tyrant, Herod, in its disgusting nature.

Mequinez, or Meknas, as the Arabs call it, was probably founded in the tenth century, though some attribute its origin to Aboo Jusef, who reigned in the thirteenth century. Its real founder, however, was Moulai Ismael, who was the first to make it a place of any importance. The population is probably rather under 50,000, and since the Court has ceased to reside here, it has greatly decreased. Having regard to the beauty of some of its buildings and the remarkable ruins in the vicinity, I consider it the most interesting town in Marocco. All around, but chiefly on the south side, are beautiful gardens and plantations, which in former days were no doubt appendant to the Sultan's palaces.

Our first afternoon we went off to do the sights, and took our nigger soldier to act as guide. He talked volubly in *Guenaoui*, the negro tongue, as he pointed out what he considered the most interesting

[1] Braithwaite's "Revolutions at the Court of Marocco."

things, but scarcely a word could we understand. Passing through the archway of the palace gate, which was supported by massive pillars, we found ourselves in a perfectly straight thoroughfare, about a third of a mile long, and inclosed on either side by walls some forty feet in height. We were informed that in the old days, when a Sultan wanted to score off a disaffected or troublesome tribe, he would invite them in friendly terms to an audience at the palace gate. When once they got inside this street all exit was barred before and behind, and armed men lining the tops of the walls soon made short work of them with bullets and other missiles. One would suppose such a trick could not be repeated very often, but they spoke of it as quite a regular occurrence. From this street we got out into a ruinous inclosure strewn with marble columns, which are said to have been brought by Moulai Ismael from Italy for his palace. Now they lie on the ground here, without the slightest attempt being made to utilize them in any way. Further on we came on a large reservoir some 250 or 300 yards in length, by 150 in width. It was dry, and—wonder of wonders—masons were at work repairing it, about the only work of public utility which we saw in progress anywhere in Marocco. Our sable cicerone waxed quite enthusiastic over this reservoir. We did not understand a word he was talking about, but gave him credit for a desire to make himself agreeable. In fact, this genial child of Ham was a little too demonstrative in expressing his affection for us, for, in the fulness of his heart, he grasped my hand and led me along the bank, chattering as hard as he could the while. The day was decidedly warm, and the palm of a nigger's hand was not exactly the place I should have chosen to place my own to keep it cool. However, I hate hurting people's feelings, and so endured it awhile.

Hard by was a large building of tabbia, in an advanced state of decay, which they said was a granary of Moulai S'liman, who reigned at the beginning of the present century. Inside, I counted no less than 400 massive arches, on which the roof was intended to rest. To judge, however, from its appearance, I should say that this building, in common with the majority of the other ruins, was never completed. Even after making allowance for the rapidity with which all things Moorish fall into decay, it seems scarcely credible that buildings of such immensely solid construction could thus have crumbled away in so short a time. The dilapidated state of these palaces, &c., is an instance of the idiotic way in which these Eastern despots went to work. One Sultan starts a palace, spends a mint of money on the requisite materials, but dies before its completion. His successor, perhaps, doesn't care about the site, or has some absurd caprice to gratify, so another building is begun, and the first left to decay, and so on *ad infinitum*.

In the evening, several very magnificent guards arrived, who, to judge from the splendour of their kits, must have been persons of rank. They brought an elegant tea-tray and service along with them; a big brew of tea was started out of our stores, and the company made themselves very jolly. Hadj Absalam joined the party, and I believe we, and the objects of our expedition, were discussed. At every town in the interior, our arrival no doubt furnished the subject of all the "coffee-house babble" of the place for at least a week.

Next day, after consulting Manuel, we procured another guide, who could make himself more intelligible to us, in the person of a diminutive Chinaman rejoicing in the name of Eno. He was a funny little personage, with blear eyes, over which he wore enormous goggles, and speaking bad Spanish with a voice like a corncrake's. What brought him to Mequinez or to Marocco at all, I forget, though I believe there was some curious history connected with him. He was said to be a Christian, but I did not examine him in his articles of faith. Probably, his religion was of an accommodating nature, like that of a certain aged Hebrew, who, when I asked him if he was Christian, Jew, or Mussulman, replied, "Sometimes one, sometimes the other; a leetle of both, 'alf and 'alf." Eno seemed charmed to look after us, and we started off on the same track as the previous day, through the palace gate, down the big street and past the reservoir. From here we walked about half a mile to the south, to visit another palace, where other and larger ruins were to be seen. Part of this palace has been converted into a stud and breeding farm, and a large number of mares are kept in it. In the other part a village had sprung up, and the little huts of the Arabs were built among the great blocks of tabbia tumbled about in every direction. A good-sized mosque stood near the entrance, which contains the remains of some of the old Sultans. After scrambling over some masses of masonry, Eno took us down into a curious tunnel, which seemed to extend underground for a good distance. The story in connection with this tunnel is that Moulai Ismael, or some other Sultan as lunatic as himself, finding his periodical journeys from one capital to another rather warm work, set his slaves to construct a subterranean way from here to Marocco city, a distance of over 250 miles, to the end that he might always travel in the shade. In proof of this we were shown apertures, some four feet in height, which occurred at regular intervals, and which effectually disposed of a suggestion of mine that the thing was in reality only an aqueduct. These apertures were supposed to be used as means of exit, and to let in the air. The Sultan, whoever he was, seems to have soon got tired of his precious undertaking, and no doubt devoted his attention to some other work of equal sense and utility. I cannot, of course, vouch for the truth of the story, but nothing appears to have been too idiotic for these Moorish potentates to have attempted, many of whom seem to have varied their leisure time between torturing their unfortunate subjects, and commencing useless buildings, which they never finished. They probably did not spend much on the labour, the work being done by slaves and Christian captives.

Close by was a huge and rather gruesome-looking building, with *tabbia* walls some seventy feet in height, which was said to have been a granary, though it seemed strangely ill-adapted for the purpose. A small boy from the village made signs to us that we could scramble up to the top. Eno ("Old Fruit Salts" H— irreverently styled him) knew better than to risk his neck for nothing, and watched us from below. Following our youthful guide in a perilous climb over the crumbling masonry, we at length got out on to what resembled a square paddock, enclosed by walls twenty feet in height. The soil had accumulated on the flat roof, and the whole was overgrown with a thick covering of grass and weeds, and we forgot for the nonce that we were at a height of some fifty feet above the ground; only the holes appearing here and there in the surface, and the tumbledown look of the walls, bade us be on our guard against falling. Old Eno watched our descent with great anxiety, and when we got down took us home by a different way on the S.W. side of the town. This led us close to the beautiful gardens of the palace, past fortresses and walls innumerable, and over a lofty viaduct. The latter, like everything else, was in an advanced state of decay, and from the numerous holes in the track, through which we could peep down at a small stream running some forty feet below, we thought it would be a bad place to cross in the dark. As far as we could judge, from our rather superficial observation, the palaces of Mequinez, with their appendages, must have been of greater size and occupied a much larger space than the Alhambra itself. There seemed to be enough masonry in the towers and walls of the palaces (none of them less than eight or ten feet in thickness), with their granaries, aqueducts, tunnels, viaducts, &c., to build a large city. Only here not a trace could we discern of beauty or architectural ornament—nothing but vast masses of brown, shapeless *tabbia,* bearing in their ugliness and deformity the unmistakable impress of the degraded minds of their creators.

It seems strange, that in the works of no other travellers do I find any account of these ruins which, if only for their size and extent, surely merit notice. Rohlfs, who stayed here some time in the garb and faith of a Moslem, had his movements so narrowly watched, that any antiquarian researches would have brought him under suspicion. Very likely, many of them have not been visited, and it was only the accident of our meeting with a more intelligent cicerone in the person of the worthy Eno that took us further afield. No Moor has any interest in antiquities or archæology of any sort. They seem to have but two answers to questions as to the origin of buildings, "Dar del Sultan" (Sultan's palace), or "The Christians did it." The latter is so far true that nearly every building of any architectural merit at all owes its origin to Christian hands. The

Koran, which rigorously forbade the representation of human or even animal form, turned the Arabs from art of every kind, so that even the beauties of their achitecture were derived from foreign sources.

We thought we had done all our sight-seeing, but were urged to visit a great wall outside the Mellah. I fear I shall be accused of "yarning" when I say that this wall was twenty-five *yards* thick, but so it was, and Hoare is my witness on the point. It was of no great length, covered with grass on the top, and an Arab had his tent pitched thereon. I stepped its width, and it was certainly well over that of a cricket pitch. The great wall of Nineveh must have been a fool to this wall in point of thickness, though what it was intended for I cannot say. This wall, like many others, was the work of Christian captives, and it is related that when any of these fainted under the work, he was immediately despatched, and his carcase used as building material for the fabric.

The "lion," however, of Mequinez is unquestionably the magnificent gate through which we passed the previous day on entering the town—one of the finest pieces of architecture in the whole country. Above the horse-shoe arch is a façade of rich tile work and exquisite Moorish ornamentation in a very fair state of repair. The stucco-work is of a delicate though not very varied pattern. At the sides are two marble columns with Corinthian capitals. It struck me as somewhat remarkable that both the capitals should be identical, but the want of symmetry and patch-work character of most Moorish buildings is exemplified here by one of the projecting side portions of the structure resting upon pillars, the other not. It is altogether a very beautiful gate, and there is nothing like it to be seen in the Alhambra. It was built by a Spaniard at the command of his lord and master, the Sultan, and a story is current as to the fate he experienced as a reward for his services. On the completion of the work, the Sultan expressed his admiration and asked the Spaniard if a better could possibly be made. The unlucky Iberian airily replied that it was nothing to what he could do if he really tried, whereupon the monarch promptly had him seized, and his eyes put out, to prevent the possibility of his gate being "capped" by another and handsomer one. There are other versions of the same yarn, but this is the one I prefer, and which is supported, so to speak, by the best MS. authority.

There is little in the town itself that demands notice. The streets are narrower and dirtier than those of Fez, and the odours more varied and overpowering. The perfumes of Araby were here to welcome us in all the plenitude of their balmy fragrance, and I agree with Leo, who says, "the towne is so durtie in spring-time that it would irke a man to walke the streetes." One universal and very unpleasant smell is that from the cookshops, where highly-scented fragments of fish, bits of liver, and other "innards" are stewed in oil, and similar delicacies prepared. The town is exceedingly compact, like most Moorish towns, and probably does not cover a quarter of the space occupied by the palaces outside.

The Mellah has little to distinguish it from the other Ghettos we had seen; hard by is the Jew's cemetery, whose low, rounded, whitewashed tombs have a peculiarly gruesome look. The denizens of this unsavoury quarter struck us as appearing even more sorry for themselves than those at Fez, though I am not aware that they are more bullied here than elsewhere. Of the disabilities under which the Jews in Marocco labour, and their persecution by the Moors, I have already spoken, but without alluding to the causes thereof. When first in Marocco, I expended much pity on these unfortunate Hebrews which, however, gradually evaporated as I became more acquainted with their character and conduct. I came to the country somewhat of an upholder and admirer of the Jews; I went back, I had nearly said a confirmed Anti-Semite. The traveller in half-civilized countries, who has observed their dealings with the natives, cannot fail to have his views on the subject moulded by what he sees. I don't think a tourist in the outlying districts of Russia would care to subscribe to the victims of *Judenhetz* in those parts. He, of course, could not justify the outrages, but he would probably regard them as the regrettable, though natural, outcome of the pent-up indignation of a half-savage population against their alien oppressors. So it is in

Marocco, where the animosity of the natives against the Jews is quite as keen, and from time to time expresses itself in acts of violence. Anything of a craven nature, such as a dog or horse without pluck, is called by the Moors "Jhudi," and the same impulse that prompts boys at school to kick their more timid fellows, makes the Moor maltreat the Jew. Their position, however, has been bettered of late years, and Sir Moses Montefiore himself made a journey to Marocco to obtain concessions from the Sultan on their behalf. That distinguished philanthropist was likewise the means of founding Jewish schools, dispensaries for medicines, and other institutions in Tetuan and other towns of the coast

Apologists for the Jews have always tried to represent them as being the victims of religious persecution. This is only natural, as nothing is more gratifying to human nature than the distinction of martyrdom. The position, however, is quite an untenable one, and has been demolished by Professor Goldwin Smith, among others, in the pages of the *Nineteenth Century*.[2] He there showed conclusively that it is *not* fanaticism that prompts outrage, but "economical and social" causes; "the unhappy relation of a wandering and parasitic race, retaining its tribal exclusiveness, to the races among whom it sojourns, and on the produce of whose labour it feeds." Their whole conduct, in fact, is one continued policy of exaspera-

[2] *Nineteenth Century* for November, 1882.

tion. While forcing their presence on an unwilling people, they retain their exclusiveness, refuse to marry or eat with their new countrymen, and actually treat as unclean the victims of their extortions.

I am, however, only concerned with the single case of Marocco, and can add my testimony in support of Mr. Goldwin Smith's contention, that native animosity has its origin in other than sectarian motives. Why, in the name of common sense, should the Moors single out the Jews as the special objects of their religious hate? Kindred alike in race, character, customs, and language, the two great branches of the Semitic stock are partners in upholding their fundamental doctrine of the unity of God. Mohammed himself was half a Jew by birth, and in character and habits of thought. His chief type and model was the Jewish prophet Moses. His religion was borrowed entirely from the Talmud and the old Jewish Gospels, and, as Professor Monier Williams[3] remarks in this connection, the first Moslem, according to Mohammedan notions, was Abraham. But I need not pursue the subject further, as it will be seen that the Moors, like the Russians, have far more solid and enduring reasons for disliking the Jews than mere religious differences. As Professor G. Smith finely says: "The oppression exercised by unscrupulous cunning, is not less grinding or less wicked than that which is exer-

[3] *Nineteenth Century* for July, 1882.

cised by force, though civilization, in its present stage, condemns the one as barbarous, and allows law to be made the instrument of the other. No cruelty, in truth, is more maddening than that of the legal vampire." The tyranny of the Jews in this country is exercised in many ways, by the small loans at usurious rates of interest, with which every country is familiar, and other methods which have gradually become inseparably connected with the word "Jew." By this means the poor peasant is gradually enmeshed, till at length he falls an easy prey. But the extortion in Marocco is by no means always "legal." The iniquities connected with the system of "protection," which will be dealt with later on, offer a fine field for the unbounded exercise of their peculiar talents. But above all, the superior brain of the Jew gives him unlimited opportunities of swindling the Moorish peasant, whom we observed to be the most gullible creature imaginable, and this results in terrible oppression. A thousand dirty tricks, most of them connected with the coinage, which would seem hardly capable of deceiving a child, are practised with complete success on these unfortunate people. In the ever-recurring famines and hard times, the Jew, who is always more or less of a capitalist, goes round the country, and by driving hard bargains reaps a fine harvest out of the dire necessities of the starving populace.

Experience shows that the number of Jews in a country is, as a rule, in inverse ratio to its material prosperity. Their rapacious instincts lead them to those places where they find the people the easiest prey. Hence Marocco, the most backward country in the world, with a population one-sixth that of England, has at least twice as many Jews. They are the descendants, for the most part, of the Hebrews who were expelled by religious persecution from Spain at the close of the fifteenth century. It should be mentioned that, in some respects, the Jews are really better off than the Moors. They are exempt from military service, having to pay a "jazial" (contribution) instead, and if a Jew is killed, there is far more fuss made about it than there would be in the case of a Moor. That clannishness of the Jews, all over the world, that makes them so powerful, prevents the interests of their suffering brethren in Marocco from being overlooked. It is a great mistake, therefore, to suppose that the Jews here can be persecuted with impunity.

The charge so frequently levelled at the Jews, that they are non-producers, cannot, with justice, be brought against all of their number in Marocco. It would be unfair to describe the whole body here as "parasitic," and enough lies at their door without this. The most skilful craftsmen in leather, metal, and other material, are to be found amongst them. In fact, the intellectual capacity of the Jew is infinitely superior to that of the Moor. Their value as capitalists is recognized by the Maroquin governors, who in some places even forbid them to depart out of their coasts. They are, of course, handy subjects for squeezing when money is required, as their money-getting instincts compel them to amass wealth, even when they know it may be screwed out of them. So it has been from time to time in European history, and various sovereigns have found it convenient to foster and encourage Jewish extortion, so as to have a large source of revenue ready to be drawn on in case of need. However, "sufferance is the badge of all their tribe," and they patiently put up with persecution rather than lose the chance of making money. They are content to bide their time, knowing well that their turn will come, and that they will in the end be at least even with their persecutors. Nor are the Moors by any means the only people who find the Marocco Jews useful. As agents and intermediaries in various transactions they are of great service to Europeans, and rich Jews are always ready to purchase a "protection," in which case their position is assured. The protected Jew, as a rule, is to be found in the coast towns. Confident in his own inviolability, he raises his head, puts out his stomach, and walks around with a sort of "touch me if you dare" look, inexpressibly exasperating. He is not slow to avail himself of the advantages his position offers, and woe be to the unfortunate Moor who falls into his clutches. His poorer co-religionists pay for this assumption on his part, being made the scapegoats of the exasperation which his conduct excites. If exceptionally fortunate, a rich Jew may even secure a

European (French) decoration for his distinguished services to civilization and humanity.

The Jews, of course, never intermarry with the Moors, but a strain of Jewish blood has been introduced by pretty Jewesses being "annexed" by the caterers for the harems of the Sultan and other dignitaries. Much has been written about the beauty of these Israelitish ladies, but I think they are a little over-praised. It is, at best, of a purely animal type, but such as it is, there is generally plenty of it. The Moors, however, seem to appreciate bulk, and the Jew who is the owner of a pretty and substantial wife or daughter, may get off a good many kicks and buffets for her sake. *Quis contemnat Hebræos qui tam decoras mulieres habent*, to borrow a well-known quotation, and the complaisance of some of these sons of Israel is truly astonishing.

Their enslaved and benighted condition renders the Jews very superstitious, and some of their beliefs are even grosser than those of the Moors. Every house in the Mellah has its cabalistic mark, to ward off the evil eye; charms, incantations, and the vilest potions are employed as cures for disease. The more disgusting the concoction, the greater their belief in its efficacy—dead men's bones, liquid filth, and other unpleasant materials, being held in high esteem. Some of these remedies are also in use among the Moors. A few Jews practise the healing art in a more rational way and keep dispensaries. They showed us one such at Mogador—

only he was said to be unable to read the names of the medicines on his bottles, which was rather a drawback.

The Jews of Marocco have, beyond doubt, much excuse for their barbarism and evil doings. Centuries of ill-usage have broken their spirit; ignorance and their foul dwellings and surroundings aid in brutalizing and debasing their morals. The above-mentioned schools, with teachers from Europe (I saw one of these at Tetuan, a bright, intelligent young fellow), are doing much good, but they are at present confined to the coast towns. In the fulness of time we may expect to see them extended inland, and then, with better education and with the advance of civilization, it is earnestly to be hoped that the condition of all the Jews may be bettered, and their opportunities for oppression curtailed, to the advantage both of themselves and the Moors.

CHAPTER VII.

Gorgeous escort—Moorish saddlery—Saraoun—Volubilis—Moulai Idrees—Saint-worship in Marocco—Its inconsistency with the true creed of Islam—Probable causes of saint-worship.

BEFORE leaving Mequinez we applied to the Bascha for leave to visit Kasr el Faraun (Pharaoh's Castle), near Moulai Idrees, where stand the interesting Roman ruins which have now been identified with the ancient town of Volubilis. The authorities made some difficulty about it, as the people there were said to be in a disturbed state, having some "question" with the Sultan. Eventually it was arranged that a soldier of the Bascha should accompany us there, and make things straight for us. On the morning of the 27th he arrived, a most gorgeous personage, got up quite regardless of expense, and putting the rather travel-stained splendour of Al Kaid Hadj Absalam completely in the shade. On his feet were bright yellow riding-boots with red trimmings, reaching to the knee, into which were tucked breeches of dark blue cloth. Above was a sea-green garment, surmounted by a *soulham* (cloak) of most spotless white, and the flowing folds of his *haik* and a fine turban, combined with the variegated trappings of his grey charger, completed a very effective picture. He carried a sword, pistol, and gun of most formidable proportions, and if we did feel any uneasiness at venturing into the fanatical domains of his deceased Holiness, Moulai Idrees, a glance at those weapons at once dispelled it. His horse's accoutrements were a study in themselves. A Moorish saddle is a wooden contrivance with a peak in front and a back behind, resting on a dozen thick blankets of various colours. I only once got into one, and soon came to the conclusion that Nature had not fashioned my body to sit on a Moorish saddle, any more than she had framed my throat to speak the Moorish tongue. Every bone I possessed seemed to meet a corresponding protuberance in the saddle, and riding as they do, with their knees almost up to their chins, soon gives you the cramp. You cannot well be thrown out, but should the horse fall, you will inevitably be impaled on the sharp peak in front. They use enormous stirrups of iron, graven in various patterns. The spur is a formidable spike five inches long; a handy weapon for disembowelling your horse, should you feel inclined. The end rests on the stirrup, so that when a Moor wants to make his horse prance or caracole, or stand on his hindlegs, or perform any of the other antics in which the natives delight, there is heard a clanking sound as of falling fireirons, a small hole is made in the flank, and the animal generally takes the hint at once. In default of the spur, the corner of the stirrup may be employed with a very fair result.

It will not make such a deep hole as the spur, but if used with skill will dig a furrow in the skin that operates nearly as well. In the *Lab el baroud* (powder play) and other displays, the horse's sides are often to be seen dripping with blood. The bit is tremendously powerful, and has a ring which compresses the chin when the rein is pulled. As soon as this has been used a little, and has established a tolerable raw, it becomes highly effective. "Shocking cruelty," the reader will say. Perhaps, yet not so much cruelty as such utter want of common sense.

The road led us down a deep valley richly wooded with orange-groves, palms, figs, poplars, and other trees. On the rocky slopes of the Saraoun hills facing us were perched several small walled towns, with their encircling groves of olives. Our route was in a northerly direction across a plain of scrub, and we were now entering on the province of Saraoun, or Sarhoun. The mountains here take a turn to the north, and the road skirts the western side of the range. By the track lay several large blocks of hewn limestone, which, we were told, were ordered by Moulai Ismael to be carried to Mequinez for building purposes; but that, on his dying in the meanwhile, the stones were left by the roadside. As many of the stones must have weighed half a ton, there must have been giants in those days. Others say that Moulai Ismael got the Devil, with whom his iniquities no doubt brought him into close contact, to carry them for him. From a comparison with the ruins at Kasr el Faraun, there can be little doubt that they were conveyed from there. Soon there appeared round a shoulder of the mountains the town of Moulai Idrees, or Saraoun, romantically situated in a gorge densely wooded with olives, and surrounded by rugged limestone cliffs. To the left were the ruins of which we were in search, and a ride of three-quarters of an hour took us to a small stream, fringed with oleanders, which issued from the gorge. The hillside here was strewn with hewn blocks of stone and bits of Roman sculpture, showing the extent of the building in former times. There is now little left standing, and owing to the frequent depredations of the natives, who remove the material for their own uses, it is probable that in a few years nothing but a few stones will remain to mark this interesting historical site.

The ruins have been described more than once, and their identity with Volubilis, a Roman colony of Mauritania Tingitana, or Western Barbary, has been placed beyond dispute. There only remains standing the ruins of two separate buildings, though the sites and traces of other houses can be seen round about. The Moors themselves can give no intelligible account of the ruins, which, in common with various other buildings, are called by the natives Pharaoh's castle. If you ask who Pharaoh was, they will probably say he was a Christian, and therefore, of course, an accomplished architect; but they will not enlighten you as to what brought him so far West as this. Leo speaks of a town called Walili, somewhere about this site, but has little to say upon the subject. In fact, modern geographers seem to be almost equally hazy concerning this locality, which is very inaccurately described on the maps. On ours I find the mountains wrongly depicted, and Moulai Idrees is put many miles to the north of its actual situation. Important places are omitted, and of the names which are given, half are unknown to the natives.

We did not visit the town of Moulai Idrees, as it is holy ground and has never been profaned by the foot of a Christian. The ancestors of the population are said to have been Christians themselves once, and the inhabitants are all descendants of the Prophet. The eponymous hero of the place is the same Moulai Idrees whose shrine is in Fez, and whose son was the founder of that city. He is the most important saint in the whole Moorish calendar —the one in whose name beggars solicit alms, and to whom everybody prays. Little is known about him, except that he was a kinsman of the Prophet, and that he came from Mecca to Marocco, where he lived and died in the odour of the greatest sanctity. He appears to have had a sweet tooth, being the patron saint of sweetmeats, and all the vendors of the sticky nastinesses one sees in various places here sell them in his name. His sanctuary, which is said to be handsomely decorated, lies at the back of the town. It is the holiest shrine in Marocco, and no Christian or Jew dare venture anywhere near its precincts. To it every Sultan must make a pilgrimage on his accession to the throne, and when he has performed his orisons at the great tomb within the mosque, wherein are laid the bones of the saint, he emerges the crowned Emperor of Marocco.

Here is a striking instance of the important part the saints play in the religion of the country. The final act of the coronation ceremony is performed at the shrine of a marabout. Few things will strike the observant traveller in Eastern lands more than the veneration paid to saints by Mohammedans. All over Marocco are to be seen the white, rounded roofs of the *kubbahs* or marabouts' tombs, and where the poverty of the people will not permit of such costly edifices, humbler monuments are reared to their memory. Here and there may be seen heaps of stones daubed with whitewash, and a stick planted in the midst with a few rags fluttering therefrom, marking the grave of some departed worthy who has been canonized in the estimation of the people, and to whom the peasants bring their simple offerings of flowers and even food. It is a species of hero worship, part of the universal instinct of admiring merit, misplaced no doubt at times, but thoroughly genuine. Sometimes these saints may have been men whose good deeds and charities live in the grateful recollection of the populace; but more often they were simply rogues of the first water, who by superior cunning and adroitness gained ascendency and a reputation for peculiar wisdom. In some cases they were even men of monstrous wickedness, of which his deceased Majesty Moulai Ismael affords an instance. There is no warrant for this saint-worship in the Koran, which inculcates that of the one true God, making

Mohammed the sole Prophet and Mediator with Him. It would, in fact, seem in opposition to the fundamental tenets of the faith, and its growth appears analogous to that of saint-worship in Roman Catholicism, which gradually became engrafted on the true faith of the ancient Christian Church. Very probably it is in both cases a survival of old pagan beliefs which have never been completely rooted out, even by Christianity. The old ideas penetrate the crust of the new faith, and crop up from time to time on the surface of the popular belief. Among Mohammedans it is also an outcome of human nature, a protest against the barren formalism of their religion, and an attempt to satisfy their longings for something nearer and more comprehensible than Allah. There are only two main ideas present to their minds in connection with Allah—that He is One, and that He is Omnipotent. With them there is no communion between man and his Creator, who is a Being released from all obligations to His creatures, and therefore hard to love. A Moor's prayers consist chiefly of a formal confession of faith and praise of Allah; they are hardly ever petitions. It is to his saint that he turns in times of sore need and distress, and to whom he ascribes any good fortune that may befall him. If the devout Moslem enters a mosque with awe and reverence, and performs his orisons there from a sense of duty, his feelings at the shrine of his patron saint are rather those of affection and gratitude.

From this point of view the idea of Allah would seem to occupy a less important place in the later developments of popular Mohammedanism. True, the name of Allah is always on the lips of a Moor. He uses it when he bruises his shins, cuts his finger, or knocks a glass off the table—in fact, pretty much as a European would an oath. He introduces it in ribald songs, and in every other sentence of ordinary conversation, and while committing trivial and even wicked actions. But this can hardly be regarded as a sign of reverence, rather the reverse. His devotion to his saint is far more genuine, and springs from a more truly religious instinct. Of course, the cult of the saints and all appertaining to them, is encouraged by the rulers, just as the Popes and other ecclesiastics of the Christian Church fostered the belief in miracles and relics, as a fruitful source of revenue. The descendants of a deceased marabout look after his tomb, and keep it in repair, and get contributions from pious worshippers thereat. Visitors to Tangier cannot fail to have seen (and heard) parties of men perambulating the place of a Friday with banners, and making day hideous with the din of their pipes and tom-toms, in order to collect subscriptions for their saint-house. Relics of their departed progenitor are also found very profitable. It would be too much to say that this phase of the national religion is leading the Moors back to idolatry, but it has unquestionably effected a very considerable modification of the faith as it existed in earlier days.

CHAPTER VIII.

Sects of Islam—Its practice—The Hadj—Fasts—Prayer—Status of women in Marocco—Faith of Islam—Beliefs concerning the next world—Superstitions—Parallelism with popular Catholicism—Spread of Islam in Marocco—Causes of its decay—Hopelessness of reform.

Marocco, where the true Arab spirit is preserved in its integrity, is the best country in the world to study Islam in its purest form, unadulterated by contact with civilization and Christianity. Here the traveller, with the recollection of the past glories of the nation in his mind, and its present depravity before his eyes, can meditate with profit on the creed which even now, in the days of its hopeless degeneration, is the guiding star of more than a hundred and fifty millions of our fellow-men. For those of my readers who are unlearned in the subject, I propose to give a sketch of the religion as it exists here at the present day; persons well read on such matters had better pass on to the next chapter.

There are three main divisions or sects of Islam, the Wahhabites, the Shiites, and the Sonnites. The order given is reverse to their relative importance. The Wahhabites are a later sect (their founder, Ben Abdul Wahhab, lived in the middle of the last century); they are the strictest of Mohammedans, the Puritans of their religion, which, with them, appears to be Islam in its most ideal shape. Their sect is confined to certain districts of Arabia. The Shiites, the Broad Church of Islam, are accounted heretical by their opponents, because they differ in their views concerning the succession to the Khalifate, a point to which they attach the greatest importance. Their principal opponents were the Kharejites, who revolted against Ali, the son-in-law of Mohammed, whom the Shiites supported. The Shiites are also more liberal-minded and enlightened than the other sects, which of course does not increase their reputation for orthodoxy. They are to be found chiefly in Persia, where the teachings of Zoroaster have not yet died out, but have left an abiding mark upon the religion of the country. The Sonnites, or followers of the traditions of Mohammed, are the only orthodox sect. They are divided into four main parties, each of whom follow the teachings of their chief Imam, or doctor, viz. those of Abu Hanifa, Malek, El Shaffei, and Hanbal. That of Malek, however, alone concerns us, for it is his system that prevails in Marocco. He flourished in the eight century, and is said to have paid great respect to the traditions of Mohammed. He was a man of great piety and learning, and was author of various works interpreting the Koran.

It must be remembered that most of the distinctions over which these sages expended so much labour and learning are on very trifling matters; distinctions without a difference, according to our ideas. It would be difficult to imagine a more unprofitable study than Moorish theology. The most trivial questions are sufficient to evoke the *odium theologicum* of the Maroquin divines; such as how one should wash, what position is most suitable for prayer, and the like. Rohlfs mentions as subjects of keen argument, whether Mohammed sacrificed a black or white ram after the first Ramadan, and the size of hell. Any discussion of the dogma itself would be accounted heretical, and, to say the least of it, decidedly imprudent. Hence the Malekitish system differs from the other three only in matters relating to the formal practice of the religion, with which I shall now proceed to deal.

The practical religion of the Moors consists almost wholly of certain outward acts, of which the following five, called the "Pillars of Islam," are the most important: (1) confession of faith in God and Mohammed, (2) to pray (and wash), (3) to keep the appointed fasts, (4) almsgiving, (5) to perform the Hadj, or pilgrimage to Mecca. It will be seen that four out of these five are purely formal, and it may be said that now the religion is entirely one of external performances. True, the Koran inculcates a holy life as necessary to salvation, but the Moor prefers to trust to his formal piety to carry him through. He keeps a sort of balance account; so many sins to be expiated by so many prayers, ablutions, pilgrimages, or fastings, as the case may be, and the latter are seldom on the credit side.

Perhaps the most important of these practical duties is the Hadj. There is some little doubt whether it was ordained by Mohammed, though it appears in the Koran, but in any case it is now a recognized duty in Islam. It is the great aim of every pious Moslem, to whom it is the crown of a religious life, the expiation of all sins past, present, and to come, and a sure passport to a blessed immortality. When he has performed it, a Moor is apt to be so satisfied with his spiritual condition that he grows lax, and gives the rein to every evil inclination. If you tackle one of these pious sinners on the subject, and ask him if he really considers himself freed from all moral restraints, he will betray great confusion of mind concerning the matter, like a certain Hadj of my acquaintance, who confided to me that he was sure in any case to go to heaven, but that at the same time he must not lie or cheat —which he did all the same, to the utmost of his ability. In fact, all their ideas on such abstruse subjects as justification by faith and by works are decidedly mixed—but then so are those of many of us Christians.

In the old days, when the pilgrims tramped the whole way, it was a tremendous undertaking. Now, however, things are more conveniently ordered, owing to the introduction of steam; and there are various Moorish Cooks and Gazes by whom the pious ones of Western Islam are "personally conducted" in gangs to the shrine of the Prophet on boats specially chartered for the purpose. At the same time considerable privations have to be endured on board these steamers, especially if disease should break out on the voyage. When I left Tangier, there was a pilgrim ship lying in quarantine in the harbour.

The Hadj may be done by proxy, just as Mark Twain did the Alps, " by agent." The rich Moor usually hires a substitute, gives him a sum of money, and starts him off. The "agent" probably goes as far as Alexandria, where he has a good time as long as his funds last, and then returns with an immense reputation for sanctity, both for himself and his principal. It will be seen that this method kills two birds with one stone. The Hadj is also performed as an office of merit for the souls of departed relatives.

Almsgiving is especially enjoined by the Koran, which directs a tenth part of a man's goods to be given to the poor, but I need not say that this is seldom carried out in Marocco or elsewhere.

The fast of Ramadan is scrupulously kept. From dawn to sunset for twenty-eight days nobody may eat, drink, smoke, or eat *haschish*. They make up for it, however, in the nights, which are of a very lively character. When the fast falls in the summer months, the heat and length of the day make it very trying, especially to weak constitutions. Every one's digestion is upset, their nervous systems deranged, and their tempers only what might be expected under the circumstances. The fast is excused to "*bonâ fide* travellers," so that a surprising number of Moors find it necessary to start on long journeys during Ramadan.

Of the three great reforms instituted by Mohammed—monotheism, temperance, and cleanliness—the two last are in danger of losing their virtue in Marocco. Their purifications are in a large measure formal, and do not extend to their clothing or habitations, and in view of the appalling filth prevailing everywhere, it cannot be said that the Moors are a cleanly people. It is to be feared, too, that, owing to European, and we must reluctantly add, Christian influence, drunkenness is on the increase. In Tangier, particularly, the low drinking-shops set up by Spaniards and Jews have already wrought much mischief among the natives. Drink, however, is one of the blessings which we must expect to accompany the march of European civilization.

Prayer is performed five times a day—at morning, noon, afternoon, sunset, and night, when the plaintive cry of the mueddin may be heard calling the faithful to worship. The prayers consist of a set confession of faith, accompanied by set gestures and positions. It is a very picturesque performance, and one which there is no difficulty in witnessing, as they always take care to go through it when there is an audience round. The mosques are used chiefly on Fridays, when a sort of service is performed and a sermon preached. The Moors take their shoes from off their feet when they enter a mosque, and they are forbidden to pray in sumptuous apparel. Herein, as Sale remarks, something is to be learned from them by the English upper classes, who make themselves so gorgeous of a Sunday that poorer folk are abashed and kept away from church. Women, too, are strictly forbidden to worship in company with men. The common belief is that women are not allowed inside a mosque at all, but Rohlfs affirms this to be a mistake, and I fancy I have seen women in the mosques myself, but I am not sure.

The charge often made against Mohammed, that he lowered women in the social scale is certainly justified by their condition in Marocco, where they are treated as menial servants, and sometimes even as beasts of burden. The Koran speaks of woman as an incomplete creation, an inferior being, who should be treated with kindness indeed, but chastised when occasion demands.

> "Use the woman tenderly, tenderly,
> From a crooked rib God made her slenderly;
> Straight and strong He could not make her,"

as Goethe says, paraphrasing the teachings of Islam. Their functions are simply to work and bear children. They are entirely uneducated, not being even taught to read, jealously guarded all their lives, and in the next world shelved to make room for the beatified houris of Paradise. Whether they will be admitted at all to the Mohammedan heaven is not quite certain, and in any case they will have no place in the common abode of men, except perhaps by special permission. It was certainly most ungallant in so ardent an admirer of the sex as Mohammed, that, while he made such ample provision for the men, who are to have seventy-two houris apiece, with, I think, eighty thousand slaves, he did nothing to secure male companionship for the ladies. Further, he once gave the comforting assurance that when Paradise was revealed to him, he saw that the majority of its denizens were the poor, but that on looking down to hell he observed it chiefly peopled with women.

This, however, is trenching on the second part of Islam, its faith, which is of equal importance with its practice. Their belief must be absolute in God and Mohammed, and in the prophets; in the Scriptures, and in the Resurrection and the Day of Judgment; in the angels, and in the doctrine of predestination. These must be accepted in their entirety, though some little latitude of opinion is allowed about trifling details connected with the domestic economy of the next world, e.g. what food will be provided (no trifle to a Moor), the exact number of houris and slaves that each true believer will have, the precise size and material of the pavilions in which they will dwell, &c., &c. Of theology dealing with the great problems affecting the destiny and welfare of mankind, there is none in Marocco. The Moors, for instance, are fatalists, like all Mohammedans, but no attempt is ever made to reconcile the doctrine of predestination with the necessity of a virtuous life. The religion bristles with similar inconsistencies, but in the degraded state of their intellects it is doubtful whether the difficulties even occur to them. Fatalists as they are, especially when their faults or shortcomings require to be excused, I never knew of their applying the doctrine in the case of their good actions. In that case, that of free-will invariably comes into play.

After death the Moors believe that they are examined in the grave by two black, livid, angels of terrible aspect, called Monkir and Nakir, who order the corpse to sit upright, and test his orthodoxy. For this reason the more orthodox are buried in a sitting posture, to be ready for the examination. It would seem that this takes place almost immediately after death, for it is the opinion of many that the soul rests but one night in the body after burial, during which pious friends often perform certain offices akin to the Roman Catholic masses for the dead. If the answers to the examination be satisfactory, the corpse is allowed to rest in peace; if not, he is beaten on the head with iron maces, and bitten and stung by venomous beasts till he roars aloud for anguish.

The Day of Judgment will be heralded by various signs, one of which is to be the coming of Moolsaa (the Mahdi), which may account in part for the frequent appearance of false prophets in the East. The resurrection will include all living creatures, according to the popular belief, though there is no direct authority for it in the Koran. The Judgment Day will last from forty years to fifty thousand years, according to various opinions, and it appears that while waiting their trial both just and unjust will be tortured impartially, though the torments of the former will be much lighter. After judgment all creatures, both men and brutes, will take vengeance of each other for injuries suffered, after which, according to Sale, the beasts will be changed into dust. This would seem to show that the prevalent idea that they have a place in the future life is a mistaken one, although the same authority tells us that certain favourite animals, such as the dog of the Seven Sleepers, and Ezra's ass, will by special licence be admitted to Paradise. Whether the exception made on behalf of the pet dog and donkey will ever be extended to a favourite wife is, as I have already said, a moot point. When all have thus taken mutual satisfaction of each other, the whole body will pass to their allotted abodes, but first every one must cross the bridge Al Sirat, which is finer than a hair and sharper than a sword. At this ordeal the wicked will grow dizzy and fall off into the pit of hell, but the righteous will pass over swiftly and in safety.

That sense of pious satisfaction which is felt by some good Christians at the prospect of the future torments of the damned is shared in a still greater degree by the Moors. Every true Moslem delights in contemplating the pleasant things in store for the unbeliever in the Mohammedan inferno. Only infidels will suffer eternal punishment; wicked believers will be punished for periods varying from 900 to 7000 years by being scorched and burnt, till at length they will be washed white in the river of life and admitted into Paradise.

The delights of the Mohammedan Paradise, with its pavilions of pearl, its flowing streams and ravishing odours, its damsels of peerless beauty, are too well known to need description. Suffice it to say that, according to Rohlfs, the conventional dark-eyed houris will, in the Moorish belief, be supplanted by "golden-haired, blue-eyed English girls, whom the Moors esteem the most beautiful of women." I trust my fair countrywomen will appreciate the compliment—as well as the prospect of assured felicity hereafter!

The Moors, like most semi-civilized people, have that craving after the supernatural which always seems associated with barbarism on the one hand, and vulgarity on the other. Necromancers and such like make a good thing out of the people, though probably much less than does a "medium" or "thought-reader" in a good way of business in England. Leo Africanus speaks of the cabalists and alchemists in his day, the latter of whom he describes as being "mightily addicted to that vaine practice; they are most base fellows, and contaminate themselves with the steam of Sulphur and other stinking smels." Volumes could be filled with an account of the native superstitions, but this is not the place to go into them. Suffice it to say that they are curiously interwoven, in some instances, with pagan and Christian beliefs, such as the mark of the cross, and the invocation of the name of Mary by women in childbirth, sacrifices to appease bad spirits, and other old heathen observances.

The inhabitants of Marocco are justly accounted fanatical, but I question whether what is called fanaticism is not very often a kind of shy dread and distrust of the Christian stranger, enhanced by the recollection of injury, rather than any depth of religious conviction. The best proof of this is the way it wears off with intercourse and kind treatment. Make friends with a Moor, and he will, especially if he be a countryman, treat you every bit as well as one of his co-religionists. Our experience went to show that the dwellers in the country districts are far less fanatical, and kindlier-natured than the townsmen.

I cannot quit the subject without alluding to the close parallelism which, as it seems to me, exists between popular religion in Islam and that on the other side of the Straits of Gibraltar, and in parts of Italy and other Catholic countries. In Spain, particularly, the traces of Moorish blood and Moorish characteristics which yet linger among the people serve to accentuate the similarity. Of the worship of the saints, and the pilgrimages to their shrines to secure their favour and blessing, I have already spoken as being common to both religions. In both is exhibited the same blind faith and reverence for their spiritual superiors—the Shereef is environed, in the popular imagination, with something very much akin to Papal infallibility—kindred beliefs in the supernatural, in miracles, and in the value of relics and charms. Self-discipline is the practice of either faith, and the flagellations and hair-shirts of the Christian ascetic have their counterpart in the self-inflicted wounds of the Aissauias and other religious orders in Marocco. Fasting is enjoined by both, though each faith has other forms of abstinence peculiar to itself, the pious Moslem abstaining from wine, the Christian monk from women. The importance of tradition in the two creeds, the formal expiation of sins, the frequent use of the name of God, belief in the interposition of Providence or the saints on trifling occasions, and certain details common to both, all these help to sustain the comparison; but the closest point of contact is, in my opinion, to be found in the blending of religion with every-day life, without necessarily making it the guide of daily conduct, and the practical separation of the ideas of piety and morality. The following remarkable passage from Shelley's introduction to his tragedy of the Cenci will, perhaps, make my meaning clearer. He says, "Religion in Italy is not, as in Protestant countries, a cloak to be worn on particular days; or a passport which those who do not wish to be railed at carry with them to exhibit." (I must confess it is very much such a "passport" in Marocco.) . . . "It is interwoven with the whole fabric of life. It is adoration, faith, submission, penitence, blind admiration; not a rule for moral conduct. It has no necessary connection with any one virtue. The most atrocious villain may be rigidly devout, and, without any shock to the established faith, confess himself to be so. Religion pervades intensely the whole frame of society, and is, according to the temper of the mind it inhabits, a passion, a persuasion, an excuse, a refuge; never a check." I cannot quite endorse all this as it stands, but for "Italy" read "Marocco," and you have an almost perfect picture of Moorish popular religion. It is really quite remarkable to see how the greatest and most palpable scoundrels here will regularly perform the ordinances of religion, and believe in their efficacy, gaining thereby, among the simple populace, the reputation of piety in their lives, and after death the honour of saints. Power and good fortune, they think, are the gifts of Allah, and will be bestowed by Him without any reference to the personal merits of the recipient.[1]

One fundamental difference, however, must be noted. In Marocco there is no priesthood, and here, it must admitted, the advantage is all on the side of the Moslem, who will not permit of any earthly intermediary between himself and Allah. They are as democratic in religion as in other matters, and any such assumption of spiritual

[1] I should have mentioned two other resemblances, viz. the mechanical aids to worship, such as gestures, genuflections, postures, the telling of beads, &c., and various offices on behalf of the dead which are held to be of merit in either system.

authority would not be countenanced for a moment. The only privileged class are the Shereefs or descendants of the Prophet.

Be the religion what it may, it has taken such a firm hold on the people as probably no other faith possesses. The labours of Christian missionaries are almost fruitless here, and those who are wisest confine their efforts to converting the Jews, and so avoid the risk of creating a disturbance and making things unpleasant for themselves and their neighbours. At the time of the Moorish invasion in 681 A.D., the Berber population had for centuries adopted the faith of their Roman conquerors, but in the days of the decaying Byzantine empire Christianity was hardly worthy of the name. Torn in pieces by trivial disputes and superstitious heresies, the Church fostered rather than restrained the universal moral depravity which had overspread its dominions. Thus the Christianized Moors fell an easy prey to the fierce warriors of Islam, whose creed was their battle-cry, and the trenchant argument of the sword soon dispelled any lingering religious doubts they may have entertained. Though they have never been animated with the same consuming zeal for Islam as filled their Arab conquerors, they have ever since remained true to their new faith. There is, I believe, no parallel instance in history of the complete extermination of Christianity in a country where it had been so long and firmly established.

The new creed spread like wild-fire along the

southern borders of Marocco, and is probably now extending its frontiers among the negro races of the interior. It reached Timbuctoo some centuries ago, and its boundaries at the present day are unknown. Probably no other religion makes so many converts. The reason is not hard to find. It is a faith comprised in the one simple and all-embracing formula—enforced often at the sword's point,—" There is no God but God, and Mohammed is the Envoy of God." Here are no subtle intricacies or mysterious contradictions to puzzle the savage mind, and so render its acceptance difficult. It at least exercises a beneficial effect in raising the blacks from fetishism and idol-worship, though it has doubtless proved an obstacle in the path of civilization by giving unity and cohesion to savage tribes that before were too weak and divided to offer serious opposition to European colonization.

But if the causes of its progress are easy to determine, those of its sudden decay are not so apparent. Surely nation never had so rapid and complete a downfall as the Moors. How is it that six centuries have wrought such a direful change in a people once the foremost in Europe in the arts of peace as well as of war—the light as well as the dread of the civilized world? While the ardour of conquest and zeal for a new faith sustained them, the Arabs were irresistible; but when these were extinguished, the religion lost its quickening power, and, having no power of advancing, relapsed into that barren formalism which was the precursor of its decay. The system of Islam from the first contained within itself the germs of degeneration. It possessed no capabilities of expansion, no possibilities of progress to meet the intellectual demands of more enlightened generations. It has been well said [1] that "Islam is an Arab religion, made by an Arab for Arabs," and again, that "the Arabic nationality is not the cradle but the boundary-wall of Islam." When, therefore, it tried to adapt itself to people more advanced than the simple men for whom it was designed—in a word, when it aimed at being universal—it lost its true character and ceased to be Islam. Civilization has advanced too far for Mohammedanism ever to render it service. It must always be the religion of the ignorant and unreflective, for its fixed and unalterable character affords no scope for intellectual development. Hence its paralyzing influence. The scientific triumphs of the old Moors, so grudgingly acknowledged by Christendom, were achieved in spite of, rather than as a result of, their faith, for they glorified learning somewhat at the expense of religion. The breach between faith and culture widened, till at last the nation fell back upon the Koran as containing all necessary knowledge. Renan divides Islam into two periods: (1) up to the end of the twelfth century, the period of intellectual growth and liberal opinions, followed by material prosperity; (2) that of decay, when fanaticism

[1] Professor Kuenen, Hibbert Lectures, 1882.

gained the ascendency, and blind faith succeeded to reason. As he says, in putting an end to scientific progress they wrought their own ruin.

The semi-barbarous Moor is indeed the typical Mussulman of to-day. Here the spiritual authority dominates everything, being indissolubly united with that of the State. Every intellectual aspiration is crushed; all must think in one groove, and you depart therefrom at your peril. As soon as a Moor has learned to gabble off a few verses of the Koran—which he probably does not understand, as the vulgar tongue of Marocco differs much from classic Arabic—a most absurd conceit takes hold of him. He thinks he has attained to the springs of eternal truth, and that no further knowledge is necessary or even desirable. Hence all scientific investigation is rigorously tabooed. The mysteries of the universe are in the keeping of Allah, and it would be impious to pry into them. The puerile fancies of the cosmogony of the Koran are sufficient to satisfy the most learned men in Marocco. It is the same with all material improvement. With the pigheadedness born of ignorance, the Moor thinks that what was good enough for his fathers is good enough for him, and will hear of no change. Lastly, while the Koran remains their sole guide, all legal and social reforms are of course out of the question, and the country must remain wrapped in barbarism.

My chief object in making these remarks is to show the utter hopelessness of expecting better things under the present system. All ideas of reforming from within the system of organized iniquity that calls itself a government should be brushed aside like so many cobwebs. Islam is going backwards instead of forwards, and has been doing so steadily for centuries. There is no possible reason for imagining that the experience of history can ever be reversed in the case of Marocco, which affords the most glaring example of the above truth. After all, the most practical criticism on Mohammedanism is the present condition of all Mohammedan countries. " By their fruits ye shall know them," and judged by that standard, Islam has been long tried and found wanting. The Moors have had their day. The sun of their greatness and prosperity, which for a while shed such a brilliant light upon the world, has set, never to rise again. Their dominion must ere long cease, to make way, we trust, for something better.

CHAPTER IX.

Obeisance to our escort—Moorish mendacity—blood-tax—Irregular proceedings of the Sultan's cavalry—High-handed oppression—Iniquities of native rule—Mirage—Beni Hassen—Dangerous neighbours—Hadj Absalam's ablutions—Distress of the people—A Kaid in irons—Sallee—Idiotic ferry over the Boo-ragrag—Rabat—Moorish sepulture—Shellah—Tower of Hassen—Mosque.

AFTER this digression I will resume my narrative. Leaving the ruins, we rode on to a village where the tents had been pitched. On the way we passed several groups of peasants, who, awe-struck at the magnificence of our new escort, rushed forward with one accord to kiss his hand—homage which he received with as much graciousness as was seemly for the wearer of such a gorgeous uniform. It was pitiable to see these poor people doing obeisance to a fellow who next morning accepted a dollar at our hands with gratitude, and, moreover, lied horribly to get it. But it is the same all over the country; the baschas, kaids, moukaddems, and all the twopenny dignitaries give themselves the airs of princes, and bully and squeeze the people, who are every bit as good as themselves. In the evening the escort kept bringing us various "presents" which he had got out of the people, till we grew quite disgusted with him. At each successive fowl or basket of eggs that he brought, he grasped our hands with effusion, as much as to say, "Just see what a treasure you've got in me, who bring you all these good things for nothing." We were so annoyed that we had a great row with Manuel in the tent, asking him why this useless individual had been brought along for no possible object except to squeeze the people on our behalf, and to pocket the money which should have gone to the villagers. The only result of this row was to afford additional proof (if any were required) of the extraordinary capacity of the Moors for telling lies. A man might be accounted a very tolerable liar anywhere in Europe, and yet fall far short of the most ordinary standard of mendacity out here. Hadj Absalam and "the escort" were confronted with each other, and each began to excuse himself, and to try and shift the blame on to the other. We gathered from it all, that the man had really come on his own account, and to collect a little tribute for his kinsman the Bascha, and he doubtless thought he might turn an honest penny by attaching himself to us.

We had a large and particularly noisy party of "warriors" at night, and the sheikh himself mounted guard with a loaded gun, which he considerately kept pointed straight at our tent as it lay across his knee. The tribe was at war with the neighbouring Kabyla of Gerouan, who were the more powerful of the two. A man out of our village had been killed two days before, and a blood-tax was as usual to be levied on the district—a rough and ready system of justice that is very effective in preserving order. A Jew had been murdered near Fez when we arrived there, and the nearest village had to pay the blood-money, though probably they had not been concerned in the crime. If our Government had only adopted the same plan a little earlier in Ireland, much crime might have been prevented. Every dog in the village was tremendously on the *qui-vive,* and barked and howled all through the night. If only the Sultan would start a dog-tax in Marocco, it would bring him in a fabulous revenue, and greatly ease the slumbers of travellers in his dominions.

The "escort" wanted to accompany us on our next day's journey, but we said we could not think of trespassing further on his kindness, and bade him adieu. He said he could not possiby accept the dollar we proffered, but put it in his pocket, nevertheless. Manuel was instructed to turn on his compliment tap, and he showered our thanks upon the dignitary in true Oriental fashion, though what they were for I cannot say. He asked us to take down his name, which we did, but I felt relieved when he did not ask for ours. We have given our cards and addresses to so many Moors, with instructions to "look us up when next passing through town," that I now live in fear and trembling lest they should actually turn up, and the arduous duty devolve upon me of trotting some inquisitive barbarian round Madame Tussaud's, the Monument, Tower, and other sights of London.

Our road lay over grass-covered, undulating country to a line of hills closely resembling the Sussex downs. The view from the top was equally similar, extending as it did over a vast plain which extended from here to the Atlantic, like the Weald of Sussex from the Devil's Dyke. We were now re-entering the Gharb province, which was evidenced by the fertility of the soil and the deep mud on the roads. On the left we passed the town of Sidi Kassim, which, being the most important place for several miles, is naturally not marked on our map. I venture to think this must have been about the site of the Roman colony of Tocolosida, mentioned by Ptolemy[1] as being four miles distant from Volubilis.

We had not pitched our tents for long in a small village when a troop of the Sultan's irregular (most irregular) cavalry rode up and proceeded to camp. They were highly picturesque, but their arrival was rather inopportune for us, as we feared they would eat up everything in the place. They had been despatched by the kaid of a district nominally under our friend the Bascha of New Fez, but he seemed here to be doing a little business on his own account, which I shall now describe. When the horses had been picketed, the kaid of the troop rode into the village and arrested four men, whom he threw into prison. I made inquiries of various people as

[1] Ptolemy, Geography, iv. 1, § 14.

to the reason, and visited the men in the small dungeon where they were confined. Heavy chains were placed round their waists, but they seemed tolerably cheerful, and evidently regarded the matter as one of the regular incidents of Moorish life. Of course there is no disgrace in such arbitrary arrests as these, and the victims are not stigmatized as jail-birds. Their crimes were that three of them owed small sums for taxes, so the kaid had seized the opportunity to imprison them, and extract eight or ten times the amount. The fourth owed nothing, but he was known to be rich in flocks and herds, and was therefore to be locked up till he should disgorge enough to satisfy the cupidity of the greedy scoundrel who ruled the district.

This piece of high-handed tyranny had hardly been enacted, when we saw a couple of boys being led along by the soldiers by a towel tied round their necks. The elder boy seemed in an agony of fear, and was throwing appealing glances round to his captors, and then to us, as if to implore our intercession. Five minutes afterwards, hearing loud cries of pain, we ran out, and saw the boy lying on the ground and a soldier administering a severe thrashing with a knotted cord. The boy's mother stood by weeping bitterly, but the soldiers only pushed her roughly out of the way. The flogging was continued for some minutes, when the soldier stopped to rest awhile, and then began again. The cause was a trumped-up charge by another Moor that he had stolen twenty dollars, a pair of slippers, and an important letter from the Bascha. The sum of twenty dollars was afterwards reduced by the accuser to half a dollar, and the letter was found on the road, having dropped out of the owner's pocket, and on his evidence alone the boy was tried, convicted, and the flogging begun, all within the space of five minutes. A very excellent specimen of Moorish justice, and an instance of what false witness can effect in this country. Our servants, and even Hadj Absalam, a soldier himself, were highly indignant. Mohammed said that if England had the country such things would not occur.

The remark rather surprised me, but no doubt the just rule of some civilized power would be welcomed by thousands of the oppressed inhabitants. Before turning-in I paid the prisoners a visit in their small, dark den, and brought them a few little luxuries in the shape of candles and some cigarettes —the latter, I fancy, they thought were something to eat. The gaoler made a touching appeal for bread for his charges, which I fetched, but on returning a minute afterwards I caught the wily fellow keeping it all himself.

The above is a fair, though small, instance of what goes on every day throughout the land. One wonders why the people do not rise against their oppressors, unless it be that their superstitious reverence for the scoundrels who rule them, "the divinity that hedges a king," keeps them quiet. The whole system in Marocco is one of robbery downwards. The Sultan squeezes the baschas, the baschas the kaids, and the kaids rob the poor—and, it must be added, the Christians and their *protégés* plunder them all. This, however, is a subject which must be reserved for separate consideration. The chief thing to be remembered in connection with the system is, that the native governors buy their posts direct from the Sultan, and do not receive any, or at best a purely nominal salary. Often the offices are put up to auction and fall to the highest bidder, who, of course, has to make what he can out of the people. As a rule, it is an investment that bears excellent interest, as it is an understood thing that he shall rob. "You can't expect all the cardinal virtues, Uncle, at thirteen dollars a month," as the Yankee said; still less can you look for scrupulous honesty in an Oriental official, salaried at the rate, say, of eight shillings a week. In England many people have the art of living on nothing a year and saving money on it; out here a man pays for his post and grows rich on the earnings.

However, the turn of the kaid generally comes at last. As soon as he has amassed a good pile, he is called upon by the Sultan to disgorge, and the accumulations of his tyranny go to fill the coffers of the superior tyrant, unless he should chance to die under the torture, and so leave the secret of his hidden treasure undisclosed. It seems strange that, with the knowledge of the fate that surely awaits them in the end, men are found to accept these posts, but the greed of money is so great as to overcome all prudential motives. It would not be difficult to multiply instances of the atrocities resulting from this system, and which must continue to occur as long as it lasts. Meanwhile the patient, voiceless populace suffers silently and unresistingly, misery and starvation staring them in the face while they are poor, torture and imprisonment awaiting them should they grow rich.

The soldiers disappeared at 4 a.m. next morning, having done a good afternoon's work, and doubtless with the intention of doing similar things in the next village. There was something delightfully casual about the whole proceeding. It was as if a squadron of dragoons should go the round of an English county, flogging this man, haling that to prison, and extorting money from every one, all at their own sweet will. To do the Sultan justice, he does not know of half the iniquities that are perpetrated in his dominions, but he makes no attempt to reform the Government of which he is the head.

We resumed our journey across the wide plain, which was cultivated in parts, or else bearing rich pasture. In places the fields were ablaze with flowers, which formed a rich carpet of gold, spangled with red poppies. We saw several curious effects of mirage in the shape of large lakes with wooded islands in their midst, and sometimes houses and hills appeared raised above the horizon. I had often read of thirsty travellers in the desert rushing forward to imaginary lakes, but I never knew before how complete was the illusion. I had a series of small bets with Hoare that the appearances were real water, he consistently backing the mirage at six to four, and winning almost every time. I forgot to mention that the previous day we forded two rivers, the second of which, the Wad el Beht, has the peculiarity of losing itself in a big marsh before it reaches the sea.

We were now in the territory of the Beni Hassen, a large and powerful tribe of Arabs, very turbulent, and always at war with the Zemmoor, a warlike clan of Berbers who inhabit the neighbouring hills inland. They cause much trouble to their lord and master, the Sultan, whose troops gave them a sound drubbing a few years back, since which they have behaved better. In these parts, everybody carries weapons all day. The people market armed to the teeth, and the ploughman drives his bullocks with his sword buckled on and his long gun laid by ready for use. The flocks are never left out by night, and in the day are tended by armed shepherds. We halted at a large village, and purposed camping outside to escape the smells and noise, but the kaid, who received us with great courtesy, refused to be responsible for our lives and property unless we came inside, as they were at war with the Zemmoor, who made nightly raids on their cattle and sheep. All the villages about here are arranged with the tents in a circle, for the purpose of watching and defence. The animals are inclosed in a sort of pound, inclosed by a mound and ditch, surmounted often by a formidable fence of cut thorn-bushes. It is anxious work at night-time for the Arab, as he lies awake with his long gun and his faithful watch-dog beside him, not knowing what moment the foe may spring upon him from out of the darkness. Thieving in general, and horse-stealing in particular, is here regarded as a fine art, a gift bestowed by Allah, which it would be foolish, nay wrong, not to cultivate. A successful horse-stealer is considered an important personage, and wears the long hair which is considered the mark of a "brave," and belongs by right to any one who excels in any manly pursuit or who has killed a foe in battle. I was rather anxious about my horse, who had belonged to a noted cattle-stealer of the Beni Hassen (whence his name, "Hassen-aouie"), as the Arabs are always anxious to regain any favourite horse they have been compelled to part with, and his great speed had often been of service to his late master in their sudden forays. Whether that estimable animal would have been willing to leave the path of virtue and good living for his old life of lawlessness and short commons, I don't know, but fortunately the alternative was never offered to him.

The natives all about here struck us as a fine set of men. The Beni Hassen are lightly built, but wiry and athletic-looking. The Berber tribes inland are among the most troublesome in the country. A glance at the map will show the round-about route we had been compelled to take from Mequinez to Rabat in order to avoid their territory, which cannot be entered by any Christian. Being semi-independent, they are a prosperous and hardy race, and with the exception of paying tribute in a rather sketchy fashion, do pretty much as they like.

A party of soldiers belonging to the troop of the previous evening arrived shortly after us, and took up their quarters close to our tents. Soon after nightfall there was a sound of wailing and lamentation outside. A poor woman had just discovered that her husband's horse had been stolen in his absence, and she was bringing the matter before the kaid, who, of course, could give her no redress. As the circumstance coincided with the arrival of the troops, it was suspected that one of their number was the guilty party. We ourselves had guards to watch our animals, but "Quis custodiet ipsos," &c., we thought; in other words, What shall we do if a "warrior" takes a fancy to one of our mules and decamps with it to the mountains?

Just as we were turning-in, Manuel, and our soldier, who were continually at loggerheads, started a tremendous row. It transpired that the worthy kaid, whose punctuality at his devotions has been alluded to before, had the obnoxious habit of performing the required preliminary ablutions in the bucket which contained our drinking-water. For this Manuel was very properly rating him soundly, but to all our expostulations he replied that the ordinances of religion must be complied with, and that our equipment contained no vessel so suitable for his purpose as the bucket. I suggested that he should use sand when there was no water handy, and quoted the Koran to that effect, which display of learning on my part, I flatter myself, impressed our servants not a little, though Al-kaid did not seem to see it. The Moors have a way of performing their ablutions in most inconvenient modes and localities. I have the greatest respect for that cleanliness which the Koran says is the "key of prayer," and an essential part of religion, but it really *is* annoying when you arrive, tired and thirsty, at the only spring within three or four miles, to find, say, three dirty Moors and a fat negress cleansing themselves therein. Whenever our soup or coffee was extra strong of an evening, we always knew we had camped near one of these natural lavatories.

From here to Rabat was two good days' journey, still across the same wide plain. Distress was everywhere visible, and the fields were filled with people digging for the ayerua root, which we saw them drying in their tents. When we left our encampments the poor women used to come and scrape together the grains of barley left by our animals, and any piece of bread given them was eagerly devoured. If we gave them money they still asked for bread in preference, which showed how pressing were their needs, and showered blessings on our heads on receiving it. Our grandfathers and grandmothers, we observed, got all the curses, and ourselves the benedictions. The difficulty of buying bread for those situated at a distance from the towns, greatly aggravates the distress, and renders charity more difficult, as, though one can give money, it is impossible to carry about large stores of bread. This is one of the many evils resulting from the want of means of communication.

We halted early at a duar near the banks of the Wad Seboo, here grown to a stream as big as the Thames at Richmond, and amused ourselves in the afternoon by practising with our revolvers. A ragged native, wearing a red jelab and long hair, and carrying a long gun over his shoulder, joined us. We exchanged weapons, and the revolving of the chambers of our pistols puzzled him immensely. He fired a shot from his own piece for our edification. It took him some time and all his strength to cock it, but having at length succeeded, he pulled the trigger, but nothing happened. A little priming was added, this time with a better result. As the hammer fell, a blinding stream of smoke and flame issued from the pan for a few seconds, till at last the thing went off with a bang about two yards wide of the mark. If a man takes a shot at you with one of these weapons, it is long odds you have time to run round the corner before it explodes, and he shoots some one else—as actually happened at Tangier. The only people I ever knew to whom a Moorish gun was a source of alarm, were the

British authorities at Gibraltar. I once brought over from Tangier what I believe to have been the longest gun in the country, and it so impressed the Custom House officers that they deprived me of it, and impounded it till I got special permission to introduce such a dangerous engine within the fortress.

Before starting for Rabat we paid off and sent back to Fez the blameless Ethiopian who had conducted us thence. We were sorry to part with him, as he was a capital fellow, very hard-working, and a considerable addition to our staff. On the way we overtook a party of soldiers, having in their custody an elderly Moor, the kaid of a district near Alcazar. He was a most respectable-looking old gentleman, and comported himself with much dignity as he sat on a mule with thick irons round his ancles—a most unnecessary indignity, as it seemed to us. The only reply we got to our enquiry as to the reason was, "By command of Sidna" (our lord the Sultan), but it needed no telling that he was on his way to be squeezed, and perhaps to be tortured. It was curious to watch the air of stoical indifference with which he bore the misfortune that sooner or later overtakes every rich native in the country.

The last ten miles of the road is along the coast, and one has the town of Rabat, and especially the vast tower of Hassen, which stands on an eminence outside, in full view almost the whole way. Rabat may be said to consist of two portions, one on each side of the big river Boo-ragrag, but the northern part is called Sallee. Approaching the northern suburb, we passed through vineyards that seemed to thrive excellently, and then under the arches of the grand old aqueduct, which has stood the wear and tear of centuries, and is still almost perfectly preserved. It is said to be the work of Roman hands, though I must say I should not have guessed it myself. Rohlfs and other travellers speak of a Roman aqueduct near Rabat, without alluding to this one, and Leo tells us that Almansor built it to supply Rabat with water. I do not know of any aqueduct of any size near Rabat (there is a small conduit at Shellah), so possibly there is some confusion with the Sallee one.

A mile of rocky road brought us to Sallee, which we simply passed through, as it contains nothing of interest. The inhabitants are very fanatical, and the place contains no Christians. The Sala Colonia of the Romans, I may mention, was not, in spite of the coincidence of the names, Sallee, but Rabat. Readers of "Robinson Crusoe" may remember that he was carried a prisoner to Sallee after his shipwreck. Of the famous "Sallee Rovers," the terror of mariners of every nation in the last century, mention is made by various travellers, as well as of their barbarity to their captives, whom they either murdered or sold as slaves in the interior. They even extended their audacious depredations to the English Channel. It was the boldness and cruelty of these Barbary Corsairs, rather than their strength, that made them feared, and, incredible as it seems,

England and other great powers actually paid tribute to Marocco to secure immunity from their raids.

The estuary of the Boo-ragrag would make an excellent harbour but for the dangerous sand-bar which blocks its mouth. These bars exist in all the Marocco rivers, and form a serious obstacle to the development of commerce, as not a single harbour worthy of the name exists on the whole Atlantic coast. We could hear the breakers booming at the river's mouth as we made preparations to cross the ferry. Of all the idiotic contrivances to be found in this benighted country, I think a Moorish ferry is the one which shows the most utter want of common sense. A flat-bottomed barge is brought as close to the shore as the shallow water will permit. The animals wade out and are expected to jump out of the oozy slime over the high gunwale into the boat. Not even a plank is provided to help them; they have simply to tumble in as they best can, barking their shins and hind-legs in the process. My horse, in particular, always had a rooted aversion to this ferry, such as was only to be expected from any animal of proper spirit, and gave much trouble. The Arabs cursed his father and mother, and belaboured him soundly, but neither reflections on the moral character of his ancestors nor the application of the stick had the slightest effect. At last several men seized his fore-legs and lifted them in bodily, and others walloped him behind to such effect that poor Hassen-aouie had to yield. Once in, all behaved quietly enough, though I thought it would have been lively work if any of them had commenced kicking in mid-stream. To think that these creatures can have been passing by this same ferry for centuries and never have found out a better method!

Rabat is by far the prettiest town on the Atlantic sea-board of Marocco. It stands high above the Wad Boo-ragrag, on cliffs of red and grey rock, and is surrounded by most lovely gardens; the river winds away to the east between high banks, the left being crowned by the great Mosque and Tower of Beni-Hassen. Seawards are imposing forts and batteries, whose antique armaments frown down on the entrance to the river, and seem to menace the European brig and steamer that are lying in the offing. Having surmounted the perils of the ferry, we ride up through the streets, thronged with a busy crowd, to find our camping-ground. A large trade is done here in the beautiful Moorish carpets, whose brilliant yet harmonious colours may be seen in the Tangier bazaars. Much harm was done to Moorish textile art by the introduction of French dyes, with their thinner and less artistic hues of violet and magenta that can easily be detected by the experienced. Their use is now prohibited by government under severe penalties, to the benefit both of buyers and producers. The town is of large extent for its population, which numbers about 30,000, including several European families. It was founded by the great Sultan, El Mansor the

Victorious, in the twelfth century, and in his glorious reign appears to have speedily grown into importance.

Passing right through, we camped on the Southern side near the sea-shore, under the lee of a large, square kasbah, which seemed to be used as a sort of drill-hall. With their accustomed kindness, the French had insisted on providing the Sultan, much against his will, with some officers to help him in drilling his forces, and this kasbah was used for the purpose. The ground between our tents and the sea served the double function of battery and cemetery. From the dates and inscriptions on some of the guns, they must have belonged to Christians, and have been more than 200 years old; others looked as though they might have been coeval with the invention of gunpowder. The cemetery was full of bones, perhaps owing to the recent edict of His Majesty forbidding their exportation. Some of them looked like human remains, which they very possibly were, as, owing to the hurry in which they bury people out here, the graves are very shallow. "O, earth, lie lightly on his head" would be a suitable epitaph for an Arab, who has only a foot or so of gravel placed over him. The system has one great advantage, we were told, as in a country where sepulture must be before sundown on the day of death, little mistakes are apt to occur, so that if your friends have been a little premature in your interment, the scanty top-dressing gives you half a chance of getting up again. The graveyards are considered holy ground, and certainly a very perceptible odour of sanctity emanates from the adjacent tombs.

During our stay we experienced much kindness from Mr. Frost, H.B.M.'s Vice-Consul, and Mr. Blake, an English merchant resident in the place. The latter took us out shooting one day on the other (Northern) side of the river. The sport was not very excellent, but I managed to burst my gun at the muzzle, which got choked with sand. However, I took it to a Moorish blacksmith, who sawed three inches off the end of the barrel, and I have made excellent practice with it since. A curious fact connected with the sport here is, that while rabbits swarm on the North bank of the Boo-ragrag, not a single specimen exists anywhere in Marocco to the South. The river was also the boundary of ancient Mauritania, but I do not know that there is any connection between the two circumstances.

The next day Mr. Blake took us to see the ancient ruins of Shellah, which lie a couple of miles to the East of Rabat, and beyond the Hassen tower. It was high tide as we rode along the river-bank, but, to judge from the water-worn appearance of the rock above us, as well as from the alleged existence of some old dockgates well above the present high-water mark, the level of the river must once have been much further up the sides of the valley. Cantering down some lanes that led through gardens and orange-groves, we soon reached the ruins. These are some of the most interesting in the country, of mingled Roman and Moorish origin (some say there are even Phœnician remains, but I take leave to doubt this), though of the Romans who lived here little is known. And yet if Sala Colonia comprised, as an eminent authority [1] seems to think, both Shellah and the site of modern Rabat, it must have been a place of great size. At present the Moorish work predominates. There is a small but graceful minaret belonging to a ruined mosque, which contains the tomb of the great Almansor, as well as those of the Sultans of the Beni-Marin dynasty, which are covered with inscriptions descriptive of the virtues and greatness of the deceased. I noticed some very beautiful tile-work and stone-carving, the latter of which must have been the work of other than Moorish artists. Hard by are numerous cupolas and saint-houses peeping out of the luxuriant vegetation, which is watered by a spring of beautifully clear water. Altogether it is a most enchanting spot. On every side but that of the river rise steep hills, while close round about are gardens and groves of oranges and lemons, and little thickets, through which runs the streamlet that can be heard murmuring as it issues out of the fountain hard by.

Riding on in a Southerly direction, we came to more extensive ruins, and passed through a large gate, and then beneath another archway with Gothic ornamentation, that must have been the work of Christian hands. On the way home we passed a

[1] M. Tissot.

large, white, barrack-like building; this was a new palace of the Sultan's, who occasionally sheds the light of his royal presence upon Rabat when passing between the two capitals. It is the only town on the coast which is thus favoured, the reason of which, we were told, is that it contains fewer Christians to pester him with complaints and petitions.

I explored the Sma Hassen and the appendant mosque by myself. The tower is a truly magnificent work, and from its immense proportions (it is of the same width throughout its height of nearly 200 feet), I am inclined to think that had it been completed, it would have been the finest specimen of its kind in the world. By the way, there are only two others exactly like it, the Kutubia of Marocco, and the Giralda at Seville, but it is the latter I have in my mind in making the comparison. That it could even have surpassed, or even rivalled, the superb structure in the Seville cathedral, is perhaps too much to assert positively, but in order to secure the due proportions, it would have been necessary to raise it to an equal height. All three towers are ascended, not by steps, but by means of an inclined plane, up which you could ride a mule, and all are said to be the work of the same Christian architect. Savants assert that the design of all these minarets is derived from Constantinople: it is exemplified in the belfry of St. Mark's, and one or two other churches in Italy.

Of the body of the Mosque there is now not much left except the outer walls, which are of *tabbia* and little more than twenty feet in height: Jackson asserts that the roof was supported by 360 marble columns, but from the look of the building, as a whole, I should have thought it had never been finished. I did not notice any of these columns, but several massive pillars of stone are still standing, one row being nearly perfect. Remains of a large underground cistern are to be seen in the body of the building, which supplied worshippers with water for their ablutions. The Mosque, if it was ever in a complete state, must have been an immense building: from a rough calculation, I should say its length was from 450 to 500 feet, its breadth about 400. Almansor intended it to be the largest and finest Mosque in the world.

The Kasbah or citadel of Rabat is worth a visit, and contains a very fine gate. A good view is obtainable from here out to sea. We used to watch the lighters, engaged in stowing and unloading cargo on board the coasting steamers, shooting the bar—an exciting and perilous occupation at the best of times, and quite impossible in stormy weather. As they near the mouth of the river, they mount on the crest of a big wave, and, pulling with all their might, trust to luck and their own strong arms to carry them over. Sometimes a cargo will be detained for weeks together before it can be shipped.

CHAPTER X.

N'zalla of Boo Z'neka—Moorish melody—A bad camping-place—Casablanca—Trade of Marocco—War indemnity—Women-flogging—Off again—Ben Rajit—Terrible scenes of starvation—Moorish appetites—Z'ttatt—Sharp frost—Hospitable kaid—Extortion by a Jew.

THE fourth day after our arrival sees us off again *en route* for Casablanca, Mr. Blake accompanying us. My diary tells me we have traversed 330 miles according to our calculations, which I believe to be tolerably accurate—little more than a quarter of the whole distance of our journey. We stay for the night at the n'zalla of Boo Z'neka, one of the kasbahs or public guard-houses built by Government for the protection of travellers at intervals along the coast. They consist of a square inclosure, surrounded by a battlemented wall, with gates that are locked at night. A small fee is charged each person using them. Our servants are very musical this evening, and even the dignified "Kaid el Hadj" Absalam bursts forth into melody. The songs are sung in a monotonous droning tone, very comical to listen to, but without any particular tune that I could make out. The kaid's ditty this evening is of a strongly erotic character (some fragments

o

would hardly bear translation), and each verse ends with the choice refrain:—

> "Twenty maids and thirty boys,
> What a sight, O Allah, Allah!"

The rest repeat the words "Oollah, Oollah" in chorus, and the song had not finished when I fell asleep.

Thursday, March 8th.—We should have been at Casablanca to-night, but a tidal river, the Wad N'fifikh, delayed us three hours waiting for low water. The result is, we have to camp at a peculiarly filthy village, in a sort of pound, where sheep and goats and cattle are penned along with us. Our tent is full of liquid muck, owing to the heavy rain which has just begun, and what some people call a "fine farmyard smell" prevails everywhere.

The next morning we rode in early to Casablanca through a storm of wind and rain. We had been commended to the good offices of Mr. Fernau, an English merchant of the place, and he received us with the same kindness that we experienced everywhere along the coast. Indeed, if we had accepted all the offers of hospitality that we received, we should never have got to our journey's end. Casablanca, or, to use its Arabic equivalent, Dar el Beida (the White House), is not an interesting place, but it is one of the most important on the coast from a commercial point of view. A very considerable trade is done here in wool and skins, and the manufacture of carpets, similar though not equal to those of Rabat, is carried on. Other exports are peas and beans and millet; maize can only be exported with the Sultan's permission. Wheat and barley can in no case be taken out of the country, and not even shipped along the coast. Free trade in all cereals is one of the reforms which has been most urgently pressed upon the Sultan, but fanaticism forbids the corn of true believers going to feed the Nazarene. A ten per cent. (*ad valorem*) duty was levied on all commodities exported and imported after the peace of Tetuan in 1860, and has been enforced ever since. By that treaty the Spaniards acquired the right of having officials of their own at the various *douanes* on the coast in conjunction with the Moorish custom-house officers. Half the customs were appropriated by Spain, in payment of the war indemnity of 4,000,000*l*. This debt was only paid off towards the end of 1884. Manuel told us there was a keen competition among Spaniards for these posts, which no doubt were very lucrative. A curious thing in connection with this indemnity is that the Sultan actually found himself richer after the war than before. The *douanes* were better administered, the universal contraband trade was checked, and by means of the ten per cent. tax the foreigner really paid the debt.

Casablanca was built early in the sixteenth century by the Portuguese, who at that time had several settlements on the coast. They had previously sacked and ruined the old Moorish town of Anfa, which stood upon this site. It has a population of about 5000, among whom is an unusually large proportion of Europeans. There is also a large colony of Jews, who share with their brethren of Tangier the unique privilege of not being confined in a Mellah. The climate is unhealthy, owing to the frequent fevers, but the soil in the neighbourhood is very rich. We heard of corn being sown and reaped here, all within the space of forty days; at Tangier I have known the land to bear three crops of potatoes in the year, which two facts say something for the capacities of the soil. Unfortunately, by the Moorish law no Christian can own land, which is an impediment to proper cultivation, though in many cases the rule is evaded by means of nominal conveyances to a Moor, who holds it on behalf of the Christian. The right of European proprietorship was conceded in principle at the Madrid Conference of 1880, but the Sultan objected that the exercise of this right would be an infringement of the precepts of the Chraa, or civil law derived from the Koran, which, being fixed and unalterable, as the laws of the Medes and Persians, could not be modified by any individual Moorish potentate.

A short time before our arrival, there had taken place the flogging of two Moorish women at the instigation of a servant of the English Vice-Consul, which created so much stir in the country. Readers of the *Globe* newspaper may remember the interesting damsel Esther Amar, "young, pretty, and with fawn-like eyes," whose sad case and "modest, gentle manner" stirred the heart of that paper's correspondent to its depths, and was the subject of several questions in Parliament. One amusing circumstance in connection therewith was that neither Lord E. Fitzmaurice nor the Royal Geographical Society knew where Casablanca was, the place being marked on the maps under its Arabic name of Dar el Beida. The rights of the matter were never fully ascertained, but the version we heard was that the young lady was no better than she should be, and suffered at the hands of the Moorish officials the punishment meted out by Mohammedan law to such characters.

We had intended to push on the following day, but pouring rain kept us another twenty-four hours under Mr. Fernau's hospitable roof. The delay was but a slight annoyance at the most, and it was more than counterbalanced by the reflection that this rain meant the prospect of food for thousands of starving people in the coming season. We had been in some doubts as to what road we should take to the city of Marocco. Those from Mazagan and Saffi further down the coast were the shorter and more usually travelled, but a desire to see as much of the interior as possible induced us to strike inland at once. As the road we took has never been described by any previous travellers, I shall do so in some detail. It may be asked why we had taken such a roundabout route from Mequinez to Marocco, but the direct road lies through wild and mountainous country, inhabited by turbulent clans of Berbers and Arabs, who will not even allow the Sultan to enter their territory, and is therefore quite impracticable for Christians. A glance at the map will show that our course now lay south-east, and as we set forth we passed through corn-fields giving promise of a good harvest, while the vegetation everywhere springing up gave glad signs of returning peace and plenty. The promised change was coming none too soon. Four bad seasons had impoverished the people, and now many of them had not even grain to use as seed, so that rich tracts were even now left uncultivated. The distress had been particularly severe in the south, and in the districts through which we were about to pass. At Benrajit, a small walled town, the number of starving poor about was heart-rending. A group of hapless wretches were huddled together in a hovel built on to the town wall, all in a state of most utter destitution. Many were half-naked, with nothing but a few rags hanging from them, and some seemed half-silly from want. Hadj Absalam was told to get five and twenty loaves to distribute among them, and we gave them a double allowance in the morning. It was pitiable to see them rush in a body on the food; tall men whose shrunken limbs and wasted bodies told of their sufferings, women and children with legs and arms no thicker than sticks, mere walking skeletons. The gallant kaid was forced to beat a retreat, and it was only after two or three men had armed themselves with sticks and knotted cords to keep them at bay that the food could be distributed at all. This may seem brutal treatment of starving people, but it was necessary else the men, being the stronger, would have got it all. Then the women crowded round and, kissing, the soldier's cloak, begged piteously each for a larger share, while the men fought and struggled among themselves for the pieces. A sharp watch had to be kept at night to see that the poor creatures did not steal our horses' corn. The sight of all this misery detracted much from the pleasure of travelling, and the thought was always present to my mind how easily things might be bettered under a decent Government. Where the food resources of a country quadruple the needs of its scanty population, it does seem scandalous that sufferings like these should continue. Everywhere may be seen wide tracts of fertile ground growing nothing but weeds, but the people have not seed to put in. Of course, ours was a particularly good season, but as the people cannot store up grain, their opportunities are only half utilized. Often they are starving in one place while corn is selling cheap in another, but transport is so slow and expensive that one cannot help the other. With roads and railways this would be obviated. Meanwhile it is the interest of the scoundrels who are over them that things should remain as they are, for ignorance, poverty, and misery are the mainstays of Moorish government. Men whose whole energies are centred in earning their scanty daily bread have little left for sedition and revolt, and as before said,[1] the Sultan pursues the enlightened policy of grinding down his subjects in order to keep himself on the throne.

The Kaïd of Ben-rajit received us with great hospitality, and soon there arrived bounteous mona

[1] p. 64.

of sugar, tea, mint, candles, meat, chickens, barley, milk, bread, eggs, and a kind of very wet, indigestible crumpets. These were for our own use, but soon there came servants bearing dishes, with their beehive-shaped covers, containing each a mountain of koos-koossoo for the servants, which made their greedy eyes glisten. Hadj Absalam particularly, who was a shocking old *gourmand*, was in ecstacies, as with us he was not allowed to indulge to such excess. His voracious appetite was a constant source of complaint with Manuel, who prided himself on his economical management of our establishment. "Me beesom² go catch 'em, buy one sheep to give maungy³ to *soldat*," as he said in his curious pigeon-English when Hoare expostulated with him on an over-large butcher's bill. I visited the servants in their tent later on, and found they had already consumed several cubic feet of koos-koossoo and other messes, but their appetites were by no means appeased. Only the soldier heaved a deep sigh of repletion and contentment, rubbed his stomach sympathetically, and faintly murmured "Bezzuf" (What a lot)! His face then assumed that expression of supremest satisfaction which can only be felt by a good man who has dined well, and in a few minutes he was fast asleep. The others indulged in frequent eructations, which here, as in most savage countries, is the form prescribed by good breeding to express gratification at the hospitality you have received. With the Moors it serves as a sort of grace after meat, and is often

² I must (*besoin*). ³ Food (*manger*).

accompanied by the exclamation "Hamdoollah" (God be praised) !

The sight of all this guzzling disgusted me, with all the miserable creatures around looking on with longing eyes at three men stuffing themselves, while they were starving. The amount a Moor can eat is prodigious.[4] We were told of a man at Fez (I never saw him myself), the capacity of whose stomach was unrivalled in the country. He could eat, they said, a hundredweight of koos-koossoo and a whole sheep—all at a sitting and without turning a hair. For his splendid powers of cramming he was reverenced by his neighbours as a saint, as indeed he deserved to be. I repeat, I never saw this individual, but simply "tell the tale as 'twas told to me."

More rain fell in the night and we had to wait in the morning till the tents dried. For some hours we passed over the same flat plain which extends in one long belt from forty to fifty miles in width all along the coast. Nothing but the golden blaze of the marigold covering the ground relieved the monotony of the landscape. Everywhere the soil was wasting its rich qualities upon the weeds which grew knee-high all around, and simply waiting for some one to come and cultivate it. A man would only have to take his plough, clear off the weeds, and Nature would do the rest. Parts here and there showed signs of recent cultivation, but the Moors,

---

[4] As Manuel put it, the Moors "eat by the eye," that is, not according to what they require, but whatever they see set before them.

after taking one crop off the ground, leave it to lie fallow, and go elsewhere. With their wretched system of husbandry they get eight and tenfold from their crops, which shows what might be done with steam-ploughs and other European improvements. Some forty miles from the coast we left the rich plain and entered on a more hilly and wilder country, and two hours more brought us to Kasbah Z'ttatt, a pretty little town consisting of a few scattered houses and the kasbah which occupied the centre. Hard by the road ran the remains of a large subterranean aqueduct, and various other remains showed that the place must have been of greater importance formerly: it was following the example of the rest of the country and falling into decay. The distress here was even worse than at Ben-rajit, and the starving people more numerous. As at the latter place, the kaid received us well both by word and deed, and was even more than usually lavish in his hospitality. On this part of our journey, where a Christian is seldom seen, we were treated with greater respect than anywhere else. All the people imagined we were officials going on affairs of State to the Sultan, a belief very much encouraged by our servants for their own sake. We heard Mohammed one night call out to a noisy " warrior " who kept singing near our tent, not to awaken the Bashador (ambassador). We took our guns and strolled in the evening round the gardens that encircled the town. There was a quiet, home-like air about the place that made it very attractive, and we thought what peaceful, happy lives these people might lead if only their rulers would allow them. We met no living creatures, save half a dozen ragged natives and a very fanatical cow, which took fright at the sight of us, and bolted like a thing possessed, giving its owner no end of trouble to get it back.

The night was exceedingly cold, and when we got up next morning the ground was covered with a thick rime. It was a sharp frost. I mention this to give an idea of the climate of the country, about which, as in many other matters, people have very erroneous notions. Two things I learnt on my first visit to Marocco : it is not a desert, but remarkably fertile; and the climate, so far from being tropical, is as temperate as any one could desire. Here were we, on the 13th of March, on fairly low-lying ground, 200 miles south of Tangier, and actually being frozen! There were very few days which we considered too hot, and I rode all across the southern plains at midday in April with no protection to my head beyond my *tarboosh*, or Fez cap.

Early in the morning the kaid's factotum, a gentleman "of most unbounded stomach," arrived to say that his master would like to see his visitors before they departed, so we repaired to his house. We found him seated outside, and after thanking him for his kindness, we prepared to take our leave, when he asked us if we would not come inside. I knew at once we were in for a heavy dose of Moorish hospitality, and regretted that we had not been forewarned of it. On entering, he received us with great cordiality and, bidding us be seated, said that the moment we had passed his doors and eaten of his bread, we were as his brothers. We passed up a flight of stairs into an upper room, and several of his kinsmen and retainers joined us at the meal. First we had chocolate, decidedly a foreign innovation, but it was not at all bad. Next the servants brought round bowls of a very trying compound, a kind of gruel highly flavoured with onions which the Moors lapped up with avidity, but which I, having just finished a hearty breakfast, could not possibly manage. However, I contrived to swallow a spoonful, explaining the reason of my want of appetite to our host, and told him it was *mezian* (excellent), which lie I trust may be forgiven me. Feeding in Moorish houses affords an apt illustration of the incompatibility of courtesy with veracity under certain circumstances. The next course was also gruel, but less highly seasoned than the last, and the Moors swallowed it with a kind of chirruping noise, such as ill-bred people make when taking soup, expressive of extreme gusto. Then came the inevitable green tea with sugar and verbena, as already described, of which we had to take three cups, the regulation number prescribed by Moorish etiquette. What with Jewish wines and Moorish teas, a man going in for fashionable life in this country should be possessed of a strong digestion. There is nothing a Moor delights in so much as these social gatherings and kettledrums. It is the form of dissipation he chiefly affects, but to myself the result of a long course of them would inevitably be an attack of tea-tremens.

Our host was very communicative, and being a man of considerable intelligence asked us a number of questions on various matters. He had performed the Ḥadj, and having been through Alexandria was particularly anxious to know all about the Egyptian war. The general opinion in Marocco appeared to be that Arābi had sunk all the British ships, and forced us to pay an enormous ransom in order to be allowed to depart out of the country. Our entertainer was better informed, and evidently viewed our action there with no small concern. He plainly had no faith in the sincerity of our intentions to evacuate when peace and order were established, and I fear I made some rather rash prophecies as to the probable date when we should retire, the non-fulfilment of which, I doubt not, will have served to confirm his suspicions. He seemed pleased to hear that Arābi was safe and being well treated, but asked whether it was not a fact that several Egyptian notables had been put to death by the English. I replied that none had so suffered except such as were clearly proved guilty of pillage or murder.

The kaid had another matter on his mind that occupied his thoughts far more than the Egyptian troubles, and which I fancied was partly the reason of his asking us to his house—possibly in the hope of obtaining some redress. It appeared that a certain Jew, under French "protection," had come to his house, and he had taken the man in and treated him well, giving him food and lodging, and had even despatched a soldier and servants with him on his way the next morning. As a reward for his hospitality the lying Hebrew had sworn that a box containing $1500 had been stolen from him in the night while in the kaid's house; a claim for that amount was sent in, and, as usually happens in such cases, the unfortunate kaid was compelled to pay the money himself. As before remarked, the wily Israelite is always too much for the Moor in this country, and in spite of the kicks and scorn he endures, the advantage rests with him in the end. The circumstance naturally preyed upon the mind of our worthy host, and he was continually alluding to it in the course of conversation. He accepted his loss, however, with becoming fortitude, and said he was sure that Allah would one day visit the crime upon the head of the guilty party, a reflection that seemed to console him, though it could not bring him back his money.

CHAPTER XI.

Fraudulent claims—Facilities for extortion by foreigners—Oppression of the natives—"Protection" in Marocco—Its abuses—Protected Jews—Malpractices in the interior—Madrid Conference of 1880—Its provisions inoperative—Proposed remedies.

THE above is a good specimen of the kind of "claims" which are continually being brought by foreigners against Moors, and which the latter are compelled to pay. It was chiefly fear of giving us an opportunity of making such a claim that made the Moors everywhere guard us with such care, and which causes the advent of travellers to be regarded as anything but a boon or a blessing to the natives. Witness the behaviour of the Bascha of New Fez to us at that place. We might have dropped a handkerchief on the road, or rather, we need not have lost anything—a little hard swearing will effect everything—and then have sent in a claim of five hundred or a thousand dollars against some individual Moor or the Government. Only, if the matter had come to the ears of Sir John Hay, we should not have got much assistance from him; but very often the unfortunate Moor pays up at once, for fear of suffering worse things if he refuse. The whole thing is as simple as possible. You have only to swear you have been robbed, or, better still, suborn a witness or two—and they will not be hard to find. Rascals are sure to abound in a country where the occasions for rascality are so numerous and remunerative. In this case I found afterwards that a low Spaniard had been bribed to swear to the truth of the story; the man, I believe, was hundreds of miles away at the time the supposed robbery was committed, but that was a mere trifle. Documentary evidence is easily obtained—for a consideration—through the *adools*, or notaries, and the wretched Moor, who very possibly can neither read nor write, is easily frightened by the display of a big paper before him. Further, the kaids themselves, partly in dread of the consequences if they refuse, but also sometimes acting in collusion with the claimants with a view to a share in the profits, aid the latter in enforcing their demands. But what is most lamentable is the part foreign legations have played in the matter; that the representatives of great Powers should permit themselves to act as attorneys, as it were, for persons sending in their little bills against the Moors. I do not mean to say that they have been always aware of all the facts connected with the foundation of the claims; but that, if only from want of proper investigation, they have aided the promoters of these unhallowed schemes is indisputable. The offender in the present case was a Jew, but it must not be supposed that they are the only people guilty of these malpractices. Indeed, they have now become so common that the manufacture of claims is described as the most remunerative business the country affords. The following remark of a European who used to keep a farm in the country was told me as illustrative of the system. My informant asked him if he had sold many cattle lately; he replied, "No, it pays me much better to have them stolen!" The beasts were no doubt worth far less in the open market than as vehicles for extorting money. The system has reached perfectly scandalous proportions, and calls loudly for reform, and I rejoiced to see certain English papers some time ago taking the matter up. The prisons are said to be full of hapless wretches who suffer the unutterable torments of those hells upon earth because they will not, or cannot, pay what they do not owe. Harrowing tales are told of unfortunate debtors being torn from their homes at the instance of European and "protected" claimants, and driven off to languish in dungeons far from their relations and friends, who alone can relieve them and save them from starvation. Innocent men are flogged and tortured, perhaps to death, to make them confess robberies that they have never committed. It is this and similar treatment, far more than so-called "fanaticism," that has caused the foreigner to be so hated, and which makes the name of Jew and Christian to stink in the nostrils of every true believer. There are, I know, honourably-minded Europeans on the coast who set their faces resolutely against these things; but there are others who do not, and the Jews are largely aiders and promoters of the system.

P

But, as before said, the chief blame lies at the door of those foreign officials who, if they have not encouraged the system, at least have done nothing to put it down.

These abuses are in a great measure the outcome of that system of "protection" to which I have often alluded, and which I shall now attempt to describe. Without a clear understanding of the subject, it is impossible for any one to fully appreciate the conditions now existing in Marocco. It sounds rather a satire upon a Government that its subjects should be compelled to seek the protection of foreigners in their own country against their own rulers, but where neither person nor property is safe from the arbitrary exercise of power by corrupt and tyrannical governors, the origin of the system becomes apparent. It has been shown that any one who has amassed wealth by any means is liable to be imprisoned, tortured, and robbed of his money at any moment. If, however, he can secure the protection and quasi-citizenship of some foreign Power, he is safe from native robbery and his position is assured. The Moors have long since learned the power of European nations, so that now the authority of the kaids is as nothing when brought in conflict with foreign representatives. Hence the great aim of almost every Moor is to denationalize himself at any cost and with what speed he may. For these reasons they are willing to pay large sums to secure the privileges of foreign citizenship, and the consequence is that the buying and selling of protections has become as universal a business as the manufacture of claims.

By the Madrid Convention of 1880 each foreign Power secured the right to protect twelve Moors, not holding official positions under Government. Further, each *bonâ fide* European trader in a fair way of business may protect two native agents to do business for him in the interior, which obviously could not be attended to by the principal himself. Were this all, there could be no possible ground of objection. But besides this legal protection, a large amount of promiscuous and informal protection goes on. A man has only to say that a Moor or Jew is his agent or partner, and no native official will dare to meddle with him. It may be presumed the kaids are not acquainted with the precise terms of the Madrid Convention. The result is that now the operation of the system is practically unlimited, as the protected agents in the interior dispense their own protection to any extent, and thus a ring of these pseudo-*protégés* is formed, who snap their fingers at Moorish law and carry on their malpractices unchecked.

Directly a native secures his protection, he becomes freed from the authority of the Moorish Government, and holds himself responsible only to the Power whose citizenship he has adopted. In vain the Sultan complained that it was impossible for him to carry on the government of his country under such circumstances, wherein numbers of his subjects can set his laws at nought, and, freed from all the restraints and duties of citizenship, plunder and rob the unfortunate natives who have not the good fortune to be of the number of protected ones. Moreover, he never knows that, in taking summary measures against rebellious subjects of his own, he may not be embroiling himself with some foreign Power by including some protected Moors or Jews among the victims. For instance, if he sits down with his army in front of some *kabyla* that will not pay its taxes, and the order goes out that heads of the recalcitrant tribesmen will be paid for at the rate of so many *okeas* a head—in such a case, if by any chance a protected Jew or Moor should happen to be decapitated with the other victims, trouble would be sure to come of it! In particular is this likely to be the case with French protection, whose ramifications are spreading all over the country. The Shereef of Wazan, the virtual ruler of a large tract, is now a French subject, so that a large tract of the Sultan's dominions is practically withdrawn from his authority, and placed under the dominion of the representative of the Republic, who will doubtless find it easy to treat any attempt of the Sultan to quell disturbances in that part as making war against a French citizen.

The Jews are the readiest and most efficacious instruments in this nefarious system; they act frequently as intermediaries between the Moors and Christians. Most of the richer Jews, however, especially in the coast towns, are under protection themselves, and directly the Jew has bought or otherwise procured the privilege, he is at liberty to do business on his own account. He can abuse his position, and send in his claims as well as any Christian. Moreover, he does a fine trade in selling the protection to the poorer Moors, by making them his agents, as already described. So anxious are the natives to secure protection, and so stupid, that they do not scrutinize closely the right of the grantor to dispense his favours, but pay up. The Jew has various other methods of raising the wind, such as selling his services to the kaid, who, acting in collusion with the Jew with a view to a share in the profits, will often compel some wealthy Moor to disgorge on the plea of a fictitious claim. While refusing to recognize the authority of the Moorish governors as against themselves, they are by no means averse to utilizing it as an engine of extortion on their own behalf. They thus get the benefits of two Governments, both Christian and native, at once; and, further, while they defy the native law, these men are often practically unamenable to the jurisdiction of the Consular Courts. In the interior, where there are no foreign representatives, they can carry on their malpractices, rob, or even murder, in tolerable assurance that the distance from the scene of European authority will secure them immunity from the consequences of their crimes. Not a tithe of the iniquities perpetrated under the name and authority of foreign Powers are ever brought to light, much less can the offenders be brought to justice.

A Moor has not necessarily got to the end of his troubles when he has secured his much-

coveted protection. He may have paid down for it a good round sum, but he has not counted with the Jew if he thinks that is all. The informal protection is not necessarily permanent, but can be withdrawn at the will of the grantor, at whose mercy, therefore, the protected person remains. Hence transactions such as the following are recorded :—
The Jew sells a protection for a sum of money down, or else gets the Moor to acknowledge himself as his debtor to a certain amount. The latter carries on a good trade, relying on the security of his position, and, while amassing a tolerable fortune, embroils himself with the kaid in consequence of his independent course of action. Here is a second opportunity for the vendor of the patent, who threatens that, unless the Moor pays up to a pretty considerable tune, he will withdraw his protection. Further, the Jew, whose knowledge of human nature always serves him in good stead, is well aware that the spirit of revenge is only less strong in the Moor than his greed for gain, and that to get an enemy in his power he will even " part." An arrangement therefore, is come to between the kaid and the Jew for a division of the spoil, and the latter sells his hapless *protégé* into the hands of the oppressor. when his fate may better be imagined than described.

It is to be hoped that such extreme cases as these are rare, but abuses, in the shape of extortions and thefts by protected Jews and Moors, are of daily occurrence. The lot of the natives would not be an enviable one were they simply at the tender mercy of their own rulers. As it is, many of them are between two fires—plundered and ground down by their own kaids on the one hand, squeezed and pillaged by Jews and Christians on the other; and this last oppression, coming as it does from the hated members of alien races, is doubly hard to bear.

At the Madrid Conference of 1880 the attention of the European delegates was drawn to these abuses, and the following complaints were made[1] by Sidi Mohammed Barghash, the Sultan's representative:—(1) That whenever a claim is brought by a Jew or Moor under protection, pressure is brought to bear on the kadis by the interpreters and other native subordinates of the European consulates, who are bribed for their services. (2) That when a European brings a claim or complaint against a Moor, the Consuls and other foreign officials often prejudge the case, and by influencing the kadi prevent justice being done to the Moor. (3) That Moorish subjects, after residing abroad, come back to Marocco, and, declaring themselves to be foreign citizens, produce what purport to be documents of naturalization, on the strength of which they refuse to submit to the Sultan's laws, escape all military and fiscal burdens, and insult the kadis and bully the people with impunity. Further, that Moorish merchants suffer at the native Sokos and auctions, as the protected people outbid them, and then, when the things have been " knocked down " to them, refuse to pay the price they offered, under

[1] Documents Diplomatiques: Question de la Protection Diplomatique et Consulaire au Maroc.

pretence that the goods are of inferior quality. By this time the seller has lost his market, as the people have dispersed, and he is, therefore, forced to take what he can get. That there was much foundation for these complaints is beyond question, and whatever force they had at that time, they possess still, as the Madrid Convention is practically a dead letter, and the abuses are more rampant than ever. Among other things, it was agreed that all irregular and informal protection should thenceforth cease, but a very brief stay in the country will show how far this provision has been carried into effect. One great difficulty must always be the verification of the patents or passports of foreign citizenship, as the native governors cannot read them, and any piece of paper that is written on and stamped will serve the purpose of the person claiming European protection in the interior.

To the part played by foreign legations and consulates in reference to protection and the abuses connected therewith, allusion has been made already. The chief, almost the sole, opponent to the system and to the trafficking in patents and the manufacture of claims is Sir John Hay, as even his greatest opponents admit. The Moors have, on some occasions, looked to him for aid against exactions by foreigners, though in such cases it is little he can do for them. In matters where our own countrymen are concerned which come before him, natives can rely on at least meeting with justice, and the former complain that their interests are not adequately supported. Hence cases of extortion by

British subjects (not necessarily Englishmen) are comparatively rare, though the utmost surveillance could not prevent abuses in individual instances, as transactions recently brought to light have shown.

The only remedy, as far as I know, which has been suggested for this state of things, is the constitution of Joint Consular Courts, or some international tribunal which alone should have the power of granting protections, and which, while rigorously investigating all claims, should severely punish persons found guilty of malpractices. It is more than doubtful, however, in view of the not entirely amicable relations that exist between the various foreign legations, whether such a scheme would work in harmony for long, and, apart from the difficulty of constituting such a tribunal, dual or multiple controls are not in much favour just at present. The one thing certain is that the present state of things is a scandal and a reproach to civilization, for now the powers and authority of civilized nations are exerted in favour of those who plunder helpless barbarians.

CHAPTER XII.

First view of the Atlas—Kasbah Boo-siri—A little learning is a dangerous thing—Ornithology of Marocco—Entertainment at Beni Miskeen—Tadla—Wad Oom R'bea—A dangerous ford—Ambassadors' mona—The Atlas—Beauty in distress—Alcala—Terrible misery—Tamilelt.

March 13th.—The kaid pressed us to stay in his town, and we could with truth express our regret at leaving his hospitable roof. As a slight return for his kindness, we gave rations of bread to the poor, and a scrimmage similar to that we had witnessed at Ben-rajit took place. The condition of these famine-stricken people was something frightful. We were naturally followed by a large crowd of beggars on leaving the town, and one fellow, whose bones seemed very well furnished, and who was otherwise in good case, received a sound leathering from Al-kaid for his importunity.

The country retained its comparatively wild and stony character, and though parts were cultivated, it did not compare in fertility with the rich alluvial soil of the plains. Topping the crest of a low hill we came suddenly in full view of the glorious range of the Atlas mountains, whose glistening summits seemed to bar our progress to the south. They were in reality more than a hundred miles from us, but the clearness of the atmosphere caused them to appear not half that distance. It was like some distant view of the Alps, except that the contour of the latter is far more rugged and diversified. We were in fact much struck with the regularity of the chain, which runs in one unbroken wall of snow almost throughout its length. We were here on the outskirts of a region almost as unknown and quite as unexplored as any in the world. Our course lay almost due south, but we had to diverge a few miles to the south-west to reach a small kasbah—the only place within many miles where we could find entertainment for the night. The place was called Boo-siri, after the name of the then kaid, a fashion they have here of naming their villages, which renders their insertion in maps a work almost of supererogation. By the time the next traveller passes the same spot, it will very probably be called by some other name. Not many miles to the west we could see where the Wad Oom R'bea flows down its deep valley between dark and gloomy mountains. A few miles higher up, the stream takes a sharp turn to the east, which will necessitate our crossing it ere long.

In the evening we took our guns and went in pursuit of quail and anything else we could pick up in the little gullies, thickly covered with brushwood, which intersected the country. In one of these I found a tall native in a starving condition plucking and eating the young shoots of the shrubs. He started at the sudden apparition of an armed Christian from the thicket, and seemed still more surprised when I gave him a small silver coin, evidently thinking there was something uncanny about it all. I managed to get separated from Hoare in the bush, and returned alone to camp with a very scanty bag. Hoare was a long time before making his appearance, but at last turned up at the tent without any quail, but accompanied by a Moor carrying a big jar of rancid butter in his hand. On asking for explanation, found Hoare had been trying his Arabic. Had meant to ask if there were any *s'menna* (quail) about, but the native thought he said *s'min* (butter), and had actually taken him to his house a mile off and made him a present of the pot! A little learning is a dangerous thing, and Hoare, who never had a high opinion of the Arabic language, now thinks less of it than ever.

Our tents were surrounded by a number of gaping natives, who evidently had not seen a Christian in their midst for many a day. The kaid was especially anxious to inspect our breech-loaders, and we had to give an exhibition of their shooting powers. The people were much poorer here, so that we were relieved at not having to accept quantities of *mona* (always excepting Hoare's highly flavoured gift!) which we did not want. Our road the next morning led us through a sterile region of hills and valleys of a somewhat forbidding aspect and wholly uncultivated. On the right, rugged glens led down to the main valley of the Oom R'bea, and the track, which here took a more easterly turn, was as bad as could be, very hilly, and covered with big stones. I should have mentioned that the previous day we had passed out of the province of Shaouia, wherein Z'ttatt is situated, and had entered that of Temsna, which is bounded on the south by the Oom R'bea. At midday we halted awhile at a most romantic spot in a deep gorge with high cliffs around, wherein innumerable pigeons and hawks and a few eagles had built their nests. A tiny streamlet trickled through it, and bright flowers were growing in clusters along its banks. The place looked like some robber's stronghold, as, indeed, it may possibly have been. From time to time our party was joined by sundry natives, among them a Jew on a donkey wending his solitary way to the capital; all were glad of the company and protection we afforded in travelling through this wild and lawless country.

On the road Hoare shot a specimen of the lesser bustard, which are pretty numerous at this season of the year, and I had a chance at a covey of desert partridge, one of the numerous varieties of sand-grouse. I got a brace afterwards on our way up the coast. Of the big bustard (*Otis tarda*) we were never fortunate enough to get a specimen, though they, too, are to be found in the country. At Alkala we saw an immense number of large hawks, and further on we shot one or two grey vultures measuring about five feet across the wing. For the ornithologist, few countries afford a finer field than Marocco; of the sport, I have already spoken. During my two visits I bagged nearly a thousand head of game, chiefly snipe and partridges, the remainder being made up of hares and rabbits, plovers, duck, wild boar, and a few odds and ends; and my rambles gave me abundant opportunity of studying the fauna of different districts. The extraordinary variety of the duck tribe is such as I have seen nowhere else, some of them being very beautiful. The number of hawks, also, chiefly harriers and buzzards, is quite remarkable. In the southern districts they abound more than anywhere else, though animal life is far scantier there. Probably, like their human congeners throughout the country, they prey on each other. In the north, small birds are as common as in England, and in the course of my wanderings I noticed many varieties that are strangers to our shores. The subject is well dealt with in Colonel Irby's "Ornithology of the Straits."

We noticed several kasbahs along the road, all in a more or less dilapidated state; and one particularly, which was totally ruined, we were told had been recently sacked by a neighbouring tribe, the inhabitants massacred, and the place deserted. Of course it was never rebuilt: and so they go on whole towns are destroyed, new ones are not built, and the population, owing to war, famine, and pestilence, is steadily decreasing. The whole country here was far barer and more thinly populated than in the north, and its wretchedness increased as we got further inland. The inhabitants are poorer and more enslaved and of inferior physique compared with those of the Gharb, doubtless owing to insufficient food. We had a short day's journey to-day, having to stop at the flourishing town of Beni Miskeen, which was the only one on the road for nearly fifty miles. Beni Miskeen is a fair-sized place, consisting of a number of houses built of *tabbia*, and a kasbah which contains the kaid's house. It lies in the midst of a rocky waste, which made us wonder why such a site should have been chosen, but its denizens had a singularly flourishing appearance, and though the name Beni Miskeen signifies "Sons of the Poor," there were fewer signs of poverty here than in any other town along the route.

Quail could be heard calling all over the place, so we took our evening walk after them; but owing to the high weeds that grew wherever they were to be found, we could not make much of them. Our only plan was to follow the sound as they ran calling before us through the rank vegetation, doing pointer's work by ear instead of nose, and in that way managed to pick up a few couple by sunset. While shooting, we were joined by a very affable individual with a high falsetto voice, who acted as beater and afterwards insisted on our taking tea with him in his house. This was a cozy little place built of reeds, and tastily adorned inside with small divans and carpets. It was rather late, and I thought our servants would be expecting us, but did not like leaving before we had taken the regulation three cups. Several Moorish ladies presently appeared, unveiled and with slightly free-and-easy manners, and assisted at pouring out the tea. This struck us as a little inconsistent with Mohammedan manners, and made us entertain grave doubts as to the moral character of our hosts; these doubts were afterwards confirmed, but one could hardly have expected such improprieties in a solitary village near the foot of the Atlas!

Suddenly a loud noise was heard outside, and a man rushed in in a very excited state, and intimated by vehement gestures that it was supposed our throats were cut, and that we should now go out at once. At the tents we found several of the kaid's retainers with mona in abundance. They said great anxiety had been felt on our account, and that the kaid had been on the point of ordering his soldiers to mount and scour the country in search of us. We apologized profusely for all the trouble we had occasioned, and expressed our thanks for the kaid's kindness. Meanwhile, our late entertainer, who had indirectly been the cause of it all, and was now standing by and looking intensely miserable, came up and begged us piteously to protect him, as he was sure the kaid would cause him to be flogged for taking us so far out in the country. Hadj Absalam was therefore sent to explain to the kaid that we were entirely to blame, having called the man to beat for us. The kaid sent back word that he had intended to whack him for his imprudence, but that "because of our countenance," *al oojak* (a graceful phrase rather hard to translate), he would pardon him. He repeated the promise next morning, but one could not help thinking it was a tempting opportunity for a little "squeezing;" and now that we knew more about the gentleman, we were of opinion that a good thrashing would do him no harm.

The kaid was a stout, hearty young fellow, about thirty years of age, and there was a frankness in his manner that quite took our fancy. We asked him if we could by any possibility visit the town of Tadla on the Oom R'bea, but he smiled, as if at the absurdity of such a request. The place lies only a day's journey to the East, as a glance at the map will show, but it is inhabited by about the most intractable set that are to be found in the dominions of the Sultan. When the latter visited it, not many years ago, they plundered his camp, killed some of his followers, and otherwise treated him with scant respect. A governor he put over the town was murdered soon after his appointment, and the place has never been visited by Europeans. I need only mention the fact that there are no Hebrews in Tadla, and if a Barbary Jew can't make a living there, that fact alone speaks volumes for the character of the inhabitants. They are very well-to-do people, rich in cattle and sheep, but they do not condescend to pay taxes if they can avoid it, and they are troublesome customers to force. They have extensive copper mines in the vicinity, from which they coin *muzounas*, or blanquillos, containing only half the proper amount of metal, and do a great business with them. The Sultan forbids their circulation, but with very partial success, as we came across them in great quantities, and at Alcala there was no other money to be got. There is a great deal of bad, or light coinage in Marocco, as the natives bore holes in the silver pieces and file them down to get off the silver, which they sell. One of the many tricks whereby the Jews "do" the

Moors, is that of buying up large quantities of these light coins, which will not pass, and getting rid of them, one by one, as occasion offers; by this means they make a profit of twenty-five per cent. Of the gullibility of the Moors I have already spoken, and it is not too much to say that it requires a surgical operation to get an ordinary Arab to see that two-and-sixpence make half-a-crown.

The coins chiefly in circulation are French and Spanish dollars. English money, begging Dr. Rohlfs' pardon, does *not* pass in the country. Of the Moorish coins I have already spoken, but it should be added that there is no such coin as an okea, or ounce; it is only a unit. They use silver pieces, worth from six to twelve okeas, but one of the most remarkable things in the country is the rapid variation in exchange. At Casablanca the dollar was worth about ninety okeas; by the time we had got fifty miles into the country it had risen twenty per cent, and at Alcala it stood at a hundred and twenty. The slow and expensive means of transport prevent equality of value. Gold coins are utterly useless in the country, as the people refuse to take them, so that it becomes necessary to carry about with you an immense weight of silver. This peculiarity recalls to mind the story which tells how the rude forefathers of these people once captured large treasure in gold, and went about asking if any one would exchange all that yellow metal for a little of the white.

March 15.—We have to cross the Wad Oom R'bea to-day, and the kaid is sending a man to assist us in the task. There is a crossing-place lower down, called the "Meshra el Halloof," or Ford of the Wild Boar, which I believe is the one usually taken, and it might well be better than ours. The Oom R'bea ("the mother of grass" or weeds),[1] is the most formidable river we have encountered: it is marked on the map as "deep and rapid," and though the turbid waters give us no clue as to its depth, the current, which is running at the rate of five or six miles an hour, certainly justifies the latter epithet. Just within a few feet of the other side, when we think we are safely over, the beasts all stumble over a big stone lying in the treacherous bed of the stream, and suddenly find themselves in four feet of water. The big mule, carrying a heavy load, was all but carried off his legs by the force and depth of the stream, but being a powerful beast he recovers himself, and, aided by the efforts and yells of the Moors, struggles gamely up the steep and slimy bank. All the animals get over in some fashion or other, and no damage results beyond the wetting of a few things, but I never was in such a bad or dangerous ford. The Wad Oom R'bea is full of shebbel, which I consider the best fish that swims; it is said to be identical with the American shad, and it is the only decent food we ever get in the country. On the southern bank we found ourselves in the province of

[1] In point of volume of water, the Oom R'bea equals, if it does not exceed, the Seboo, which is generally accounted the largest river in Marocco.

Seraghna, and we are out of the jurisdiction of our friend the Kaid of Beni Miskeen. There are about twenty different provinces in Marocco, but their boundaries, except where, as in the present case, a river forms the division, are very loosely marked out, and have no influence on the form of government. A kaid may possibly exercise jurisdiction over parts of two or more different provinces, and in fact the lines of demarcation appear to be quite arbitrary. A heavy shower of rain overtook us here, and we were all pretty well soaked when we arrived at the duar where the kaid had recommended us to camp. A knot of Moors were seated outside on the ground, quite regardless of the wet, and on our announcing our intention to pitch our tents, they all began to make objections. The sheikh himself did not seem so much averse (he was no doubt afraid), but several of the villagers made such a clatter as only Arabs can, when they disagree. There was one ill-favoured fellow, astride of a tiny little donkey, with a big jar of *s'min* [2] in his hand, who was particularly loud in his remonstrances. They would not give any reason, but it was no doubt because of the mona and the other causes, which have been already detailed, of their dislike to travellers. They were playing a rather dangerous game, as the sheikh doubtless knew, for had we reported their inhospitality to the authorities, the latter might have made it warm for them.

[2] Rancid butter is a favourite article of diet. A Moor thinks that, like wine, it improves with keeping, and regards a jar of tolerably putrid *s'min* much as we should a bottle of fine old port.

We learned afterwards that some ambassadors and their suites had been through the place the previous year on their way to the Court, and no doubt recollections of enforced mona on a large scale had embittered their minds against Christian travellers. This, again, is another source of native ill-will against Europeans. The system of reciprocal hospitality which prevails amongst themselves, by which one man who is host to-day may be guest to-morrow, is fair enough, as the benefits are equalized in the end, but the fashion of entertaining Christian strangers becomes a terrible tax on their slender resources in the case of ambassadors and the large parties that accompany them. It is not too much to say that the march of some of these embassies leaves behind it redoubled misery and starvation. It is, no doubt, very pleasant to take one's friends on a novel and entertaining sort of picnic in the interior of a little-known country, but considering the loss it entails on the poverty-stricken inhabitants, the practice of making up large parties on the missions is greatly to be deprecated. It must be borne in mind that every member of the suite requires several attendants, muleteers, tent-pitchers, &c., and a still greater number of animals; besides which, there is probably an escort to conduct the legate with safety and becoming state—all of which have to be fed, and well fed, gratis. Add to this such peculation as can only go on where Moors are concerned, every greedy underling requiring to have, not only his belly filled, but a good share in the pickings, and you may fancy what a drain the total becomes on the hapless natives. Sir John Hay alone takes care to have his retinue as small as is consistent with the dignity of the mission; it generally consists of eight or nine persons, and accounts are taken regularly of the mona which comes in, which minimizes, if it cannot do away with, the evils of the system.[3] The amount of mona which is sometimes demanded is prodigious. I much regret that I have not by me the exact figures of the supplies which had to be given to the French embassy one year at Casablanca: except that I might incur the imputation of drawing upon my imagination. Instances have occurred where Christians have openly sold the mona and simply pocketed the proceeds. Captain Trotter tells[4] one such story of atrocious extortion and oppression, followed by the cruel flogging of eight, and the death of two innocent men, which is well worth reading, as an example of what goes on

---

[3] On this subject Captain (now Colonel) P. H. Trotter, in his excellent work, "Our Mission to the Court of Marocco in 1880," says, p. 24: "Strict measures are taken by Sir John to prevent oppression and peculation on the part of his own native headmen and servants, who would render the march of so large a party more like the advance of a horde of licensed robbers than the peaceable progress of the Mission of a friendly power. Well would it be for European prestige in this Empire of Marocco, if such humane and thoughtful precautions were enforced by representatives of other nations, who visit the Court of the Sultan; our ears would not then be made to tingle by tales of violence and extortion, consonant enough with Moorish ideas, but hardly to be expected from the delegate of a nation which boasts a high rank in the civilized world."

[4] ib. p. 80.

in the country. It is to be hoped such flagrant cases are not of every-day occurrence, but sufficient iniquity of a similar sort is perpetrated to make one utterly sick and disgusted with the doings of these precious products of our latter-day civilization and philanthropy.

The difficulty was settled in the end by the villagers drawing lots as to which of three neighbouring duars should be burdened with our presence, and the lot fell on the sheikh of a village an hour's march further on. Every one seemed in a state of blank ignorance as to where this duar was situated, and I began to think it was merely a dodge to get rid of us. Meanwhile, black thunder-clouds filled the sky, from which descended tall columns of rain, which swept by one after another, the greater part being drawn off by the Atlas mountains to the south. However, we got another drenching before a small collection of huts was pointed out as our destination. The first thing I noticed, was the carcases of a number of horses and mules that had died of starvation during the drought. I counted a dozen quite close to the tent, which showed how great are their losses of live-stock in these times of scarcity. With all the facilities afforded them by climate and soil, the Moors never make hay, a provision for the future which would, I suppose, be at variance with their notions concerning unalterable destiny. Hay-making, I trust, is one of the improvements which they will learn before many years are over, and it will add largely to their resources. The sheikh made no objection to our pitching the tents, and if he had we should have been compelled to disregard them, as no other camping-place offered itself. The people were too poor to provide us with mona, which disgusted our servants immensely, but we managed to procure a few necessaries.

When we rose next morning, a dense, leaden mist hung over the plain, but the rain of the previous day had cleared off. Above, masses of white, fleecy clouds floated lazily over the Atlas range, obscuring them from our view. Suddenly, through a rift in the rolling vapour, there appeared the deep blue sky beyond; the rift widened, and therein stood a glistening, snow-white peak, cut off, as it were, from the earth, by the leaden pall which filled the valleys, and appearing to be suspended in mid air. Another and another peak followed, as one by one the mists retreated before the augmenting power of the sun, till at length the whole chain, a vast wall of glitering snow, 200 miles in length and 12,000 or 13,000 feet in height, stood forth in all its glorious majesty. The mountains were now about forty or fifty miles distant, and it was a picture such as I have never seen in any other country. In Switzerland the whole country is one mass of mountains, grouped together in confusion round the central chains of the Alps. Here a plain, fifty miles in width, as flat as a billiard-table, stretched away to the foot of the mountains, which rose, seemingly, in one direct ascent from the lowest level, and continued in one unbroken line throughout their entire length. As a matter of fact, there are numerous foothills at the base, and the topmost peaks stand several miles back from the bottom of the range, but the aspect from the plain is that of a steep wall of snow.

For an account of the Atlas I must refer my readers to "Marocco and the Great Atlas," by Sir Joseph Hooker and Dr. Ball, wherein they give an account of their adventurous tour in these mountains, during which they ascended one of the highest passes and one of the more Westerly peaks. They may claim the distinction of being the only Christians who have ever penetrated to the heart of any part of these great mountains, though, of course, nearly the whole of the range still remains unexplored. From their observations, the average height of the chain appears to be between 12,000 and 12,500 feet, and they say that the range, throughout a length of eighty miles, possesses a mean elevation exceeding that of any other of equal length in Europe, and indeed, with two or three exceptions, of any chain in the world. There are few peaks that rise far above the level of the chain; the Jebel Glaoui, and a mountain marked in the maps as Miltsin, though no native has ever heard of such a name, which lay respectively S. and S. S.W. of us, appeared to be the highest, but the above-named authors are of opinion that no peak exceeds, or probably even reaches, the altitude of 13,500 feet.

Such being the case, and the Atlas being so essentially a chain, it is curious that it should have been supposed by all the ancients to be a single mountain, on which the world rested: none of the old writers seem to have had any idea of its being a range. Pliny speaks of it as a mighty, solitary peak, rearing its majestic crest out of a wide expanse of sand that environs it on every side. A "religious horror," he says, steals over the beholder who sets his eyes upon this awe-inspiring mass for the first time, while at night it is lit up with lurid fires, and re-echoes with the notes of flutes and the clash of cymbals and the sound of drums, and is the scene of gambols of Fauns and Satyrs. The elephants, crocodiles, hippopotami, lions, and other wild beasts, which, he says, infested the country, have now disappeared, with the exception of the lions, of which a few specimens are killed by the natives every year. The Atlas is inhabited by independent tribes of Shelluhs, who no doubt retired to these mountain fastnesses, like their kinsmen of the Riff and other hill countries, at the time of the Arab invasion. It will be observed that the Atlas runs nearly parallel with the coast, with wide plains between it and the seaboard, a characteristic which it shares with most other mountain ranges of Africa, and which has had no small share in keeping the mysteries of the interior of the Dark Continent so long undiscovered. The Berbers call the Atlas Drarn, or Daran, and it is noteworthy that Pliny speaks of it as bearing the name of Dyrin among their ancestors.

As we were on the point of starting, a girl came up to petition a favour of us. It appeared that her father had been one of the men appointed by the sheikh to act as "warriors" for us, but apparently not caring to sit out in the cold all night on our behalf (wherein I cordially sympathized with him), he had refused to come. Whether he suffered from rheumatism, or was afflicted with the hollow cough peculiar to all persons of the "warrior" class, I cannot say, but his refusal had not been countenanced by the sheikh, who had imprisoned him, and his daughter now begged for our intercession on his behalf. It was obviously impossible to resist the appeal of beauty in tears, even when urged by a rather homely village wench, so we told the sheikh we should be very sorry that any one should be imprisoned on our account, and begged him to release the man. He acceded to our request, and a soldier was despatched for the purpose. Of course, the soldier had to be bribed —nobody "does nothing for nobody" gratis in these parts—but for the moderate sum of half a franc I purchased his liberty. In this country, if a man is "run in," he must pay the constable for taking him there. He will be wise, also, to fee his gaoler periodically during his incarceration, and must give him a substantial *douceur*, on obtaining his release. The gratitude of the damsel was quite affecting to behold. She followed us a good mile, vociferating her thanks at the rate of sixty to the minute, and calling upon Hadj Absalam to convey them to me, which, I need not say, he was quite incapable of doing. "Ah, Sid el Hadj!" she kept calling out, as that imperturbable functionary paid little attention to her; then, running up to me, she presented to my lips a can of milk with a big pat of *s'min* (rancid butter) floating about in it to enhance its richness, and insisted on my drinking it off. It was quite a revelation to her that a Christian could be anything but a monster; she said that had she only known that the Nazarenes were such a good lot she would have brought us presents of milk and eggs and fowls, and all sorts of good things, and she hoped we would stay at their place on our way back. I assured her I would make a point of calling upon her when next passing through the village, and bade her adieu with a very unpleasant flavour of *s'min* on my palate, but with a sense of satisfaction at our having done something towards getting the Christians a better name in the country

From the duar we got on to the flat, scrub-covered plain, and made straight for the town of Alcala, which lay some five-and-twenty miles to the south. The road was a most deserted one; we sometimes never met a single caravan or travelling party for days together. As before remarked, the more usual route is that of Moulai Booshaib, the road from Azamoor, or that from Mazagan. Here and there a ragged Arab or two could be seen digging for roots, but hardly a soul cultivating the ground. Further on, but quite close to the track, stood a good-sized town, not in ruins, though the roofs were off some of the houses, which had been completely deserted the year before owing to the famine. The last inhabitant had left or died (the words are synonymous in the euphemistic Moorish language) a few weeks before, and the houses and streets were now as silent as the grave. Everywhere around the soil showed signs of recent tillage, but the cultivators were either dead or gone elsewhere. If you ask the reason of this, they will tell you that the ground will not bear two crops in succession, and certainly, with the vast tracts of virgin soil that has never felt the plough, there is no need to overtax its capabilities. However, with the use of manure and proper cultivation, and above all, by a system of rotation of crops, this could easily be altered. Add to this the magnificent opportunities for irrigation afforded by the streams, which, fed by the eternal snows of the Atlas, flow unceasingly down and could easily be distributed over the plain, which is on a gentle slope, by means of conduits. Not that I suppose for an instant that this will be done for many a long day to come; I am only speaking of what might be, and meanwhile the people are starving, and will continue to starve. It made me sick at heart to think of the terrible existence passed by thousands of the denizens of this unhappy country. Simply dependent on the seasons, it is certain that at least one-fourth of their lives must be one long struggle with famine. The over-sufficiency of good years cannot be laid by without its being liable to be stolen by the greedy scoundrels in high places who grow rich and fat on the oppression of the poor. Hence every bad season finds them unprovided with the means of subsistence during its continuance, and leaves them without seed for the ensuing crop.

It is absurd to attribute this round of perpetually recurring misery to the idleness of the people, or to their lamentable "fatalism." They are idle because industry is useless in a land where the labourer has the fruits of his toil torn from him; they are fatalists because they have never had a chance of being anything else, partly owing to the teachings of their religion, partly to bitter experience, which has taught them to bear the buffets of ill-fortune with patience and resignation. As Rohlfs observes, the Moors are fanatical because they are barbarous, not barbarous because they are fanatical.

What we saw was but the fringe, as it were, of still greater distress prevailing elsewhere, and it must not be thought that there was anything abnormal in the circumstances under which we visited the country. The same is bound to occur periodically. In 1878 the famine caused far more terrible suffering, and it is pleasant to know that the grateful recollection of English relief still dwells in the minds of many of the people.

The plain near Alcala is copiously irrigated by small streams drawn off from the Wad Tessoot, which, with the Wad el Abid and the Wad el Akdour, are the principal affluents of the Oom R'bea. Their united waters could form an excellent irrigation scheme. At three in the afternoon we reached Alcala, a mud-built town of some size lying at the foot of a range of hills running North-West, and partially concealing the Atlas from view. The kaid's hospitality was unbounded, and his mona at once the last and biggest we received. He expressed himself as being glad to see us, "because of the Sultan's countenance," under whose gracious protection we were travelling. At the tents a man came up suffering from lung disease and spitting blood, and asked us for medicine. Our stock of physic was not extensive, though it included several of those patent medicines which, as they are warranted to cure every ill that flesh is heir to, ought to have included his case; but his complaint seemed to be beyond human skill, so that it would have been cruel to hold out hopes of recovery which must have proved illusory. Moreover, if the man had died, they would have said that the Christians had killed him, the inevitable result of unsuccessful treatment by a Nazarene physician. It is strange the love all uncivilized people have for being doctored, though most of the Moors have more faith in the efficacy of charms. They fancy that all Christians are doctors, which arises from the idea that because Christ possessed the gift of healing, therefore all His followers must have a share of it likewise. For the diseases of Marocco—not a very savoury subject, as they are mostly of an unpleasant character—I refer my readers to the works of Drs. Rohlfs and Leared.

The sight of the famine-stricken wretches in this place was awful—quite the worst we saw anywhere. We intended to distribute bread, as at S'ttatt and the other places, but the rush of starving men and women was such that we had to lock the gates of the inclosure where we were encamped, and give it them over the wall. The worst of this plan was that the stronger despoiled the weaker of their share, so that those who most needed it got none. When the mob had partially dispersed, we walked out with a few loaves to give to any we might find who had not received a portion, and these were not a few. Among the pinched and glaring faces around, there was one figure in particular that attracted our attention, as much by her pitiable appearance as by the feeble moan with which she begged for help. It was that of a woman, emaciated almost beyond description, who, too weak to walk or even to stand, had crawled to the gate in the hope of getting relief, which she, of course, had not found. I gave her a piece of bread, which she put to her lips, but she was too far gone even to swallow it, and one could only hope that death would soon put an end to her sufferings. "Bread, bread, for God's sake, give us bread!" was everywhere the cry, but what could one do? It was like some horrid nightmare to stand there surrounded by this crowd of one's fellow-creatures, begging for help one could not give, but which was their only chance of escape from the most fearful of deaths. I am not squeamish, and do not mind the sight of corpses particularly, but there is something in that fixed, glassy stare in the eyes of a starving man which, once seen, can never be forgotten. When we left next morning we were followed by such a crowd of these poor people, surrounding each one of us, clinging to the stirrups and imploring aid, that we had to spur our horses and gallop through the throng.

Continuing our course to the south, we passed through a narrow glen in the hills, and at length emerged into the plain beyond. Here we saw that the range, which the map depicts as an offshoot of the main Atlas chain, is in reality in no way connected with it, but sinks into the plain some distance away from the foot of the mountains. Once in the plain, we turned south-west, arriving, after a short day's march of about eighteen miles, at Tamilelt, which appears to be some six or eight miles only from the Atlas. We strolled through the town and into some gardens outside in quest of game, which we did not find. There was a corpse lying in the gate, but nobody seemed to take any notice of it, or to be in any hurry to bury it, and it was still there when we left next morning. One cannot help being struck by the remarkable indifference to disease and death, which is one of the results of the conditions of existence in all countries like Marocco. Familiarity, I suppose, breeds contempt in this as in other matters.

Sunday, March 18th.—Up at five in time to see the first rosy flush of dawn overspread the immense snows of the Atlas—a lovely sight. We have a long day's march before us to-day to reach Marocco City, and our route at first lies N.W.W., nearly parallel with the Atlas, but slightly drawing away. There is a howling wind blowing, and the mountains become rapidly clouded. We pass over some stony bits of ground, with hills on either side, and get a glimpse of the first sign of the city in the shape of the lofty tower of El Kutubia, the principal mosque. Other minarets and cupolas soon come into view, till at length, above its encircling palm-groves, we see the quaint old town, with its antique towers and battlements, in its entirety.

R

CHAPTER XIII.

Palm-groves—Marocco—Entry into the City—Description and history of the place—El Kutubia—Soko and auction—The Sultan's army—Lynch law—Tame sparrows—El Kantra—Lepers' Town—Moulai Hassan and his Grand Vizier—Power of the Sultan—The palace and its appurtenances—Sunset in Marocco—The City by night.

Two and a half hours from the town, hard by a large saint's tomb with a mosque attached, we forded the Wad Tensift and entered the forest, or grove of palms, one of the chief glories of Marocco, which extends from here almost to the gate of the city, encompassing it round on almost every side except the South. The palms are not indigenous to the soil, as is proved by their not being found elsewhere in the country, but they were introduced from beyond the Atlas. Emerging at length from the forest, we entered the city by the Bab el Debagh, or Gate of the Tanneries, and threaded our way through streets narrow and tortuous even for a Moorish city, scowled and stared at by the natives as we passed. Now and again we were shocked by the spectacle of soldiers in brilliant but very un-Moorish uniforms, consisting of breeches, tunic, Fez cap, and slippers, and armed with European rifles. These were the *askar* or regular troops of the Sultan, of whom we were to see more afterwards. We made our way straight to the house of

Kaid Maclean, the generalissimo of the army, to whom we had letters of introduction. Kaid Maclean was an officer in the English army, but having taken service with the Sultan, now holds the post of Chief Instructor of the Imperial forces. He received us with the greatest possible kindness, and it was indeed a pleasure to set eyes upon an English face again after the wild journey we had just made. With some difficulty he procured us a house on the outskirts of the town, where our men and animals located themselves. Hoare and myself were entertained by Kaid Maclean, and we paid periodical visits to our servants to see if things were going on right, which in our absence they very seldom were. The master's eye is indispensable in any work the shiftless Arab may be engaged on, or everything will be left to take care of itself. Our house was outside the city walls, being built just within the wall which encloses the Sultan's palace and pleasure-grounds on the South-West side of the town. We had five *askar* appointed to guard our belongings, who always rose and saluted us with fixed bayonets whenever we entered the house. The words of command, such as "Attention!" "Present arms!" &c., are always given in English, which sounds very comical from Arab lips. They never allowed us to go outside without an escort—more for appearance' sake, I fancy, than for protection. These people are such sticklers for etiquette; indeed, persons " of quality " ought not to be seen walking about the streets, as riding is so much more dignified. The escort's chief function seemed to be to chivy and thrash the small boys who cursed and burned our grandmothers as we passed, and they kept him fully occupied. I thought he would have consulted our dignity better by letting them alone.

Marocco, or Marakkesh as the Moors call it, is a great contrast to Fez, and though covering a greater extent of ground, it has little more than half the population. This in ordinary times is probably about 60,000, but when, as at present, the Sultan is there his court causes a considerable increase. There is an air of desolation about the place, as of a city of the past, which is very different from the bustle and stir of Fez, where trade is brisker and the citizens are richer and work harder. It is a more rambling place, dirtier and meaner in appearance. The streets are mostly narrow lanes, often half-choked with muck-heaps and rotting carcases lying about; the houses are chiefly of one story, with miserable entrances, and devoid of all external ornamentation. There are no picturesque corners or remains of arabesque work such as are to be seen here and there in the northern capital—all is bare, uncouth, and unlovely. Dirt and decay are undoubtedly important elements in the picturesque— were they the sole ones Marocco would be the most picturesque city in the world—but after a while one wearies of the fearful squalor and wretchedness, the endless rags and dirt and poverty, the disease, deformity and dilapidation that everywhere meets the eye. Many of the buildings are in ruins, and much of the space within the walls is taken up with waste ground, rubbish, and extensive gardens. Manuel told us we could get shooting in the heart of the city if we liked. Some of the finest gardens are those in the neighbourhood of the Kutubia, which was the first object of interest to which we directed our steps. The Djemma el Kutubia, or Mosque of the Booksellers, has already been mentioned with reference to its great minaret, which was built by El Mansor on the same lines as those at Rabat and Seville. This tower, which is of red sand-stone and some 250 feet high, if not equal in height to the Giralda,[1] or even to what the Hassan minaret would probably have been had it been completed, is still a grand structure, and incomparably the finest piece of architecture in the city. The stone is crumbling away, and most of the fine tile-work which formerly adorned its walls has fallen off. It is a mistake to say this tower is the only stone building in the city, as two or three fine gateways, through which we passed daily on the way to our house, are of that material. The body of the building is not remarkable, except it be for its dilapidated condition. Rohlfs says the interior resembles that of the Karubin Mosque at Fez, and under the floor is a large cistern used by worshippers for their preliminary purifications. Other large mosques in Marocco are those of Ben Yussoof

[1] The Kutubia is the one perfect specimen of a Moorish minaret existent, and shows us what the Giralda must have been like before the incongruous additions made to it by Christian architects.

named after the founder of the city; El Mouezzim, and El Mansowry, but they are by no means striking.

Marocco, like Fez, is magnificently situated, though here again the character of the scenery is totally different, and the surroundings of Marocco are far grander. It lies in the centre of the great plain, 1500 feet above the sea-level, environed by its groves of palm-trees, and with the Atlas rearing their snow-clad crests some twenty miles to the south. Northwards is a range of rugged hills, about 4000 feet in height and almost destitute of vegetation. The city is of later origin than the northern capital, but is of some antiquity, having been founded in the year 455 of the Hegira, or 1073 A.D., by Sidi Yussoof Ben Tesfin, who commenced by erecting a Mosque and a kasbah on the spot. From these small beginnings the city grew at a most startling rate, if we may trust Leo's account, as in the days of his son and successor, Ali, an enlightened and pacific monarch, it contained no less than 100,000 houses. Its decay, however, was scarcely less rapid, as in the time of the same author it had already lost its importance. Leo attributes this result to the "injurie of continual warres and the often alterations of the magistrates and Commonwealth."

The great El Mansor left the impress of his genius upon Marocco as on so many other cities of Africa and Spain, causing among other things the building of the Kutubia. From 668 to 785 A.H. it was ruled by kings of the Marin dynasty, who came from the district which is now the province of

Dukkala, and these tyrannized greatly over the people. Under them, as in Mansor's reign, the kingdoms of Fez and Marocco were united. In the days of the city's prosperity, there existed a college which was of such repute, that parents from afar sent their children here to be educated, and many learned men were congregated in the place. Among others Averrhoes of Cordova, the great philosopher and commentator on Aristotle, lived some time in the city, having been invited over from Spain by El Mansor, and he ended his days there.

In Leo's time the number of students had dwindled down to five, who, he says, were ruled by "a most senceless professour, and one quite voide of humanitie." Early in the sixteenth century the college was closed, and the libraries which gave its name to the Kutubia have likewise vanished, along with all the other glories of the city.

Some writers have tried to identify Marocco as the approximate site of the ancient Roman town of Boccanum Mite (βόκκανον ἥμερον) alluded to by Ptolemy,[2] though I cannot see on what grounds. Certainly the position he assigns to it (9° 20′ long., 29⅓° lat.) would make it far to the South-West and beyond Tarudant, nor did I hear of any Roman remains in the town or in the vicinity. There can be little doubt that the Romans did penetrate as far as this, and probably the Imperial eagles waved in places where now no Christian can venture. Dr. Ball[3] is of opinion that the expedition of Suetonius

[2] Geography iv. 1, § 15.
[3] Journal of a Tour in Marocco, p. 383.

Paulinus, described by Pliny, was to the south of the Atlas, in the direction of Wadnoon, but it does not appear to have led to any permanent occupation. Sala (Rabat) is generally spoken of as the most southerly of the Roman colonies of Mauretania.

On the second day we rode with Kaid Maclean to a beautiful garden of Sidi Mohammed's, the late Sultan, a mile or so outside the walls to the west of the city. It contains many fine trees and shrubs and a large lake. In the afternoon we made the round of several Sokos that are held within the walls, and visited also some shops and the auction, where we made some purchases. The principal trade seemed to be ornamental leather-work, some of which was very pretty. Most of the shopkeepers seemed anxious enough to "taste our money," as the Jews say out here, but such a pitch has fanaticism reached, that one fellow actually refused to sell to us because we were Christians! I could not help inwardly respecting him for this sacrifice of pocket to principle, for, with all their contempt and hatred of the Nazarene, the Moors seldom carry it so far as to refuse his money; they rather regard the traveller as a sort of orange which is made to be squeezed thoroughly, sucked dry, and then thrown on one side.

The throng of marketers in the Sokos struck me as being more motley and diverse than at Fez, and we saw several specimens of the queer-looking "sandies" or carroty Moors. Every type of feature and shade of complexion had examples here. Here, too, were the same familiar figures and scenes, the snake-charmers and jugglers, quack doctors, water-carriers, street-preachers and story-tellers, surrounded by their rapt audiences; single-stick players who, for a few mazunas, will whack each other about the head and legs with astounding good-humour. One hears more different languages spoken; Shelluh or Berber predominates almost over Arabic, and the queer lingo of the negroes now and again attracts one's attention. There is also a startling variety of costume, both as to colour and quantity, from the metaphorical postage stamp of the Haussa black to the thick cloth and ample folds of the Moorish merchant's jellabia. In the auction mart all this heterogeneous mob is huddled together in a narrow space; rich and poor, "velvet and rags," side by side; sleek respectability jostles with the most utter indigence, and every one is on an equal footing with every one else. It struck me as an excellent place to get one's pockets picked, or to catch leprosy, or small pox, or some other loathsome complaint, but fortunately none of these contingencies came to pass in our case. They do not employ an auctioneer as in European countries, but the seller perambulates the place, calling out each successive bid he receives for the article on sale; there seems to be nothing to prevent him making fictitious bids.

We saw, several times, Kaid Maclean's troops at drill, and were struck with the way in which they have profited from the constant pains he has bestowed upon them. He has been eight years in the Sultan's service, during which time he has seen many strange sights, and had many strange experiences, which should form a most interesting narrative, could he be prevailed on to publish them. Some of the regiments were decidedly smart, and from an undisciplined militia he has reduced them to a highly-trained and efficient force. Others, on the contrary, are very much the reverse of the above, as will be seen presently, but Kaid Maclean is far from being responsible for all such as may be seen in uniform on certain occasions. Moreover, he told us that his best troops were absent, drafts of picked men being continually sent off to quell disturbances in distant parts. One day there was a parade of the forces, and after it was over we stood and watched them as they marched past back to the town, and were not a little amused at the very sketchy way in which, their commanding officer's eyes being now off them, they came by out of line and step, no two of their rifles in the same position, and the whole lot jabbering away at the rate of sixty to the minute. And a very scratch lot they were; venerable grey-beards side by side with boys of twelve, miserable starvelings, wall-eyed and semi-blind creatures, lame, and in every stage of collapse. Talk about boys in the English army! Some of these were infants who seemed scarcely strong enough to carry their rifles. The word "uniform" is rather a misnomer for the startling variety of costume in which they were arrayed, which suggested the idea that the purveyor for the army must have done an extensive business in the old clo' line. Nor was there a less striking diversity in the rifles which they carried, though I fancy the best troops are all armed with the Martini. Between two companies there marched a batch of prisoners in chains, linked together, and their hands heavily manacled. The fact is, that H.R.H. the Moorish Commander-in-Chief is paid according to the number of men in uniform he can cause to march past the Sultan on Review days; hence it is not surprising that the lame, the halt, and the blind should be periodically pressed into the service, and apparelled in garments of similar cut but very varied hues, to serve for the occasion. The number of *askar* is said to be about 6500, but this, no doubt, includes many of the infantine and decrepit warriors whose peculiar evolutions we had just witnessed. At the same time there must be a considerable reserve of smart and serviceable troops, and besides the regulars there are the Maghaseni, or Gheesh, irregular cavalry and militia, a large force which might be turned to good account were they properly armed. They showed the stuff they were made of in the Spanish war of '59, when, though badly led and armed only with the flint-lock of the country, they fought with the greatest desperation. The finest corps in the army are the Bokhari, the Sultan's guard of picked negro troops—or "Black Watch," as the French newspapers would doubtless call them. Discipline is enforced by flogging, which is administered impartially to officers and men alike. A foot-soldier's pay is four okeas (about 6*d*.) per day, and he has to feed himself; a horse-soldier gets six okeas, out of which he has to maintain himself and his horse, but they supplement this scanty pay by robbery of various kinds. As might be expected, incompetence and peculation are the order of the day in everything connected with the native military administration. Army officials have control of all supplies and the pay department, and of course do not fail to utilize their opportunities for their own benefit.

We considered it our duty one day to visit the sons of Israel in their unsavoury quarter, but the stench was so great that before getting half through we were compelled to beat a retreat. The Jews of Marocco are sufficiently industrious, and have many skilful silversmiths and other craftsmen amongst their number. In the afternoon, while looking out of the window of Kaid Maclean's house, which opens on the Soko for grass and charcoal, we saw an unfortunate man beaten almost to death by the mob. He had been detected in the theft of a loaf of bread, and this is a kind of lynch law which is always carried into effect when a man is caught in the act of stealing. Sometimes the delinquent is mounted on a donkey and led through the crowd, who belabour him with sticks. This poor half-starved wretch paid very dear for his fault, but the system is justified on the grounds that it is the only possible means of preventing theft from becoming too common, especially in times of famine. The distress was very great in the city, and beggars proportionately numerous and importunate. Many of these wretched creatures were maimed or deformed, and all seemed to be suffering from opthalmic diseases, which are extraordinarily prevalent in the country: half the population seems to be semi-blind or to squint in an extraordinary degree. There was a donkey-boy I knew who had one eye skewed further round than I should have thought possible. When he was about to be paid for his services he would face round and pretend to be absorbed in the beauties of the distant landscape, whereas I knew he was eyeing me intently, and calculating the amount of backsheesh he was to receive. I never liked this, because when I was at school there was a master similarly gifted by nature, who used to catch me drawing pictures and in similar malpractices when I thought he was looking the other way. Hosts of flies take up their abodes on these poor creatures, and never seem to leave them, except to repair now and again to the adjoining refuse heaps for change of air. Travellers will be wise to keep these insects at a distance, as they may convey the poison.

The prisons in Marocco are pretty much the same as in Fez and elsewhere—foul, dark dens, filled with half-starved wretches. There is said to have been a *morstan*, or madhouse, in the Jewry, but I am not aware if it is still in existence, and there is also a separate prison for women in the same quarter.

One very pleasing feature in the place is the tameness of all wild creatures. At Kaid Maclean's dinner-table there were always a number of little birds hopping about on the cloth, which at first we thought were pets of the family, till we were told they were the sparrows of the city. They picked up the crumbs under your very nose, and boldly perched on the bread and the edge of one's wine-glass, a familiarity which at times I found had its disadvantages. They are held sacred, and being thus preserved from injury are perfectly fearless and domesticated. This bird, which is called *tabib* (doctor), is quite different from the European sparrow, being of a red-brown colour with pretty markings, about the same size, but of a less stout build. When I woke of a morning there were often one or two of these little fellows on my pillow, and others perched on the end of the bed. The stork enjoys everywhere similar immunity from molestation[4] in his enormous nest on the housetops and minarets.

Friday, March 23rd.—We had a very pleasant ride to-day, passing out through the Sok el Khemis, or Thursday market, and on through the palm-groves to El Kantra, the Moorish bridge over the Tensift, some five miles to the north of the town. There is nothing remarkable about the bridge, except that it is one of the few specimens of its kind in Marocco, and that it is in excellent repair, but we had some lovely views on the way of the mountains and the town. We stopped awhile in an open space in the wood to enjoy the prospect. A large caravan of camels had halted to rest in the shade and formed an excellent foreground to a very

[4] Ali Bey (I. 127) mentions a hospital in Fez which was richly endowed with funds for the sole object of curing sick, and interring dead, storks; these the natives believe to be men from far-distant islands, who at certain seasons take the form of birds in order to visit Marocco. Hence it is murder to kill a stork.

striking picture. The white cupolas of some Marabouts' tombs peeped here and there through openings between the stately palms, which also gave us glimpses of the walls and towers of the city, with the snows of the Atlas glistening through the dark-green foliage against the cloudless sky. Returning by a different path we rode along the city walls on the Western side. The present fortifications, which consist of *tabbia* walls some twenty-five feet in height with towers at intervals, were built in the middle of the last century by the Sultan Abd Allah. At the north-west corner of the town, we passed El Hharrah, or the Lepers' Town, a village of *tabbia* houses which is set apart for lepers. These unfortunate creatures are not allowed to mix with the outside world, but they intermarry amongst themselves, and it is said that the children of leprous parents are not necessarily afflicted with the disease. The Moors show great hardihood in associating with lepers, and seemingly have no fear of contagion (the belief is growing among physicians that the disease is not contagious), but Hoare and myself thought we would rather not go inside the place. Rohlfs says these people have their own mosques and schools, with priests and teachers who are lepers. Some of them are well-to-do, and own much land and cattle; in fact the community has a life of its own similar to that of any other town. I only once saw a real leper that I know, and I don't want to see another if I live to be a hundred. On that occasion I passed within a foot of a lady in an advanced stage of the disease, and it took me a week to get over the shock. She was just like a four-days-old corpse well chalked over, and I thought how apposite is the phrase that describes it as a living death. As, however, it is said that some lepers have no outward indication of the disease, I may have seen others without knowing it. In El Hharrah there is also a Mellah for leprous Jews, which I should imagine must be a nice sort of place.

Passing on, we tried to enter the town just before midday by the nearest gate, but found it locked, and so had to remain outside. This we found was owing to a curious superstition of the Moors, arising from an ancient prophecy, to the effect that on a certain morning of the Mohammedan Sabbath, the Christians will gain possession of the city during the hours of morning prayer. Therefore every Friday they go through the ceremony of closing the gates, all of which are kept locked from 10 a.m. to noon, to prevent the fulfilment of the prophecy. Looked at from a Mussulman fatalist's point of view, I call this a most unwarrantable attempt to interfere with the decrees of unalterable destiny.

In the evening we had a small card-party at Kaid Maclean's, being joined by M. Erkmann, a French officer who holds a similar appointment in the Moorish artillery to that of Kaid Maclean in the regular army. Neither he nor our host understand the other's language, so that they meet on common ground in Arabic; I spoke French with M. Erkmann, and Mrs. Maclean being a Spanish lady, we sat down to a strangely polyglot loo, English,

French, Spanish, and Arabic being all mixed up together. If anybody asks me the Arabic for "Pass," or "Take the miss," I cannot tell him. Probably the language does not provide for such expressions, as gambling is forbidden in the Koran in at least two passages, though in a rather qualified manner. I may mention that chess is allowed, and it is a favourite pastime of many Moors.

We were never gratified during our stay by the imposing spectacle of the Sultan parading the streets under the shade of the Shereefian umbrella, nor did we have an audience of his Majesty, not having any occasion therefor, and being unprovided with suitable presents, which are indispensable for an interview. The proper thing appears to be to make the guileless monarch a gift of some inexpensive novelty, some toy of such quaint and ingenious construction as will captivate his barbarian fancy, and to get a horse, or mule, or other serviceable quadruped in exchange. At present, however, his Majesty is a little shy of receiving strangers, as he always expects they want to get something out of him (which, indeed, is usually the fact), and his Government has been sadly taken in by various Christian adventurers. "Once bit, twice shy," and the Moors have been bitten very much more than once. One day some disinterested people will take a contract for the supply of rifles for the army, warranted not to go off, or to burst if they do; next comes a gentleman, who has, of course, nothing but his Majesty's interests at heart, with an infallible system of coinage, which will surely enrich the Sultan. Whether the latter finds his pockets better filled may be questioned, but the inventor certainly does. Every improvement or innovation must, of course, come through European hands, and unless the Government are fortunate enough to meet with disinterested counsellors, their ignorance makes them an easy prey to clever schemers. The money to pay for these novelties has to be raised somehow; the screw is put on, and it is the helpless people who are the sufferers in the long run.

The present Sultan, Moulai Hassan, is the fourteenth sovereign of the dynasty of the Fileli, or Shereefs of Tafilet, who have occupied the throne since 1632. There is no law of succession in Marocco, and though the Sultan on his death-bed has the right to name his successor, it does not follow that his nominee will be accepted by the Shereefs and grandees who have the chief voice in the matter. The consequence is that the Emperor's death is generally the signal for great revolutions and disturbances. The authority of the law is relaxed and anarchy reigns till the incomer has established his right by fire and sword. The sceptre does not descend lineally in all cases, and often a brother or cousin is preferred to a son of the late Sultan. Moulai Hassan came to the throne in 1873. He is about forty-five years of age, and is described as a tall, handsome man, of commanding appearance; he has negro blood in his veins, but, as already explained, that is far from being a matter of reproach in this country. From all accounts he would seem to be a kindly-natured man enough, and anxious to do right, according to his rather imperfect lights. But what can he do? He cannot know of half the scoundrelism that goes on in his "blessed country," as the Moorish officials, with unconscious irony, call Marocco, the plunderings and oppressions of his subordinates, who, though there is a nominal limit put upon their arbitrary authority, are, during their term of office, practically unrestrained in its exercise. For instance, they have not the power of inflicting capital punishment, but they may flog or imprison at will, and if the victim should happen to die from the effects of the one, or be starved in the other, that of course is not their fault: in the matter of exactions they have their own way, as long as they send sufficient grist to the Imperial mill. Further, the Sultan is but a puppet in the hands of his Grand Vizir, through whose hands all business must pass before it reaches him. This official of course gains his place by favouritism, or the caprice of the ruling monarch—anything but personal merit—with the result that any idiot or ruffian may be raised from the gutter to the supreme office of the realm. The present occupant of the post, who is described as being the incarnation of pig-headedness and fanaticism, is a worthy representative of the system which promoted him. He is all-powerful at Court, and having his spies and emissaries all over the country, each kaid and native governor is kept under his thumb, and is liable at any moment to feel the effects of his displeasure, which are apt to be serious. Being animated by an abiding hatred of Christians and foreigners, he is the chief obstacle to all internal reform, which his instinct tells him would weaken his position, and deprive him of many of the dubious means by which he makes a good livelihood. Constant pressure cannot be brought to bear on the Moorish Government, as the foreign representatives live at Tangier, far from the Court, and though on their occasional visits to his Majesty they may extract from him vague undertakings to reform, as soon as they are gone he is tackled by his Vizir, who causes him to repent of his rash promises, and things remain as they were. A great contrast to the Vizir is the Foreign Minister, Sid Mohammed Barghash, a man of rare integrity and comparative enlightenment, who resides at Tangier.

The Sultan divides his time between Marocco and Fez, spending two or three years at either capital. Mequinez used to be a favourite residence, but of late it has not been favoured by the presence of Royalty. The shifting of the Court is an affair of great moment, requiring vast preparations, and the journey usually takes six months or more. He is accompanied by his army and a following of some 40,000 men, and with these he moves hither and thither, not travelling in a direct line, but inflicting chastisement on all such of his subjects as may have raised the standard of revolt or refuse to pay tribute. The movements of so large a body are necessarily very slow, and as the commissariat department is not very highly organized in the Moorish army, the troops are often starved, and the very officers have not enough to eat. When he wishes to "eat up" any rebellious tribe, his usual method is to sit down opposite it with his army and to command them to submit and bring in their taxes. He gives them a short time to think over it, at the expiration of which, if they still prove refractory, he lets loose his soldiers; neighbouring tribes are invited to join in the work with a promise of a share in the plunder, and the heads of rebels are paid for at the rate of so many *okeas* per head. Sometimes he gets the worst of it, as already mentioned at Tadla, and there are tribes in the heart of his dominions that he has never thoroughly subdued. "Where the Sultan's horse treads the grass ceases to grow," says the Turkish proverb, and the march of the Shereefian troops is as though an army of locusts had passed over the land. We in England, who are accustomed to receive without emotion the intelligence that our Queen has left Windsor for Balmoral, can hardly conceive of a state of things in which the Sovereign has to fight his way from town to town, spreading ruin and desolation in his track. The numberless ruins we passed on our way bore silent witness to the misery thus inflicted, and the line,

"They make a desert and they call it Peace,"

might well have been written of this enlightened Government in its dealings with its unhappy subjects.

The Sultan's authority over the mountaineers of the Rif, most of the Shlohs of the Atlas, and the Berber tribes on their southern side, is purely nominal. In Tafilet and other places on the confines of the desert, he is represented by a kaid, but the latter's jurisdiction is at best over a very limited area. Most of these tribes are quite independent, each electing its own rulers and councillors, and their condition, even if they have not the same opportunities for acquiring wealth, is a far more enviable one than that of their brethren who have to bow beneath the grinding yoke of Moorish tyranny. They may respect the Sultan as a Shereef, but their recognition of his temporal power shows itself at most in the payment of occasional tribute. The Mohammedan system of government being essentially a theocracy, the spiritual and temporal power are always united in the same person. Hence the Sultan is not only Emperor of Marocco, but Head of the Church in Western Islam, which causes his name to be held in reverence by many who would resist to the uttermost any attempt to subdue them by force of arms. This dignity has been enjoyed by his predecessors ever since the expulsion of the Moors from Spain, when a Shereef for the first time ascended the throne. But the Sultan claims a wider ecclesiastical authority even than this, and in common with every other member of the Arab race he disputes the legality of the Turkish Sultan's title to the Kaliphate Islam is essentially an Arab creed, and the Turk, besides being of alien blood, lacks the most indispensable requisite for the honour in Arab eyes—descent from the Prophet. Ottoman supremacy over the religious world of Islam has its sole sanction in the possession of superior force and the guardianship of the sacred city of Mecca, and with the proud consciousness of their high lineage the Sultans of the West consider themselves far the superiors of their rivals on the Bosphorus.

The proximity of our house to the palace did not in any way assist us in getting a sight of the Imperial residence and grounds. The latter must be of great extent, judging from the length of the enclosing wall, and his Majesty, who is a man of retiring habits, seldom appearing in public except on his visits to the mosque of a Friday, takes daily exercise therein. Close to his palace is the Imperial treasury, and adjoining it the harem, which is said (and it may well be believed) to be much better stocked than the treasury. The Sultan probably does not know how much he is married, but he unquestionably is so to a very large extent, though of legal wives he has but four, the number allowed by the Mohammedan law. The only Moslem who was ever permitted to exceed this limit was Mohammed himself, but then he had an obliging friend in the angel Gabriel, who always came down with a special dispensation from Heaven when the Prophet had need of any little indulgence on his own behalf. As to his Majesty's progeny, I am told it is not his fault if the population of Marocco is on the decrease, and princes of the blood royal must be almost as numerous as in Russia. The ladies are looked after by numerous eunuchs, but it seems certain these creatures have no influence in state affairs, a point worthy of notice as being a redeeming feature compared with other Mohammedan governments. Rohlfs, who was often in medical attendance on the Sultan's ladies, and gives a most amusing account of his experiences, says that all the eunuchs have strongly fragrant, aromatic names, among which he cites those of his friends Mr. Camphor, Mr. Musk, Mr. Otto of Roses, &c. Never having been privileged with the society of any of these gentlemen, I cannot say if they are deserving of these appellations; if so, they must differ strangely from the large majority of their countrymen.

The Moors are all so absurdly jealous, that one is always in danger of sinning against the strict code of etiquette which is established as an additional barrier to intercourse between the sexes. I often wished to mount on the roof of Kaid Maclean's house, so as to survey the wonderful panorama around, and to get a bird's-eye view of the city, but such a proceeding would have been considered the worst possible "form," and might have given rise to a suspicion that I had designs on my neighbours' domestic peace. I therefore had to content myself with the prospect afforded by the less central position of our own house. Of many glorious scenes which it has been my good fortune to witness in various countries, none is so indelibly imprinted on my memory as that of sunset in the city of Marocco. Westwards the eye roves over the uninterrupted expanse of plain which drops on the horizon as upon the shore of some illimitable ocean. As the sun sinks, the cloudless heavens are flooded with a gold and crimson blaze, sometimes mingled with other brilliant colours, which gradually suffuses the whole landscape. It first fills the wide plain, then falls upon the feathery tops of the palms, the white roofs and crumbling battlements and minarets of the great city, and last, catches the glittering summits of the giant Atlas towering 12,000 feet above. The hues of sunset upon the snow are sometimes followed by the lovely "after-glow" familiar to Alpine tourists. Here, however, the strange and southern surroundings, and the African vegetation below, render this glorious phenomenon doubly impressive.

As the fiery orb disappears, there rises from twenty steeples the solemn call to prayer, *El Maghreb*, or the evening mueddhin. It commences with a low, plaintive, wailing sound; then the strain is taken up by voices on the surrounding minarets, now swelling in a grand inspiring chorus, now dying away in soft musical cadence—all in the most perfect harmony. It is the simple Mussulman confession of faith, commencing with "There is no God but God, and Mohammed is the Prophet of God," and in the morning they add, "Prayer is better than sleep, come and pray." Six times a day the hour of prayer is announced, and the mueddhin serves to tell the people the hour of the clock. The time is taken from the sun at El Dohor, or the midday mueddhin at 12.15 p.m.; astronomy is the one science of which any vestige remains in the country, but I do not know if they are equal to calculating mean time. It was always pleasant to listen to the mueddhin, and it inspired me with far more devotional feelings than the jangle of those church bells which Rabelais, I think, speaks of as being, from their number, the most remarkable things in England. I wish some of our clergymen would take a hint from the followers of the Prophet and break up their bells and start a crier from the steeple. If any one would do this I could promise him one towards a congregation.

When the last rays of sunset have vanished there succeeds the brief twilight of the South, and then all is speedily wrapped in the profound silence of night in an Eastern city—in strong contrast with European towns, where the hum and roar of the streets continues till far into the night. Being seized with a desire to see what the city looked like at night, I once arrayed myself in Moorish costume, and sallied forth at midnight on a tour through the streets. It was probably not a very wise proceeding, but no harm came of it. Indeed, for awhile I saw no living creature, save an occasional dog gnawing the carcase of a dead donkey or committing acts of cannibalism on those of his own species. There were no watchmen or policemen about, though in olden times "the force" is said to have been partially organized. The only preventives of nocturnal crime are, first, the fact that scarcely any one goes out at night, and secondly, the closing of the gates of all the different quarters at sundown, so that marauders cannot get from one part of the city to another. Burglary is not developed into the fine art it now is in England, and the construction of the houses, with the windows all opening into the courtyard inside, is decidedly against it. Suddenly, on turning a corner, I heard the beating of tom-toms and pipes, and came on a party of revellers, who were celebrating a wedding at this unseemly hour. One of them accosted me, and though I answered in my best Arabic, he did not seem to know quite what to make of me. The only other sound was the occasional discharge of guns from the sentinals in the *askars'* quarter, who have this peculiar method of showing their officers that they are on the *qui vive* and not sleeping at their posts. Apart from these disturbances the streets were untenanted and still and silent as the grave.

CHAPTER XIV.

En route for the coast—Numerous guard—Ain el Baida—Onkh el Jimmel—A thaleb out of work—Argan forest—Sok el Tletta—Mogador—Highly scented Mellah—Sus and Wadnoon—Independent Jews—Soudan trade—Slave trade in Sus—Flooding the Sahara.

Saturday, March 24th.—Having spent five very pleasant and interesting days under Kaid Maclean's care, it is with genuine regret that we turn our backs to-day on the city *en route* for Mogador. Outside the gates we pass the parade-ground, where our host is hard at work on his charges, and we bid him farewell. We ford the Wad N'fys, a good-sized river that is now reduced to a trickling stream. Passing over the plain near the city, we noticed several mounds of earth, which on closer inspection turned out to be water-conduits arched over to protect the water from the sun and consequent evaporation. In many of these ducts the masonry had fallen in and the work rendered useless, but a moderate expenditure of labour might effect a complete system of irrigation for the plain. We camp at Kasbah Ouadaiah, a large fortress about twenty miles from Marocco. There is a large guard of at least fifty "warriors" sitting in rows round our tents to-night. This is no doubt due to the fact of the Sultan being so near, as the country is perfectly safe; the kaid probably thinks that if any harm came to us, his Majesty would be certain to hear of it and to make matters unpleasant for him.

Sunday, 25th, Easter Day.—Up at six; the poor people crowding round the places where our animals had fed, to pick up the grains of corn, and even the horse-dung is collected by them for the same purpose. The Atlas look very grand in the morning sun, but present quite a different appearance here from what we saw of them at Beni Miskeen and the province of Seraghna, and their sides, which then seemed so steep, are now seen to be gently-sloping, intersected by valleys, which are said to be very fertile. It is not my intention to describe this part of our route at any length, as it has been more often travelled, among others by Dr. Ball and Sir Joseph Hooker in their journey to the Atlas, and it contains little that is interesting. After encountering a heavy shower of rain, which drenches us all, we camp at Ain el Baida (White Spring), a village of conical huts such as are to be commonly seen in this part of the country.

Monday, 26th. In two hours we pass Sheshaoua, a village in a fertile spot watered by the river of the same name. So far we have been travelling on an absolutely dead level ever since leaving Marocco, but presently, at about fifty miles from the city, the road ascends between some curious flat-topped hills, with steep, or even precipitous sides, which bear the name of Onkh el Jimmel, or Camel's Neck. They might just as well have called them haystacks or windmills, as far as the resemblance goes.

Manuel is in great doubt about our getting provender for the beasts, when by good luck we meet a Moor with a donkey loaded with barley which we buy of him. Descending from the Camel's Neck, we lose sight of the Atlas for the first time, and late in the afternoon arrive at Sidi Mokhtar, a collection of about seven dilapidated mud hovels. I notice this place is marked on all the maps—probably because there is nothing else to mark in this most forsaken country. By the way, I have taken the liberty of altering on my map the relative distances of the villages on the road, which are inaccurately given in most maps, especially in that of Sir J. Hooker and Dr. Ball.

Tuesday, 27th. We enter the province of Shiedma to-day. On leaving the village a young Moorish *thaleb* (schoolmaster), with his slate slung over his shoulder, accompanied us. Catching me alone a short way behind the caravan, he came up and in a rather shamefaced way asked for bread. I gave him part of my lunch, and as he ate it he poured his tale of misfortunes into my ear—how the famine had come upon the village and the people had died or left, while those who remained had not money to send their children to school, so that now he was left penniless and absolutely starving. Poor fellow! He has a bright, intelligent face, and it seems hard indeed that he cannot earn enough to keep the wolf from the door, but from the condition of the very few children we saw in the village, I can well understand how it is so. Nothing, indeed, is sadder in these times of scarcity than to see the effect of want on the children of the poor; their little limbs shrunk to a pitiful thinness, while their stomachs are distended to a most unnatural size from the grass and other green stuff that they are compelled to eat to keep body and soul together. The crying of the starving little ones at night in some of the villages is very distressing also.

The next village on the road is Ain Oumast, situated, as the name denotes, near a large fountain, which makes it a convenient camping-place. As, however, it is yet early we push on, and after getting another soaking we arrive at the confines of the large forests of Argan trees which abound in this part of the country. The Argan tree is the "local representative of the olive," according to Sir J. Hooker, and is not found north of the Tensift, or indeed in any other country of the world. It is a very picturesque object with its gnarled trunk and twisted branches, and dense dark-green foliage. It has a fruit from which is made a bitter and nauseous oil, which the natives, however, consider delicious, so that it ranks as one of the staple products of the country. The scenery here changed its character completely, and Hoare and myself remarked simultaneously on the very English look it bore : all around the country was undulating and well-wooded, reminding me strongly of parts of South Warwickshire. The sight of these trees with their rich foliage was most refreshing after the barren, scrub-covered plain, and we felt inclined to wander about in the dark recesses of the forest.

At four in the afternoon we reached Sok el Tletta, or Place of the Tuesday Market, a rather flourishing village, near which we noticed a good-sized kitchen garden. We strolled out in the evening with our guns in pursuit of bustard, which we failed to get near, and dined off a very tough fragment of a he-goat which had just been immolated for our benefit.

Wednesday, 28th. Off early through the Argan woods. The road presently emerges into open ground, well cultivated and more thickly populated. A good many of the people wore black *jellabias*, and we were told these were members of the neighbouring Berber tribe of Ouled Boo Sba, though no reason was given for their adopting a distinctive costume. Close to the road we were struck by the spectacle of a crowd of women gathered round the massive trunk of an ancient Argan tree; it was a Soko of females, without a man amongst them, for cloths and cotton stuffs and household requisites. Hard by were other Argan trees with goats jumping about in the branches in quest of the fruit, which most animals are very fond of, and completing a rather curious picture. Our arrival was the signal for the clatter of numerous tongues among the women, and all business was stopped for the time. The province of Haha begins here, and extends to the south as far as the Atlas. The Argan woods gradually cease, giving place to scrub; we mount the line of sandhills which extend all along the coast, and get our first sight of the Atlantic and the town of Mogador, while the snowy tops of the Western Atlas come also into view. Mogador lies on a flat promontory or spit of sand running out some way into the sea, and we had two hours' abominable ride through the deep sand, which a high wind drove in blinding showers in our faces. We wondered why on earth any one should have chosen such a spot for a town, surrounded as it is by miles of sand on every side. The port, however, is a consideration, and doubtless determined the site. This is formed by an island a mile from the mainland, but, regarded as an anchorage, it must be considered a failure, as the waves burst in with such force in bad weather that vessels have often to stand out to sea. The town is only 120 years old, having been founded by Abdallah, the same powerful and energetic Sultan who built the fortifications of Marocco. The name Mogador comes from the adjacent shrine of Sidi Mogdal, but the Moors call it Soueirah, which, freely translated, means The Beautiful. Population about 15,000, nearly half Jews, with about 200 Europeans. We found it a fresh and breezy place, and residents here told me that the heat in summer is far from being oppressive, and that on a visit to England, they found our August weather hotter than their own. It claims to be the healthiest town in Marocco, and Dr. Leared, who gives a long description of it, speaks highly of its climate for chest diseases. Personally, were I consumptive, I think I should prefer a short life and a merry one in England to prolonging it in Mogador, but that is a matter of taste.

We camped on a grass plot inside the town, near

the port. Our tents soon attracted various members of the hawk-eyed Hebrew race on the look-out for a chance of " tasting our money." We had a letter of credit to a Jew here, who obligingly supplied us with twenty pounds' worth of dollars so old and worn as to be considerably below their proper value. Far more welcome visitors presently arrived, in the persons of Mr. Payton, H.B.M.'s Consul, and Mrs. Payton, who, with every kindness and offers of hospitality, pressed us to leave our tents and stay with them. In fact, we are beholden to the English residents of Mogador for the same courtesy that was shown us elsewhere on the coast, and it was only the fact of time pressing that prevented us remaining.

The next day we made the tour of the town, which is well built and clean looking for the most part, with wide streets and a general air of prosperity. Only the Mellah here beat everything. In search of curios, we invaded some of its most highly-scented recesses. We thought that after our lengthened and extensive experience, we were tolerable connoisseurs in Moorish stenches, but now we were forced to confess ourselves mistaken. Talk of Coleridge's " seventy-two stenches, all different and well-defined, and as many separate smells," there were twice as many here; those of Alcazar were as eau-de-cologne and the Mellah of Marocco otto of roses in comparison. In the former places the filth was at least left to evaporate as best it might in the open air; here they have small drains just under the paving-stones with traps thoughtfully placed at intervals of every few yards, so as to throw it up well under your nose. What is most astonishing is the fat and blooming appearance of the denizens of these unsavoury alleys. Manuel gravely assured us that this atmosphere afforded nourishment to the Jewish constitution out here, and his theory really seems borne out by the fact that the Ghetto in Rome is at once the filthiest and healthiest quarter of the city. I observe in Dr. Leared's book, in his description of Mogador, the statement that "the use of the bath is unknown among the Jews," and I certainly am not prepared to contradict it.

The country to the south of Mogador is little known beyond a certain radius. In Haha the Shloh element predominates among the people, and in Sus they are wholly Berber, though Arabic-speaking tribes are to be met with here and there. The men of Sus, of whom many may be seen in North Marocco, their energetic character leading them to seek their fortunes further afield, are a clever, active, and intelligent set, more apt than the Moors at learning the arts and habits of civilization. In their own country they are turbulent and dangerous, and not many years ago they murdered an Austrian traveller who had just set out on a journey from Mogador. Though within the Sultan's dominions, they have long been semi-independent, the mountainous nature of the country aiding their warlike nature. The present Sultan is the first for many years who has tried to assert his authority over them by force of arms, and in the summer of 1882 he made an expedition into their territory. Considered as a military promenade, it was an undoubted success, but probably it has not led to any permanent result. The effects of the famine prevented the natives from offering effectual resistance, but the sufferings of the Imperial forces were terrible; the troops were starved and six hundred animals died of drought in a single day.

Beyond Sus is Wadnoon, a country inhabited by the most dangerous and fanatical tribes in North Africa, into whose territory even the intrepid Rohlfs did not dare to go, and who are responsible for the murder of more than one European traveller. Our head man, Manuel Correa, who had lived all his life in the country and spoke Arabic like a native, had spent twenty-two months in Wadnoon, having been despatched there to negotiate with the Sheikh, who held captive a number of shipwrecked Spaniards whom he treated with the greatest brutality. Probably no other European could claim to have such an intimate acquaintance with the interior of this almost unexplored region. He lived and dressed there as a Moor, and even held himself forth as a Shereef to the people, knowing well that the Saint business is the most lucrative native industry in these parts. He thus saw much of the manners and habits of the natives, and much of his information was most interesting. I had of course little means of verifying it myself, but having always found him intelligent and trustworthy, I saw no reason for doubting its accuracy. The Sheikh of Wadnoon he described as a great scoundrel, but of much power in the country, his influence extending a long way into the interior. I imagine the inhabitants must be chiefly of Berber extraction, but he spoke of Arabic being the prevailing language. The most curious thing in the country seems to be certain tribes of Jews who are semi-independent, not confined as elsewhere to the towns, but *agriculturists*. I do not know of Jewish agriculture existing anywhere else in the world. They are respected by the natives, and being on an equal footing with them, they wear the same dress, the only distinction being a black cap. They appear to have abandoned many of their Judaic customs and observances and to have adopted the life and habits of the Moors. They are industrious and not "parasitic." Each tribe is under the protection of some powerful sheikh who dwells in an adjoining fortified kasbah, and insults and wrongs against the Jews are avenged by him as if they had been committed against his own people. In that part of the country fortified dwellings are almost universal. Manuel expressly denied the existence of warlike Jews, which was asserted by Davidson and other writers, and indeed a bellicose Hebrew would seem to be a strange anomaly.

Considerable trade seems to be done there with the Soudan, a large item thereof being ostrich feathers. The ostriches are hunted by the natives, on the confines of the Sahara, on fleet desert horses; they ride after the birds up wind till they are tired down, when they knock them on the head with thick bludgeons.

Manuel also said he had been to Timbuktoo, but several people have claimed to have reached that favourite goal of the African explorer, whose pretensions will not bear the test of examination. At the same time, I am not prepared to say it was not the case. He once went so far as to offer to personally conduct us to the "Queen of the Desert," the fabled home of the voracious cassowary and other legendary characters. He suggested that Hoare should go as a *hakim*, or medicine-man, and myself as a deaf and dumb lunatic, a character he seemed to think would fit me admirably, and would ensure me the respect and veneration which they pay to all such personages. A person who retains his speech and sanity is accounted very small potatoes in these parts. As, however, I had no fancy to go jibbering for forty days across the Sahara with the prospect of having my throat cut at the end of the journey, we did not put his sincerity to the test. The distance is some 1200 miles, the oases few and far between, and the people for the first part of the journey the most blood-thirsty. A better way is to start from the coast south of Wadnoon, where a more tractable set are to be found and the distance is much less. The trade with Timbuktoo and the Soudan is at present entirely in the hands of Moorish and Berber merchants, some of whom reside in the city, and their fanaticism and jealousy of foreign, and especially Christian, competition form the chief obstacle to opening up the country.

Slaves are the most important article of commerce with the Soudan, and Marocco forms the chief market for the traffic in human flesh. Once stop the trade here, and the chief inducement to kidnapping will be gone. It is true that the slaves are treated well in the country, being protected by law as propounded in the Koran, and they may even rise to the highest offices in the realm, but here as elsewhere it is not so much slavery but the slave-trade which is objectionable. The sufferings of the caravans in that terrible journey across the Great Desert must be very great. It does seem strange that in these days of freedom, when the traffic is suppressed in the remotest quarters of the globe, slaves should be openly bought and sold within twelve miles of the shores of Europe.

Considerable efforts have been made from time to time to promote trade in this part of the world. A short time ago the Spaniards, after much bullying, made the Moors give them a port on the Sus coast, now called Puerto Cansado, in accordance with the eighth Article of the Treaty of Peace in 1860, and much good may it do them. Nobody seems to have known where Puerto Cansado was; the Sultan procrastinated in true Moorish fashion, and tried to fix on a spot where nobody could land on account of the surf, and now it seems he has generously made them a present of what is not his to give. It is always impossible to say what are the exact frontiers of Marocco, which are purely arbitrary, and advance and recede according to the power of different Sultans.

A company which was promoted and formed by Mr. Mackenzie, and now has a settlement at Cape Juby, some three hundred miles south of Mogador, has enjoyed a very fair measure of success. This

Mr. Mackenzie is best known as the promoter of the scheme for flooding the Sahara, which, though it attracted a good deal of notice some years ago, now seems to have dropped out of the public mind. Whether any of us will live to take return tickets by passenger steamer to Timbuktoo is doubtful, but the idea which sounds so wild is probably feasible. It seems clear that El Joof, the immense depression in the Desert, is well below the level of the ocean, and that were the few intervening miles of sand cut through, what was probably once the bed of a vast sea would again be submerged with the waters of the Atlantic.

Encouraged, perhaps, by the success of Mr. Mackenzie's company, another was recently set on foot for trade in Sus. They appear to have settled there in the Sultan's territory, going through the rather antiquated farce of getting a grant of land from the "local chief," who, I believe, is generally on such occasions the first ragged native that is met with on the beach. They came to an untimely end, being attacked by the natives, and their stores pillaged. I observed that in winding-up the concern, Mr. Justice Pearson refused an application for a stay of proceedings, because, as he said, the chief assets seemed to be of a "rather uncertain nature," consisting as they did of a claim against the Moorish Government. Very uncertain indeed, I should say. Increased modes of communication and greater security for life and property will be necessary before any such undertaking can hope to meet with success in that part of the world.

CHAPTER XV.

In the plain of Akermout—Journey to Saffi—Fat women—Status of the sex in Marocco—The barb—Dukala—Lovely flowers—Numerous ruins—Zaouias—Marketing in Azamoor—An upright Bascha—Rabat again—Excursion up the Boo-Ragrag—The Zair tribe—Moorish yarns—Mehediah—Journey up the coast—A would-be embezzler—Larache and El Khemis again—We meet an old friend—Boar-hunting extraordinary—Back at Tangier—Our impressions of Marocco and the Moors.

Friday, March 30th.—At last we are off on our homeward journey, but some four or five hundred miles yet lie before us. We keep to the sea-shore for a couple of hours, then strike inland through hills and dense thickets, and emerge into the wide plain of *Akermout*, or "figs," in the Shloh language. On our right are the Jebel Hadid (iron mountains), a range some 2000 feet in height. There are said to be remains of mining works on these hills, and the earth and water in the plain are strongly impregnated with iron. On their summits are several holy sanctuaries where, in Leo's time, pious and ascetic hermits had their abode. He gives the natives of this district the character of a faithful and peaceable nation, which I fear could hardly be said of them now. However, they are very civil to us in the little village of Gragrag where we encamp.

Saturday, 31st.—We have taken a great fancy to our quarters at Gragrag, which are pleasantly situated in the middle of the fertile plain, and make up our minds to remain a day. Some of our servants, too, are ill from over-eating, and we have taken the opportunity to dose them all, with surprising effect. Hoare and myself spend a quiet day, shooting and botanizing in a very amateur way, and I am fortunate enough to bag a couple of the beautiful desert partridge, or small sand-grouse. There is something very pleasant in these quiet days in the country, with pretty scenery around, and in the company of the primitive peasantry. The nights, too, are fine and warm, and one can sit out with comfort and observe the cloudless heavens over a pipe. There are shooting-stars innumerable to-night, which the Moors, if they knew their Koran, would tell us were bits of red-hot iron flung by good angels at evil spirits who approach too near the Empyreum or verge of heaven.

Sunday, April 1st. The road takes us to-day still through pretty country, hilly and well-wooded, but goes winding about all over the place. Every ten yards we meet some obstruction on the path, probably placed there by the people to prevent travellers walking over the arable land, but which suggests to us the idea that April-fooling is not confined to Europe. We descend into the valley of the Tensift, some six miles from the sea, and ford it without difficulty. As we approach, I suggest a bathe, but the Moors say the water is too muddy, and indeed, were it much thicker, it would cease to run. However, they drink it with avidity. I read in Jackson that the water of this river is esteemed highly salubrious, and aids the powers of digestion, but these people have queer stomachs. Our chief amusement during the ride is trying to shoot quail off our horses' backs, a process that Hassen-auie resents far more than should an animal who, in his time, has had much powder burned off his back in native warfare, and has distinguished himself in the *Lab el baroud*. I got a right and left in this way this afternoon, a feat that nearly resulted in my tumbling off on to my head.

Monday, 2nd.—Following the valley, we draw nearer the sea, passing some large and picturesque ruins [1] on the opposite bank of the Tensift, then strike away to the right through woods carpeted with flowers, and descend by an abominable path to the sea, where the breakers are booming loudly on the iron-bound coast. Two hours more we reach Saffi, a pretty, compact little town of the regulation Moorish type, only more picturesque than the generality of coast towns. It lies in a bay, sheltered on the north by a lofty headland a short way south of Cape Cantin. The ground is broken here, and the kasbah is built on a steep eminence, with a ravine descending to the sea at its base. There exist also the remains of a large Dar del Sultan (Sultan's palace) of the sixteenth century. The origin of Saffi is shrouded in obscurity, but it has a sufficiently stirring history, having been the scene of many

[1] Possibly these ruins may have been part of the old town of Rabat Koos, which is mentioned by former geographers as being at the mouth of the Tensift, but which seems to have disappeared, though they are too much inland

sieges and battles. The Portuguese had possession of it in the sixteenth century, and have left traces of their occupation in the fortifications, but the difficulties of holding the place, and the repeated attacks of the Moors, caused them to abandon it in 1648.

Walking through the streets, we saw the Bascha of the town, a most venerable figure with a long white beard descending to his waist, and a saintly air that I rather fear belied his true character. Further on I was attracted by the sight of a lady so fat that she could barely walk; she wobbled along like some huge human jelly-fish, and looked as proud as possible of her proportions. The Eastern love for fat people is well known; in their admiration of beauty, and on the principle, apparently, that you cannot have too much of a good thing, the Moors encourage large developments. There is no reduction on taking a quantity in the marriage market out here; rather you must pay so much per lb. Directly a woman is engaged, she goes in for a process of cramming, just as a pig is fed up for a show, *koos-koossoo* and other fattening food being swallowed in large quantities. All this sounds very comic, but I doubt if it is more absurd than our contrary practice. We admire small waists, and so encourage our women to squeeze their bodies and internal organs out of the shape and position in which Nature designed them, to the serious detriment of their health. The Moor, on the other hand, prefers a waist he can barely encircle with both his arms. He has as much right to his taste as we to ours, and the cramming process does not strike me as a bit more foolish or repulsive than tight-lacing. It is, perhaps, consoling to find that savages are not less slaves to fashion than civilized people. The Maroquin ladies sometimes wear a good deal of jewellery, but otherwise their adornment is of an inexpensive character; a Moorish milliner's bill would, no doubt, be a source of envy and delight to many a European husband. They tattoo their chins with cabalistic marks, and stain their finger-nails with henna, and their eyes are blackened with *kohl*, as may be seen any day in Tangier.

In spite of these economies, and those resulting from the denial of social gaieties to the fair sex, the Moor finds marriage a sufficiently expensive luxury, and the large majority have only one wife. With the Berbers monogamy is the rule even among the rich. Divorce is very common, and may be obtained for trifling causes, such as "incompatibility," etc., by the husband, but by the wife only for the same reasons as in England. Adultery is not visited with the same severity as in former days, though it is said that among the Mohammedan negroes of the Soudan the punishment of stoning is enforced, in accordance with the strict letter of the Sonna.

The life of an Arab woman cannot, all things being considered, be a happy one. In the towns she is imprisoned in the harems and in the country she is treated more as a beast of burden than anything else. I have seen men loafing along without a thing on their backs, with their wives carrying enormous burdens at their sides; but after all, one sees the same thing in Scotland and other European countries. Low as women are held in the social scale, the genius of the sex asserts itself at times, and I have heard Arab ladies rating their husbands as soundly as in any civilized household governed by "Home Rule." Rohlfs says that among the Berbers the influence of women is much greater than with the Arabs. In some tribes women have even the right to reign, and their social position generally is equal to that of European women. One sees very few pretty women in Marocco, the best being confined in the harems. Those who appear in public, do well to cover up their faces, as they often conceal thereby features it would be anything but a pleasure to look upon, and display their most attractive ones, their eyes. Their want of comeliness does not prevent them being most absurdly particular about concealing such charms as they possess. Out shooting I have come suddenly on wrinkled old hags who on seeing me would clap their hands and a fold of the jellabia to their mouths as if seized with the tooth-ache, till I longed to tell them my intentions were strictly honourable and that there was no cause for alarm. It is curious, though, to observe how indifferent they are about displaying any other portions of their persons, as long as their faces are covered. I once watched a bevy of women crossing a deep river, with their faces all religiously veiled, but otherwise making a sad *exposé* of themselves to avoid getting wet.

Tuesday, April 3rd.—Leaving Saffi, we strike somewhat inland and traverse a fertile but flat and singularly uninteresting country. We are now in the province of Abda, famed for its breed of horses, which are the best in Marocco. The barb is too well-known an animal to need description, but I cannot pass without saying a word or two in defence of the hardy little nag whose near kinsman, the Arab, has had so much mud flung at him lately in England. If those who scoff at him only knew the difficulties attending horse-breeding and rearing in these countries, or at least in Marocco, they would rather wonder that they are as good as they are. In the first place, the prevailing system of official robbery is a principal hindrance to keeping up the breed. The Moor knows that if he gets a handsome foal, it is liable to be stolen from him by the kaid, or some agent of the Sultan's; he therefore naturally prefers to breed an inferior animal, which he may reasonably hope to be allowed to keep for himself. Hence the owner of a valuable mare very often puts her to a common stallion, so as not to get a foal likely to tempt the cupidity of the native rulers. They will even disfigure a good-looking colt in every possible way to prevent its being stolen. They have a curious fashion of firing their horses in various places, which they think is a sovereign remedy for every complaint, but besides this, I have seen horses branded and scarred in the most ridiculous way simply for disfigurement. Consider, too, their hard and scanty fare, and the hardships they have to undergo. Put an English horse on the same short commons, and tie him up outside in the cold, damp nights, without covering of any sort, and see what would become of him. I doubt very much if he would show the same pluck and endurance under similar circumstances. It has been said that the Arab breed deteriorates as you go further west, but in the opinion of competent judges the barb is at least the equal of the Arab in power and endurance; he is certainly superior in point of size and weight. Abda, too, which breeds the finest horses, is decidedly a western province.

The next day we entered the province of Dukala, once the territory of some of the most powerful princes in the country. At present these southern districts are the most miserable in the empire, and their inhabitants the most poverty-stricken and degraded, and with an inferior physique to that of the Northerners. One may travel for miles and miles without seeing a human being or habitation, only ruins innumerable. We passed to-day the shell of a large town, nearly half a mile square, a truly melancholy object. We got inside the walls and explored the place; it seemed difficult to believe, as we scrambled about among the fallen blocks of tabbia, that probably not very many years ago this deserted enclosure was a populous city, and the grass-covered mounds streets teeming with human life. The only thing that enlivened the route were the lovely flowers, whose number and brilliancy exceeded everything we had witnessed before, nor do I expect ever to see the like again. They far exceeded anything of the kind in the Northern provinces. Hard by the road were acres of a pale forget-me-not blue spangled with crimson poppies; in other places were large patches of violet, mauve, pink, gold, orange, and scarlet—flowers of every colour of the rainbow, mingled together in dense clusters, and extending for miles without a break. From these glorious combinations of hues the Moors doubtless learned the lovely harmonies of their embroideries and textile art. Not a fiftieth part of the land was under cultivation, and the fertile soil, forced to grow something, produced weeds. In the evening we camped at another ruined town of smaller size than the last. This, they told us, was knocked to bits in '66, in the reign of the last Sultan, or, as the Moors would say, "in the days when our gracious lord Mohammed was sheltered beneath the Shereefian umbrella." The kaid was killed and the people put to the sword or sold into slavery. So they go on, towns are burned for punishment and never rebuilt, the country wasted, and the peasantry despoiled of all their property, and then they wonder why the place isn't prosperous. They make a desert and call it peace here with a vengeance. If those uncouth walls could speak, what tales of violence and bloodshed they could tell, what records of aimless brutality and hopeless and undeserved suffering! Of the Sultan's *modus operandi* on these occasions, I have spoken in my chapter on Marocco.

Thursday, 5th.—Off early on our rather melancholy journey, with a view to get it over as soon as possible, and to arrive at a more cheerful region. The only person who did not seem to feel its monotony was our muleteer, Mohammed Santo, whose high spirits found vent in songs and cracking jokes all the way along. At every joke his enormous eyes glistened and threatened to start from their sockets, while the corners of his ample mouth made tracks for the back of his head. These Moors have trudged more than 800 miles on foot, besides doing hard work loading and unloading the mules, tent-pitching, &c., &c., and are much fitter and more cheerful than when they started. Another small diversion was the eccentricities of a *baghala,* or she-mule, we had bought in Marocco. This animal's great delight was to rush off into the middle of a ploughed field and commence kicking like mad till all the baggage came off, and then it was a tremendous business to catch her, for woe betide the man who approached within "measurable distance" of her tail! She did her best to maim our staff of servants, three of whom received severe kicks on various parts of their persons. Her skull, when tapped, sounded perfectly hollow, and in the midst of her greatest transports she always wore a blandly idiotic smile, which caused the Moors to affirm she was "hhamka" (mad). Barring these small diversions, we were beginning to find it rather slow. The chief features in the landscape were the white domes of numerous *kubbahs* and *zaouias,* or sanctuaries, which were dotted about here and there. These *zaouias* are important institutions in Marocco. They are larger and finer, as a rule, than the *kubbahs,* being erected over the tombs only of great guns among the canonized dead, while a person of only moderate sanctity may hope to gain the minor distinction of a *kubbah*. Only the most important of these are sanctuaries in the sense of affording refuge to persons fleeing from the vengeance of their enemies, but once inside such an one a man is safe even from the arm of the law, which cannot enter and violate the holy place. At the same time, there is nothing to prevent them from blockading the place and starving you out. However, they are of service in preventing the immediate execution of summary vengeance and giving time for reflection and negotiation. Private feuds are often settled by paying blood-money. The Marabouts, who inhabit and look after these holy places, of course make a good thing out of the pilgrims who visit them in the hope of cures and other good fortune, and the dignity, with its accompanying emoluments, descends to the eldest son.

A very holy gentleman was that buried at the first town where we strike the coast, Azamoor, or Moulai Boo-Schaib, as the Moors call it, after the saint's name. His chapel is hard by and is of great repute. Azamoor is picturesquely situated on the high southern bank of the Oom R'bea, which falls into the sea here. It is the only town on the coast where there are no Europeans and very few Jews. The people seem a fanatical and rather ill-conditioned lot, which no doubt is the reason. Soon after arriving, I went with Manuel through the town to the Soko, taking the *baghala* with us, to buy corn; and as he had other business to do, I undertook, in a weak moment, to take it back alone. A sackful was placed on the mule's back and I mounted on the top, after the way of the natives, but before I had proceeded many yards, my amiable steed came to a sudden stand, stuck her forelegs out, and with the pig-headed obstinacy peculiar to her species, refused to budge an inch. This being a form of equestrian exercise to which I was wholly unaccustomed, I felt myself powerless, and there we stuck, in the most undignified manner; the infidel mob began to jeer, and I feared might follow up their scoffs with something harder, till at last two very small boys came to my aid, and rescued me from a position of some peril and great ignominy by one taking the brute in tow in front, the other whacking her from behind. The Moors have a peculiar way of piloting their beasts by the tail, as with a sort of natural rudder, but I thought I wouldn't have held that *baghala's* tail for fifty pounds. I shall not go marketing alone in a Moorish town like that again in a hurry.

Saturday, 7th. Crossed Oom R'bea in same peculiar fashion as the Boo-ragrag, but less dangerous than our previous passage of the same river. Large caravan of the Sultan's camels crossing from the North: animals look strangely starved, considering that the owners pay nothing for their food. Two days along the flat, monotonous coast-line to Casablanca. Passed another town ruined by Sultan Sidi Mohammed. S. M. seems to have given his subjects a rather warm time of it, and Mohammed

Santo speaks in most disrespectful terms of that departed monarch and Shereef, whose murderous propensities seem to have vented themselves particularly on this region.

We spend three days at Casablanca, again enjoying Mr. Fernau's hospitality, and have an amusing day's bustard shooting, of which there are a good many about here. There has been a change of Governors in the town since our departure, and Mr. Fernau tells us that the incomer has already signalized his arrival by acts of high-handed extortion. It appeared that on his instalment some of the leading merchants of the town, wishing to be first in the field and to gain his good graces, waited on him with presents of handsome carpets. These were graciously accepted; but the donors were rather disgusted on being told that the carpets were charming, but that he would thank them to raise a sum of 1000 dollars amongst them, and further, to compose a document expressing their deep satisfaction at his appointment, and to forward it to His Majesty. This was a little more than the worthy merchants had anticipated, but the only answer they got to their remonstrances, was that they had their orders and could act as they pleased. What the sequel was I do not know.

The retiring Bascha seems to have been a great contrast to his successor, being a rare specimen of probity and uprightness in high places. He had several times asked the Sultan to relieve him of the post, which he said was a thankless one, and his appeal, which had often been refused, was at last granted. Some money derived from the customs was owing to the Government, so he made out his accounts with scrupulous honesty, and awaited his Sovereign's command to pay what was due. To the surprise of every one, a letter arrived from the Sultan commending his integrity, and not only telling him he might keep the money himself, but making him a handsome present besides. It is pleasant, after the never-ending stories of peculation and extortion one hears, to be able to relate one of a contrary character, which shows not only that just men do exist among the Moors, but that uprightness is appreciated at Court.

Thursday, 12th.—En route for Rabat by the same route as before when going South. We pass the ancient Kasbah Fedala and the bridge, the only one on the coast, neither of which I mentioned before, and camp again in the n'zella of Boo Z'neka, reaching Rabat the next day. We enter the town by a new way, passing through lovely gardens and orange-groves, and find our friend Mr. Blake. He organizes a trip for us on the next day, and in the morning we embark in a good-sized Moorish boat, furnished both with oars and sails, and start off on a sail up the Wad Boo-ragrag. We have our tents and a certain amount of baggage, having the intention of camping on the bank of the river. Three hours' steady progress brings us amidst the most lovely scenery—high crags rise sheer from the water's edge on the right, and further on the hills descend in steep, richly-wooded slopes on either side. In parts it reminded me strongly of a Devonshire combe. High up in the rocks were curious caves, which suggested the idea that they may have been the abodes of those remarkable people, the Troglodytes, or cave-dwellers, described by Hanno in his Periplus, and alluded to by various writers. Certainly they would have to climb down the precipice, or lower themselves by ropes, but that would have been a mere trifle to people who could run faster than horses, and lived after the fashion of beasts in the mountains. We sailed placidly on some miles further, enjoying the most enchanting views, till we came to a spot in the hills where the river ceased to be navigable. Here we had expected to find Mr. Frost, and sure enough there was his tent, so we disembarked and encamped, and a very jolly party we had. At our feet the stream opened out into a sort of lake, shut in by hills covered with grass and wood; above it issued out of a narrow ravine, at the mouth of which fishermen from Rabat had set their nets to catch the shebbel, which are numerous here. At the tents we noticed a wild-looking Berber fellow, armed with a long gun, who we were told was a hostage sent by the neighbouring savage Berber tribe of Zair as a security that they would behave properly and not attack the fishermen. It should be explained that we were here on the confines of a most dangerous part of the country, inhabited by these Zair, who are *par excellence* the worst people in the Sultan's dominions, and whom he has never been able to tame. They are true chips of the old block, or stock, of their Gætulian ancestors, the

Autolali, who harried these parts in the days of the Romans, and were the most dreaded of all the tribes in the district. It is impossible to thoroughly chastise them, as they always escape to the vast recesses of the Mamora forest, which is hard by. This Mamora forest is the largest in the empire, and owing to the robber bands which infest it, nobody dares to venture inside. It is the rumoured home of lions, panthers, hyænas, and other wild beasts, and fabulous tales of adventures with these and still more fearful creatures are told by the natives. Mr. Blake told us several things illustrating the daring and cruelty of these Zair in their depredations. Not long ago, a party of them had followed a caravan of mules inside the city walls, and while they were encamped by night on some open ground they murdered the men in charge of the animals, buried them before daybreak, and made off with the mules to their own country. At Rabat there are large open spaces near where our tents were pitched, which would render such a feat quite possible.

We had a very jovial evening at the tents, the only thing to temper our hilarity being the alarming intelligence conveyed by the Zair hostage. He assures us there is an enormous lion "as big as an ox," fooling round in the neighbourhood, and seems to think we may all be eaten before the morning. This statement, combined with the savage nature of the spot where we are encamped, set us all talking about wild beasts and other terrible things, and with the able aid of our Zair guard some most astonishing yarns circulate. Hoare, not to be behindhand, and to keep up the credit of our party for invention, tells of the terrible mosquitoes we met down South, who when they could not get inside the tent, perched on the top and bit him through the canvas, and I am sure our Mohammeds are quite ready to swear to the truth of the story. I often wonder these fellows don't choke, what with their awful language and the atrocious lies they tell. There is a rower of our boat, who wears long black hair and a most villainous expression of face, who swears he has killed seventeen men, and on Mr. Blake asking him how he did it, he said he lay in wait for them by night and killed them as they passed. I often thought of the Carlylean description of the noble sons of the desert as an "earnest, truthful kind of men," whereas, from habit and other causes, most of them are utterly incapable of speaking the truth. As an incubator of unfounded rumours the Desert is only rivalled by the London Stock Exchange.

Sunday, 15th.—Up early. The king of beasts has failed to put in an appearance, and we all have whole skins. Possibly the rain, which is falling in bucketfuls, may have damped his majesty's ardour, as it certainly has ours. We have rather a business getting down the river, owing to a strong wind right in our teeth, but arrive at Rabat at a sufficiently early hour to allow me to visit again the Hassen Mosque and tower.

Monday, 16th.—We cross the Boo-ragrag this morning, and make our way to Mehediah, a pretty little town with Portuguese fortifications, on a hill overlooking the mouth of the Wad Seboo. At the beginning of the sixteenth century, it was the scene of terrible carnage, the sea being dyed red with Christian blood, but in spite of their heavy losses, the Portuguese eventually gained possession of the place, which they held for some time. Considering its position on the largest river-mouth upon the coast, Mehediah ought to be a place of much greater size and importance than it now is, and probably when Marocco is opened up, we may expect to see it develop. It is on the road between Tangier and the South, and near the caravan-route to Fez and Mequinez, and its commanding position on a rocky hill renders it a very strong place, so that, both commercially and strategically, it is a site that ought not to be overlooked. Crossing the Seboo, we follow its right bank for about five miles, and camp in a duar. From here the road follows the monotonous coast-line, which is flanked by sand-hills throughout its length. We are now again in El Gharb, as the green grass and increased fertility of the soil remind us. The heat is never oppressive, as a breeze springs up at midday, and we travel, as we have done hitherto, without even halting at noon. On our right are the long lakes, or lagoons, of Ras ed-Daura, full of frogs and wild fowl. Judging from the older maps, these lakes must be much smaller than in former days, and from what I saw and heard in the country, I suspect that a slow process of dessication is going on in the lakes and rivers. The wholesale destruction of timber probably has contributed to this by altering the climate.

Thursday, 19th.—We camped last night in a duar ruled by a Shereef who owns a Marabout's tomb near at hand, and to-day we expect to reach Larache. Manuel had bought some eggs and milk of a Moor in the village, and had given him a five-dollar piece, with injunctions to bring back the change. It is getting late now, and the man is nowhere to be found, so Hadj Absalam is sent off to look for him. In about a quarter of an hour back comes our redoubtable kaid, leading along a sturdy Arab bound securely with cords, and looking very sorry for himself. He had coolly gone off with our money, and was engaged in ploughing, so we announce our intention of taking him off to Larache and delivering him over to the tender mercies of the Bascha, which makes him nearly green with fright. While this goes on, another Moor comes up and, throwing himself on the ground, embraces the knees of Hoare's horse, and remains in that position. It is the man's brother, and this is a form of supplication that we will have mercy which prevails among the Moors. Another curious custom they have is that of cutting a sheep's, or even a fowl's, throat in presence of a person in authority when they have a favour to ask. We also have the pleasure of drawing the Shereef from his lair—a very ill-looking personage—and he joins in the request for the man's release. As we only wanted to frighten the fellow, we let him go, much to Hadj Absalam's disgust, who hoped to take him to Larache and squeeze something out of him.

Manuel estimates that our clemency has cost the kaid about three dollars, and the Bascha of Larache something more, which would have been the price of the Moor's being restored to his friends. We get off about ten, and travel as fast as we can; only that *baghala* is very much on the rampage again, causing much heat and profanity among our servants.

The country on the road to Larache consists chiefly of rounded hills covered with grass and ferns, and we see a good many bustard about. We pass through the picturesque old town, and get down to the ferry over the Wad Koos. It is pouring with rain, a stiff breeze blowing, and we hear the surf roaring on the bar, and at first cannot get any one to take us across. At last some boatmen, pluckier than the rest, come forward and, for extra pay, undertake to ferry us over. They had tremendous work, and the passage took more than half an hour, but we all arrive at last on the other side in safety. From here we make our way up the familiar road to our old camping-ground at El Khemis, and I insist on having the tents pitched on the exact spot of the previous year. The country looks charmingly pretty and green after the rain, and its beauty is heightened in our eyes by contrast with the hundreds of miles of uninteresting ground we have traversed of late. In the evening we see our old friend Boo el Kheir, who comes and sits in the tent, and we have a long chat together. He seems astonished at our long journey, and, raising his hands to the level of his head, exclaims in solemn tones,

"Hamdoollah la bas, La bas Hamdoollah" (Praised be God, you have come to no harm), at the idea of the manifold perils of sickness, of rivers, of robbers, and assassins, through which his Oriental imagination pictured us as having passed. He had brought his son with him to the tent, a sturdy, bright-eyed boy about fifteen years old, and a negro slave of the same age, who was the latter's constant companion. This slave was a new acquisition of Boo el Kheir's, which he had bought in deference to the boy's wishes. The old fellow seemed to have had considerable doubts about the matter, but, like a fond father anxious to gratify his favourite son, he had given in to his entreaties. The price had been forty dollars, and he was very anxious to know if I thought him a good bargain. I told him I was quite unacquainted with the fluctuations of the slave-market, having never done any business in that line myself, and from the cursory inspection I had made of the youth I was not qualified to offer an opinion. I added, however, that it was the same price as we had paid for our fractious *baghala*, and that we would be very glad to "swap horses." He then confided to me that the little nigger really was cheap as dirt, but that, food being so dear, the slave-market was very flat at the time. The boy did not seem to mind in the slightest hearing his qualities appraised in this open manner, and as I looked at the merry little chap, with his fat cheeks and laughing eyes, I could not help thinking that a great deal of sentiment is wasted on the condition of slaves in this country.

The conversation then turned on more general

subjects. We spoke of the misery and decay we had everywhere witnessed, and he then broke out into bitter complaints against the Government, saying that the country was a magnificent one, but that nothing could be done under the scoundrels who ruled them. He was "protected" himself, and I asked whether he would like to see the Christians come and establish a better system. He replied emphatically, "No," but he would like to see a good Moorish Government. I did not say what I thought, that he would have to wait a long time for that, and the subject changed.

A noteworthy characteristic of the Moors is their propriety of conversation when in the presence of kinsmen, and more especially when younger members of the same family are in hearing. At most times they are not particular, as might be expected, but in the presence of a son or nephew, even if he be past his teens, they will order their talk as more civilized people would when in the presence of the other sex. I notice that the same was the custom of the ancient Africans in the days of Leo, who were most particular as to what was said before youths. The wisdom of the saying "Maxima debetur pueris reverentia" seems to be thoroughly known and appreciated even among these not over-refined Moors.

The next day we spent in strolling about our old shooting-grounds, and in the evening we made arrangements for a boar-hunt on the following morning. Before turning-in I tried a pipe of "kif," or Indian hemp, which is smoked in large quantities by the Moors, and whose effects are said to be almost identical with those produced by opium. My anticipations, however, of any startling results from my first experience of the "pernicious drug" were doomed to disappointment. I had expected to have my perceptions and senses etherealized, to be wrapped in delicious reveries, or see weird visions peopled with the fantastic creations of a disordered brain, but nothing ensued beyond a slight drowsiness, so that I am inclined to think the bad effects of the drug are much exaggerated. Mohammed, the best and smartest Moor we had on our staff, was an inveterate *kif* smoker.

The boar-hunt was a great failure, like our other experiences of the same sport in this place. The hunters did not understand their work, and withal held the Father of Tusks in too great dread to oust him properly from his lair. Being dissatisfied with my luck, I determined to try lying out alone in a different part of the forest, and asked the sheikh for advice on the subject. He tried hard to dissuade me from the project, saying that no Christian could venture by night into such a lonesome part of the forest, as it was peopled by *jins* and robbers, and that if I went I should not know how to set about it. In the first place, he said, in order to succeed you must strip and go to work in your skin, as the boar has such a keen sense of smell that he is sure to wind your raiment, when he will make off in a twinkling. I ventured to suggest a clean shirt as a means of meeting this novel difficulty, but it appeared that such things were not known in the country. He insisted that I must go *au naturel*, or not at all. The Moorish peasant wears his *jellabia* night and day, and when he dies it descends to his heir, so that by the time that it has been in use in this way for two or three generations it gets a trifle strong. There is said to be a great annual wash-up of all clothing at the feast of Aid-el-Kebir, but I fancy it takes a Moorish washerwoman a good while to make a fortune. Hence it is likely that any pig of moderately refined taste would, on finding himself to leeward of the ambushed sportsman, clad in one of these hereditary garments, clear out of the premises in a hurry.

Disregarding the sheikh's singular advice, I waited till the snores from our servants' tent assured me they were all asleep, and then enveloping myself in an ulster and macintosh I stole out of the camp alone. Walking on for about a couple of miles through the forest, I finally ensconced myself in some bushes near a marsh where the tracks showed that the boar were accustomed to come and drink. The night was fine and fairly warm, and a full moon shed its beams on the not far-distant Riff mountains with a peculiarly ghostly effect, while, except for the slight shivering of the breeze in the thicket, a weird stillness prevailed, broken only by the occasional shriek of the night-hawk or the jackal's piercing, semi-human cry. Here I lay expectant till dawn broke over the hills, without seeing the ghost of a boar and chilled by the damp mists to the bone. After waiting another hour, I began to think it was hardly good enough, and accordingly turned my steps homewards. Resting a moment on the way in a small gully clothed about its sides with thick brushwood, my ear caught the sound of rustling in the bushes as of some large animal moving through the thicket. "Now," thought I, "my patience is going to be rewarded," and crouching down, I cocked my gun and made ready to fire the moment the beast should make his appearance. This he did a moment afterwards in the person, not of the Father of Tusks, but of a tall Moor who, carrying a long gun, was cautiously stealing through the thicket, evidently bent on the same fool's errand as myself. It was almost worth sitting out six hours in the reeking dew to see that Moor jump as I called out in solemn tones, "*Shcoon hada*" (who goes there?), and stood forth in my very un-Moorish get-up. I wished him good morning and hoped he had had good sport, to which he replied by jibbering and gesticulating after the fashion peculiar to these natives, and for the next few minutes we carried on an animated and interesting conversation, both talking at once and neither understanding a word the other said, and then parting went our respective ways. On the whole, I regard boar-hunting by night as a much overrated pastime, as a chance of a pig is very remote, and if you are not stalked and shot by some other sporting lunatic, it is long odds that you get a bad cold or rheumatism for your pains. My conscience pricked me at the thought of the many "warriors" we had caused to sit out in this fashion during our journey, and the fear came over me lest a just Providence should smite me with the hollow cough peculiar to all members of the warrior class.

Two days more would see us at Tangier, and our long travels would be at an end. The first day afforded us a charming ride through the woods on the steep hill-sides, where flowers, mosses and ferns were springing up in profusion after the rain. The only incident worth mentioning was a sad mischance that befell Hadj Absalam. He was riding on some fifty yards ahead of the party after his wont, and was in the act of crossing a small stream, when suddenly horse and man disappeared from our sight. On riding up we saw the horse's head appearing out of a large sand-hole in the river, the whole of his body being submerged, and the kaid, who had managed to scramble off, was tugging away at the bridle. It seemed that he had gone a short distance upstream to let his horse drink, and had got engulfed in a sort of quicksand. It was with great difficulty that we got the horse out, when he presented a shocking appearance, all the kaid's smart accoutrements being covered with a thick coating of slime. Some well-to-do Moors, travelling to Larache, were seated on the bank, and looked on at the catastrophe without making the slightest offer of assistance, regaling themselves with copious doses of snuff the while, as if to show their contempt.

On the evening of Monday, the 23rd of April, we arrived at M. Bruzeaud's hotel in Tangier, bronzed and bearded and travel-stained, but man and beast all well and sound in wind and limb, despite the length of the journey, their hard work and exposure to the vicissitudes of the climate. For ourselves, we were not altogether sorry to get back, as the *ennui* of the long trudge up the coast, where there is less of novelty and interest to beguile the tedium of travel, had begun to tell upon us. In the interior, on the other hand, all was strange, fresh, and entertaining. The varied impressions produced by all one sees renders boredom impossible in this extraordinary country, where everything combines to alternately delight and disgust, to shock and amuse, the observant traveller. Delighted he cannot fail to be at the sight of so much beauty and natural fertility, while the scenes *en route*, the camp life at night, and the quaint ways and customs of the people, are a never-ending source of entertainment. Disgust, on the other hand, possesses him at the waste and squandering of nature's best gifts, mingled with pity for the hard lot and degradation of the people, and indignation at the misrule and barbarity which is the cause of so much needless suffering.

Concerning the Moors themselves, I have little to add. If I have spoken ill of them, in common with every other traveller at all competent to form an opinion, and in view of hard facts it is impossible to do otherwise, it must be remembered that their faults are in a great measure the outcome of education—or the want of it—and the conditions under which they live. They are not bad people, according to their lights, and the fact that those lights are not very brilliant ones can hardly be imputed to them for blame. A distinction, moreover, must always be drawn between the official Moor and the Moor in his private capacity. The official Moor one gets to regard as a sort of dual personage—first as the grave, courteous, and hospitable individual he appears before you; secondly, in his other character, what training and circumstances have rendered him —fanatic, bigot, and despot. The town Moor is the least favourable specimen of his race, being slothful, avaricious, bigoted, and ill-disposed towards Christians. The peasantry, on the other hand, possess many good qualities; they are brave, hardy, frugal, patient, good-tempered, and, though inert as a rule, not indisposed to work if it is made worth their while. They are true children of nature, which gives a charm of manner even to the humblest, and they possess an inexhaustible fund of Paddy-like humour, that rises superior even to the severest misfortune.

If they hate us Christians and are occasionally uncivil, have they not cause? They do not understand us, and the treatment they receive at Christian hands is not always calculated to evoke a deep or abiding affection. Further, they feel that the sword of the Nazarene is hanging over their heads, and must one day fall, so that each traveller is regarded by them as coming to spy out the land,

and in a way as the harbinger of a new order of things, when the European will elbow out the Moor, and a Christian civilization will take its stand upon the ruins of Moslem dominion.

The chief conclusion to which one arrives from a study of the people is, that they are a race made *to be ruled, not to rule.* Patience, submission, and reverence are characteristic Semitic traits, while power brings out their brutality, dishonesty, avarice, and all the other evil passions of their nature.

As a nation, I can never cease to regard the Moors with interest, and, I had almost said, with affection, and to deplore the hard fate which must always be theirs till brighter days dawn upon their unhappy country. The recollection of the many real acts of kindness received at their hands will last as long as that of the novel scenes and experiences through which we passed. Our journey has opened up to us, as it were, a new world, to which fancy often transports me back, and then, as I travel the way over again in imagination, I feel that the days spent in that quaint land, and among its simple people, can never wholly fade from my mind, but must always remain among the pleasantest memories of my life.

CHAPTER XVI.

General description of Marocco—Its climate and resources—Historical sketch—Government and laws—Trade—Political affairs—British interests in Marocco—Gibraltar *v.* Ceuta—Marocco a possible basis of our food supply—Sir John D. Hay and his critics—Suggested embassy at Fez—The chief reforms needed in Marocco—Probable results of the introduction of civilization—Desirability of a speedy settlement of the Marocco question.

Marocco, El Maghreb el Aksa (the Extreme West), as the Moors call it, the sole independent Mussulman state of North Africa, is a country whose superficial area has been variously stated. The ordinary estimates of 220,000 and 250,000 square miles must be considered as being over the mark; including as they do large tracts which are quite outside the Sultan's authority, and which cannot therefore be deemed properly within the Empire. The frontiers of Marocco, as Said Pasha said of those of Egypt, " *sont très élastiques,*" and advance and recede according to the power of individual Sultans. The most convenient boundary line to the South, and the one which probably best describes the limits of the Sultanate at the present moment, is the Atlas chain, but this would exclude a large part of the country generally included under the name Marocco.

The coast-line is of great extent, as a glance at

the map will show, but the shore of the Atlantic is flat and sandy, and entirely without harbours, unless we except the so-called port of Mogador and the mouths of the Seboo, Boo-ragrag, Koos, and Oom R'bea rivers. All of these last, however, have dangerous bars, and are at best navigable for ships of small burden only. It is doubtful if these barharbours could ever be utilized for large ships. The sand continually drifting in from the Ocean, and the mud-deposits brought down by floods, would make adequate dredging operations very difficult and expensive, and the work would have to be frequently renewed. The estuary of the Seboo, which for its size and its position near the junction of several of the main trade-routes should be the chief water-highway of the country, is never used for ships, though the tide is felt thirty miles from the mouth, and the channel is of considerable depth. The wretched little town of Mehediah ought some day to become the site of a considerable trading port. Tangier, which has advantages both of situation and the anchorage afforded by the bay, must always be the chief outlet of trade.

The climate of Marocco, hardly to be surpassed anywhere, is beyond question the best in North Africa. Cooled on one side by the fresh Atlantic breezes, on the other the everlasting snows of the Atlas form a bulwark against the burning sand-winds of the Sahara, such as neither Algeria nor any other country on the South Mediterranean seaboard possesses. Hence the heat is never intolerable, and not only in climate, but also in its water-supply and the area of cultivable land, Marocco has the advantage over the French colony.

The population is supposed to be somewhere about 6,000,000, probably an over-estimate, though it is a ridiculously small number compared with the area and the food-producing power of the country. Nevertheless, famine, wars, disease, and oppression are bearing their legitimate fruits, and the numbers are steadily on the decrease, as is shown by the innumerable ruined towns and buildings, the waste lands and gardens, and the absence of new ones. In the Southern districts a few mud-hovels here and there take the place of flourishing townships which were to be found at frequent intervals in the days of Leo Africanus. Of the decay of education and civilization in the country enough has been said, while the sufferings of its handful of inhabitants seem to point to a no less remarkable decrease in material prosperity.

To the agricultural resources, and the way in which they are squandered by the natives, allusion has been made. Besides the various kinds of corn mentioned already, there are fruits in abundance, and vegetables thrive in so remarkable a manner that market-gardening could be made a profitable industry. Cotton was largely exported in Leo's time, but now it is scarcely grown at all. In some places the soil is peculiarly adapted for vines, but the natives do not understand how to cultivate them properly. Other undeveloped industries are the growth of tea, coffee, and indigo, which, as has been suggested, would probably prove worth trying.

Yet, despite these varied resources, the country does not produce enough food for the proper maintenance of its own scanty population.

It is supposed that minerals exist in large quantities in Marocco, but the country is not sufficiently explored to estimate their extent with any accuracy. The grounds of this belief are the geological formation of the country, resembling that of the metalliferous regions on the opposite side of the Straits, the remains of old workings, and the testimony of ancient writers. Coal has been found, copper and antimony in abundance, and silver and lead no doubt exist; gold-mines are said to have been formerly worked in Sus; traces of iron-workings exist in the South, and the soil in their neighbourhood we found strongly impregnated with iron. Salt-mines, we were told, are a great source of profit to some of the Moors.

The decline in the material resources of Marocco is parallel to, and the outcome of, the demoralization which has overspread her people. Their history for the last three centuries is comprised in the sad story of their gradual debasement and decay; the records of the latter-day Moorish empire are the ruin and desolation that everywhere meet the eye, the poverty, misery, and oppression of the mass of the population—a shameful tale of suffering and wrong that are written in letters of blood throughout the land.

A brief sketch of all that is known of the history of Marocco may not be out of place here. In the earliest times of which we have any certain record, the country was inhabited by wandering tribes of Gætulians, or Berbers, the description of whose habits, as given by Virgil and other ancient writers, corresponds more or less with those of their descendants at the present day. Gibbon alludes, in several passages, to their barbarism and extreme poverty. The subject of other prehistoric races having possibly inhabited the country, and the legendary accounts of the origin of the Berber family, has been dealt with in a previous chapter. The old Berbers lived under a patriarchal system, each tribe electing its own rulers, and though these clans were occasionally consolidated under the strong hand of some potentate of commanding influence, such as Bocchus in 110 B.C., and later on by Juba, as the representative of the Cæsars, as a rule they were without unity or cohesion of any kind. The Phœnicians formed the earliest civilizing agency in the country. Various colonies were planted by them, and Hanno, in his celebrated voyage, founded towns at intervals on the coast, the remains of some of which are still existent.

The Romans interfered little in the affairs of Western Barbary till, in A.D. 42, the Emperor Claudius annexed it to the empire as a province, under the name of Mauritania Tingitana, which corresponded roughly to the modern Marocco, except that the Roman province was bounded on the West by the river Moloya, where the French now wish to place their "rectified" frontier. The country flourished under the Roman dominion and numerous colonies were founded. Until the Arabs, the

Romans were the only civilized people who had penetrated to the interior, and the ruins at Volubilis are enough to show that their authority extended a considerable distance inland. Christianity was afterwards introduced by them and adopted by the Berbers in the same half-hearted way in which they afterwards embraced the religion of their Arab conquerors. Religious faith always sits lightly on the Berber. North Africa was at this time the home of the Donatist schismatics, who, setting all authority at defiance, established no less than 170 episcopal sees in Mauritania alone. The discontent and rivalries of contending factions and sects paved the way for the Vandal invasion, and in 429 A.D. Genseric, at the invitation of Count Boniface, crossed over from Spain. The tardy repentance of the Count was too late to save the country from the horrors of the Vandal attack, who with fire and sword and every kind of atrocity ravaged the land. Tangier formed the Western limit of the dominion of the Vandals. One hundred and four years later Belisarius drove them out, and the country was once more plunged into the chaos of internecine strife and barbarous warfare characteristic of the Numidian people, and which has always proved the bane of their race. Various writers speak of the miserable state to which they were reduced, the coarseness of their fare and their utter indigence, and their barbarism, unrelieved by even the smallest veneer of civilization. In this state they remained till in 698 A.D. the tide of Mohammedan conquest, which had swept over North Africa carrying all before it in its resistless course, burst upon Marocco. Eleven years were required to overcome the stubborn resistance of the Berbers, who, however, when once conquered, submitted with a good grace and embraced the new creed with a facility entirely in accordance with the adaptive nature they still exhibit. Mingled bands of Moors and Arabs passed over into Spain, under Tarik and Moossa, and by the defeat of Roderic at the battle of Guadalete in 711, the foundation of their Spanish empire was laid, on which was afterwards raised the magnificent fabric of the Western Khalifate. This is not the place to dwell on the glories of their dominion, the prowess of the Saracen arms, the attainments of their learned men in the arts and sciences, the splendour of their palaces and temples, the knightly courtesies and refinements of their domestic life; which, surpassing all contemporary Christian enlightenment, illuminated Europe with the light of the highest civilization then existent, and raised the Moors to the proud rank of the first nation of the world.

Suffice it to say, that a reflection of this glory extended to Marocco, where the libraries and universities of Fez and Marocco City told of the learning introduced by wise men, Moorish and Christian alike, who pursued their studies without fear of interruption on the score of religious belief. The Moors in the days of their greatness, be it observed, were far more liberal-minded than the Spanish Catholics afterwards showed themselves, and allowed Christians to practise their own religion in their own places of worship—in striking contrast to the fanaticism of their descendants in Marocco at the present day. Numerous Spanish captives passed over into the country, and brought with them the knowledge they had acquired in their own country, of which their new masters reaped the benefit. Thus, as has already been mentioned, many of the chief buildings of Marocco, notably the towers of Hassen and El Kutubia, and the beautiful gate at Mequinez, are the work of Christian hands.

The intervals of repose under the rule of powerful and enlightened monarchs, during which the above-mentioned institutions flourished, were, nevertheless, comparatively rare, and the general history of Marocco during the Moorish dominion in Spain seems to have been one monotonous record of strife between contending tribes and dynasties. Early in the tenth century, the Berbers got the mastery of the Arabs, who never afterwards appear in the history of the country except under the general name of Moors. Various principalities were formed, of which the chief were Fez, Marocco, and Tafilet, though now and again, and especially under the Marin dynasty, in the thirteenth century, the two former were consolidated into one kingdom.

In the fifteenth century the successes of the Spaniards caused the centre of Moorish power to shift from Spain to Marocco. In the declining days of the Hispano-Moorish empire, and after its final extinction, the Spaniards and Portuguese revenged themselves on their conquerors by attacking the coast-towns of Marocco, many of which they captured. It is not improbable that they would eventually have possessed themselves of the entire country, but for the disastrous defeat of King Sebastian in 1578, at the battle of the Three Kings, on the banks of the Wad El Ma Hassen, near Alcazar. This was the turning-point in Moorish history, and an African Creasy would have to rank the conflict at Alcazar among the decisive battles of the Continent. With the rout and slaughter of the Portuguese fled the last chance of civilizing the country, which from that period gradually relapsed into a state of isolated barbarism. A brief semblance of their former vigour was displayed by the Moors in the period immediately following upon the battle, but it was of short duration. The Moorish refugees from Spain settled in the coast-towns, and the reins of Government getting into the hands of this effete race, the prosperity of the country has from that time been steadily on the wane. Three centuries before the Moors had reached the zenith of their greatness, and now they were well advanced in the last of the three stages of their career. From idolatry they had embraced a fanatical creed which inspired them to make great conquests and found mighty empires; to this had succeeded a period of learning, liberality, and refinement, and now they had sunk back once more into fanaticism, but a fanaticism that was at once blind and effete, and devoid of the energy, vitality, and perception which had made them such a power in the earliest stage of their development.

For 250 years the throne has been in the hands of members of the Shereefian family of Fileli, who have remained practically undisputed masters of the whole of the empire. All this time, as in the earlier classical ages, Marocco has been practically shut out from the world. A variety of causes have contributed to this result. Except by the Arabs, she has never been thoroughly conquered, and such colonization as has been done, has been almost entirely confined to the coast—Volubilis and a few other Roman colonies forming the sole exceptions; the fact that the attention of European colonists has been concentrated upon more distant regions, and, above all, the fanaticism of the native rulers, whose instinct tells them that complete isolation is their only hope of retaining their independence, are other principal reasons. The only intercourse which the Sultans have, till lately, condescended to hold with Christian countries was in the making of treaties and the ignominious payment of tribute by the latter to secure immunity from the raids of the Barbary pirates. England has been in communication with the Court of Marocco from an early date, and in the reign of Queen Elizabeth envoys were despatched to the Sultan. Our brief occupation of Tangier, which terminated with the ill-advised evacuation in 1685, is sufficiently well known, and the circumstances connected therewith are related in the pages of Pepys' Diary. The chief events of importance in Moorish affairs in the present century were the defeat of the Moors by the French at the battle of Isly, near the Algerian frontier, in 1844, and the subsequent bombardment of Mogador and the coast-towns, and the Spanish war which terminated in 1860 with the peace of Tetuan. These reverses taught the Moors the power of European states, and brought about a great improvement in the position of Christians in the country.

The Government of Marocco is in effect a kind of graduated despotism, where every official, while possessing complete authority over those beneath him, must render absolute submission to his superiors. The supreme power is vested in the Sultan, the head of the State in all things spiritual and temporal, though the Court Ministers, and especially the Vizir, have in fact a large controlling influence. After the Ministers there are only kaids, the extent of whose authority varies greatly, who are appointed and removed according to the caprice of the ruling sovereign. All men are considered equal at birth, and the maxim that " one man is as good as another, or even better," holds good here, if anywhere. From the dregs of the populace, a man may aspire to rise to the highest offices of state, but then a single turn of the political wheel may drag him down to the gutter again, or to the still lower depths of one of the Sultan's subterranean dungeons. Co-existent with this sentiment of equality we observe an abject and almost superstitious deference to the holders of power, and a patient submission to tyranny that may well strike one with wonder. If ever there was an instance of the compatibility of despotism with democratic sentiments it is in the Moorish political system.

Law and order are enforced by a sort of rude

justice which, though repugnant to European notions, is more or less suited to the turbulent people under the Sultan's sway. The levying of general fines for robberies, and the blood-tax for murders are defensible enough on the score of public policy, but the indiscriminate burning of towns and villages, and the destruction of crops for the misdeeds of a few, are hardly conducive to the moral or material welfare of the people. The system of taxation, or the irregular and graduated process of squeezing which serves as such, has been sufficiently indicated already. The chief duties are a tax of ten per cent. on all exports and imports, as well as on everything sold. There are also gate-duties and taxes of from two and a half to five per cent. on all domestic animals and agricultural produce, but, as may be imagined, they are levied in a very arbitrary and irregular fashion. The governor of a province makes a valuation of the crops at the beginning of each season, and imposes such tax as to him seems good, or the people will stand. The baneful system of farming the taxes, which has brought about the downfall of more than one civilized Government, is in full force in Marocco, and is the fruitful source of grievous oppression.

The land system is a highly developed one for so barbarous a country, being derived, like all their civil law, from the Shraa. The tenure is feudal in its nature, but there is no such thing as a fee-simple. The land is held for limited periods, and military service in the *maghaseni*, or militia, has to be performed in respect thereof. Each occupier has his own documents of title, and an excellent system of registration obtains, while the simplicity of the formalities of conveyance might well be an example to us in England. No Christian can own land, a disqualification which, it may be hoped, will ere long be removed.

Trade is at present inconsiderable, being choked by excessive imposts, fiscal monopolies, and the extortion of officials, but it would doubtless be capable of large expansion. Exports and imports both amount to less than 1,000,000*l.* in the year, but the ten per cent. duty levied on both alike is not calculated to encourage commerce. It would be difficult to make the Sultan see that he would be the richer for the removal of an excessive tariff through the increased trade which would no doubt follow. The chief trade is done with England, France being a good second on the list. The exportation of most kinds of corn is rigorously prohibited, Moorish fanaticism forbidding that the wheat of true believers should go to feed the infidel. This prohibition of what should be the principal export is the chief reason why the magnificent properties of the soil are left unused and undeveloped.

It remains only to deal with the political aspect of affairs in relation to Marocco. It may seem a remarkable thing that in the general "scramble for Africa" among European Powers, Marocco, which should form at once the handiest and most valuable stake in this game of diplomatic grab, has hitherto preserved her territory almost intact. As it is, she is the last surviving specimen of an independent Mussulman State in North Africa. Of the ultimate dissolution of the Moorish dominion, there can be little doubt, and signs are not wanting now of a cataclysm which will shake it to its foundations. At the same time the Marocco question is a dangerous one to handle, and the interests involved are so numerous and complex that the final collapse may be long delayed. European States have long had their eyes upon it, but the same mutual distrust and jealousy which preserves the decaying fabric of the Turkish Empire has hitherto done the like for Marocco, whose Sultan serves the same purpose on the Straits of Gibraltar as the Turkish Sultan does on the Bosphorus. In the summer of 1884 the action of France gave good reason for supposing that the examples recently set in Tunis, Madagascar, and elsewhere were to be followed in Marocco. M. Ordega, the then French Minister at Tangier, and a sort of would-be Marocco Roustan, conceived the idea of setting up the now rather faded sanctity of the Shereef of Wazan as a counterpoise to the authority of the Sultan, and by taking him under the protection of the Republic it was hoped that a French subject might become a rival claimant to the throne, or at any rate, by fomenting rebellion in the country, pave the way for French interference. The acquisition of land by a Frenchman in the Riff country, where, as the

Moorish authority is but nominal, his safety could not be assured by Government, was likewise used as a pretext for picking a quarrel. Owing to the energetic representations of Sir J. D. Hay and the other foreign representatives at Tangier, these designs were happily frustrated. At that time France had more than enough on her hands to keep her fully occupied, but now, with her Chinese difficulty arranged, she is free to act, so that we may any day look for a revival of her aggressive schemes. The first step will probably be the "rectification" of the Algerian frontier by substituting the Moloya for the present boundary, which would place the French within striking distance of Fez. In fact, but for the interposition of other States, the frontier would have been rectified long ago. It may be observed, in passing, that when a Moor appropriates to his own use any property belonging to a Frenchman, the chivalrous Gaul can seldom be got to regard it as a "rectification" by the Moor of his deficiency in the property in question; on the contrary, he probably sends in a very heavy bill to the Sultan, and "demonstrates" with much effect until it is settled. Herein, however, lies all the difference between barbarism and civilization, and the Moorish Government is powerless unless backed by foreign aid.

As regards other Powers, Italy is of course jealous of French pretensions, and has always, through her energetic representative at Tangier, taken a prominent part in Moorish politics. As for Spain, it might be thought that a country that has not yet developed its own resources, and the majority of whose industries are still in the hands of foreigners, need not be ambitious of further colonial extension. Spain, however, still believes her future to lie in the territory of her ancient foe, and the old cry of *Guerra al Moro* has not yet lost its force or significance in the Peninsula. The acquisition of Puerto Cansado on the Sus coast, which would be valueless unless she has some ulterior objects in view, and the recent formation of a Hispano-African Company, nominally for the development of trade in the same region, point to the interest taken by Spaniards in the country. Germany has hitherto taken little part in Moorish politics, but it is not to be supposed that Prince Bismarck or his successors would remain unmoved spectators of any large acquisition of territory by France or any other Power.

Our own interests in Marocco (apart from the trade, which is at present inconsiderable) are easily described, but of consummate importance. They may be summarized as follows:—The safety of Gibraltar, our command of the Mediterranean, and the keeping open of our road to India. Yet it has not probably struck the majority of Englishmen that the fate of Marocco is, or ever could be, a matter of concern to us, and indifference to our interests there, both commercial and strategical, is not confined to politicians of any particular party. We have heard the leader [1] of the party which claims to make foreign politics and British

[1] Lord Salisbury in the House of Lords, February 26th, 1885.

interests its especial care give vent to the strange and gratuitous observation that "Marocco may go her own way," if only we are allowed to have our way in Egypt. Taken in connection with the rest of the speech, this meant that France might be allowed to annex the country in return for leaving us free to act as we please in Egypt. Surely, however, there is some absurdity in our lavishing our blood and treasure in the deserts of the Soudan, the ultimate justification of which is, I take it, to keep open our way to India, if we are tamely to allow a possibly hostile power to dominate the Straits of Gibraltar, the first link in the chain of communication.

A glance at the map will show the impossibility of our allowing a Power like France to hold the southern shore of the Straits. Gibraltar is wholly dependent on Marocco for its supplies,[2] which is enough of itself to show how essential it is that the latter should remain in neutral hands, while the establishment of a fortified port at Tangier would be a standing menace to our fortress and rob us of our command of the passage. As Captain Colville well puts it, "If Gibraltar is the key of the Mediterranean, Tangier is the key-guard," and Lord Nelson frequently declared that Tangier was absolutely essential for the safety of the fortress in a maritime war. If that was true then, it is doubly so now that Gibraltar has grown into a large

[2] As late as the present century our Government had to subsidize the Sultan handsomely to procure permission to export corn and cattle to Gibraltar.

and flourishing colony. Various governors have tried to repress the growth of the civil population, but chiefly owing to financial reasons they have failed, and the place is now an important commercial centre. Consider the position of a fortress with a garrison of 6000, and a civil population of nearly 20,000, with its only source of food-supply cut off! Yet this would be a very probable situation with the French at Tangier; and were Spain to side with France against us (not an improbable contingency, as history shows), Gibraltar would be untenable, and our route to India cut off at the point nearest home.

It is at least a question whether, under existing circumstances, Ceuta would not be a more desirable possession for us than Gibraltar—a sadly heretical doctrine, I fear, in the opinion of most Englishmen, but one that has good arguments to support it. The subject is ably treated in a pamphlet[a] by Captain Warren, R.N., to which I refer my readers. The principal arguments there brought forward are as follows: (1) Gibraltar is not a good harbour, and an entirely insufficient coaling-station. (2) It does not command the Straits (without a fleet, it does so no more than Dover does the English Channel, though many even well-informed Englishmen are unaware of this fact). (3) The anchorage and town are within easy range of guns on Spanish territory, where our fire could do them little injury; our ships and coal-hulks would be exposed to the

[a] "Gibraltar: is it worth holding? and Marocco." Edward Stanford: Charing Cross.

attacks of torpedo-boats from Algeciras on the opposite side of the bay, and we should have Ceuta also to deal with, only twelve miles distant, were Spain to side against us. Were Spain neutral, Algeciras would be a neutral port open to the enemy's ships. In short, we require a secure harbour and coal depôt in the Straits, and Gibraltar does not answer these requirements. (4) The national ill-feeling between Spain and England would cease, and a strong temptation for her to join our enemies, in the event of a war, be removed. (5) Ceuta is in a splendidly fertile country, and we should be "exchanging a fortress for a fortress and territory, and take a new Gibraltar to its supplies." (6) We should "have the nucleus of a colony in Marocco, which would expand under our genius for colonization until we had at our very doors a corn-producing country which would render England, with even a doubled population, independent of the rest of the world."

That Marocco will ever become a British colony seems hardly within the bounds of possibility, though a more valuable one she could not possess; but in any case, at Ceuta we should have a better standpoint for resisting French aggression, and pressure could more effectually be brought to bear on the Sultan to induce him to institute those internal reforms which are so urgently needed. England, the great civilizing agent of the world, could surely be engaged in no worthier task than taking the lead in getting this magnificent country opened up to European enterprise and capital. It is not difficult to show how both the natives and the outside world would benefit by such a work. I have repeatedly alluded to the fine qualities of the soil, and the way in which agriculture is neglected, as well as to the fact that the exportation of corn is prohibited. Were this restriction removed, as well as that which forbids Christians owning land, and the country opened up as suggested, vast tracts where now only weeds and flowers grow in rank profusion would be brought under cultivation. The facilities which the country affords for irrigation could easily be utilized, and a constant supply of water would thereby be secured for many places. The food-producing power of the country being, as I have shown, vastly in excess of the needs of the inhabitants, a large surplus would be available for exportation. The benefit England would reap from this change can hardly be overstated. Much has been said of late about the danger of starvation overtaking us at home in the event of a war with a maritime power, and few will deny that this is a real and terrible danger. England can never hope to be self-sufficing, but must always depend on others for her supplies. Hence it must always be a matter of great moment that the sources of those supplies should be as numerous and, above all, as near at hand as possible. At present the cry is all that the navy must be strengthened to guard against the possibility of our having our food cut off. Strengthen the navy by all means, but do not let us stop there; let us also increase and facilitate in every possible way the means whereby we obtain that food.[4] The bulk of our corn now comes from India and America, of which the nearest is 3000 miles distant. Captain Warren, in the pamphlet alluded to above, points out with much force that with Marocco as the basis of our food-supply, within four easy days' sail of our shores, we could make three voyages for one we can at present. In other words, we could throw three times the amount of food into the country in any given time, with a corresponding diminution of the risk of capture on the way; and by giving our navy less to do, and so leaving it freer to act elsewhere, our position would be materially strengthened. North Africa was the granary of ancient Rome, and we have it on the authority of Pliny that Marocco grew some of the finest wheat in the world. Why should she not now be made one of the granaries of England? For this purpose the country need not pass into any other hands than those of its present owners; all that is required is that it should be opened up.

It has been said that this would pave the way for French aggression, and that after the railway comes the army of invasion. In my humble opinion, it would have just the contrary effect, as the new

---

[4] The growth of the doctrine that bread-stuffs may be treated as contraband of war, as exemplified by the recent action of France in the Tonquin war, causes the question of our food-supply to assume a yet more serious aspect. We may protest against this as being in violation of International Law, but it is by no means certain that respect for a more or less doubtful principle will induce our enemies to abstain from striking at us in what they well know is our most vulnerable point—our food-supply.

interests which would be created by the development of commerce and agriculture would render other States more jealous of her pretensions. Of the ultimate civilization of Marocco there can be no doubt; the present state of things cannot last for ever. The question is, who it is to be done by, and how long it is to be delayed by the petty rivalries and jealousies of European nations. The first step in the matter is that public opinion should be directed to the subject. Were this done, England, who has the greatest influence at the Moorish Court, could take the lead in the work. It is a pity that something could not have been done during Sir John Hay's term of office, but this is, unfortunately, fast drawing to a close, and the task of inaugurating a new era of progress and reform in Marocco must be left to his successor.

The present seems a fitting opportunity to say a word about our Minister at Tangier, whose connection with Marocco, commenced in his childhood and continued throughout his life, is now about to cease. Born and bred in the country, where he succeeded his father as consul, speaking the language as well as his native tongue, a hard and thorough-going sportsman, imbued with a keen sympathy for the natives, he is probably the most popular and influential Christian among the Moors that ever lived in the country. In all these respects Sir John Hay has possessed an immense advantage over other foreign Ministers, and being the trusted friend and adviser of the Sultan, his influence at Court has been proportionately greater than theirs. Occupying such a commanding position in the country, it was only to be expected that he should arouse the jealousy and enmity of many. He has been bitterly denounced as a reactionary, as a stumbling-block in the path of progress; by men who forget that he has not been free to choose his own course of action. It is certainly to be regretted that British policy in Marocco has been so consistently directed towards maintaining the *status quo;* but as this policy has been dictated to Sir John from home, he has not been a free agent in pursuing it. It has been said that he neglects the interests of British traders in Marocco, and much of the hostility he has excited arises from his unwillingness to support the claims preferred against Moors by British subjects in the same indiscriminate fashion in which other foreign representatives enforce those of their compatriots. The other view of the matter (and my own) is that if there is one thing which redounds to the lasting credit of Sir John Hay, it is his resolute opposition to that system of protection, and the claims arising thereout, which I have endeavoured to describe in a previous chapter. Readers of that chapter will probably agree with me in saying that there has been far more need of some champion of the rights of these unfortunate Moors than of any additional machinery for applying the screw. Sir John's Moorish sympathies and his sense of justice have caused him to stand forth as such a champion, and it is much to be regretted that some settlement of the protection question could not have been arrived at before his retirement.

It is all very well to indulge in vague charges of discouraging British trade and neglecting British interests, but until our Government decides upon some more vigorous line of action in Marocco, an English Minister there must always be at a disadvantage with the representatives of other Powers. It is easy enough to advise and admonish the Sultan, but good advice is thrown away upon an Oriental unless backed by something else more convincing to the Eastern mind, and the Moors know very well that our advice is never likely to be so backed. We never threaten war or bombardment if our requests are not complied with, our navies don't "demonstrate" in order to wring, under threats of the thunder of British guns, money payments from recalcitrant debtors who very possibly owe nothing. Hence it is not surprising that our advice should be disregarded by the Moorish Government, while the demands of France and Italy are satisfied.

Questions of policy apart, one thing is certain, that during his long and honourable career Sir John Hay, by his sense of justice as much as by his force of character, has maintained among the Moors, not only the influence, but, even more, the good name of England in a manner which it has been given to few other Ministers in their sphere of action to equal. Foreigners, and among them his bitterest opponents, admit this, and if, as is said, the Moors "love" us, while they "hate and fear" the Spaniards and French respectively, this result is mainly due to Sir John Hay.

One change in connection with the foreign legations in Marocco is urgently needed, viz. that Ministers should reside, for some part of the year at least, at the seat of the Court, which is alternately at Fez and the City of Marocco. In every other country the foreign representatives reside at the capital as a matter of course; in Marocco, out of deference to Moorish susceptibilities and the bigotry of the ruling class, the Ministers are one and all located at Tangier. Now Tangier is the one city given up to the Christians. The Sultan and his advisers never go near the place, and the Moorish officials there have not the ear of their royal master. Under these circumstances it is impossible to bring adequate pressure to bear upon the Government for the institution of the required reforms. The two capitals are distant from Tangier 160 and 400 miles respectively, and the missions of envoys to the Court to which they are accredited occur on the average about once in two years. On these rare and solemn occasions there is much picturesque pomp and display, courteous speechifying, and mutual entertainment; the various members of the mission enjoy a novel experience and an agreeable picnic, and probably return home enriched with a passable Barb horse or other quadruped at the expense of the Imperial exchequer. The practical part of the business, as a rule, consists in showering good advice upon the guileless Monarch, who on his side is equally profuse in his promises of complete and immediate reform. Directly, however, the legate's back is turned, the Court officials and harem favourites get hold of their royal master and speedily make him recant, and the moral and restraining influence of the ambassador being removed, things go on exactly as before.

Nothing will ever be done under the present system. To expect the Moorish Government to reform of its own initiative is, as has often been pointed out, utterly futile; but they should be compelled to do so, by the urgent representations of foreign States. Obstacles would no doubt be encountered at first in the fanaticism of the people and the self-interest of the ruling class, whose instinct tells them that the civilization of the country means the doom of their authority. Once, however, make it plain to the Sultan that Europe was in earnest, and this opposition would soon be overcome. Among the principal improvements required, the following may be suggested: the reform of the native administration and security for life and property; the free ownership of lands by Christians and natives alike, and liberty to export corn and cattle and every other kind of produce; the lowering of the duties, and the removal of the various cramping restrictions on trade; the development of a proper agriculture and the opening of mines; the making of roads, railways, bridges, and irrigation works; and the establishment of a postal system. Capital would flow into the country without fear of a satisfactory return, and the present are not the times when we can afford to despise any fresh outlet for commercial enterprise or the development of a new market.

In gratitude for thus opening up his country, the Powers would doubtless display the same paternal solicitude for the Sultan's welfare that they do for his rival on the Bosphorus, and beneath the sheltering wing of a Multiple Control, or some similar diplomatic arrangement, he could rest secure from the aggressive designs of France or Spain. By thus bolstering up the tottering fabric of his power, the question of what is to become of Marocco at the dissolution of the Moorish dominion could be staved off indefinitely, and the main object, the civilization of the country, effected.

From a humanitarian point of view the gain would be immense. At present we see a great corn-producing country, rich in all the elements of material prosperity, with its splendid resources unused and wasted; a fine people, whose industry is crushed by an inhuman rule and the extortion of taxgatherers, shamefully bullied through the agency of Christian Powers, and periodically starving in the midst of possible plenty. It might be easy to paint a too glowing picture of the benefits which would accrue from the introduction of European influences and the enforced teachings of civilization, but they would beyond question be very great The establishment of proper means of communication alone could not fail to better the condition of the people, especially in the southern provinces, where they are sometimes starving while there is a superabundance of food in other parts. At least, the present frequent recurrence of famines would be made impossible, and travellers would be spared the spectacle of the peasantry trooping every morning out of their villages to gain like beasts a bare subsistence from the roots and grasses of the field. Waste lands would be put under cultivation, and tracts now uninhabited be rendered populous. The horrible state of the prisons, and the iniquities perpetrated by the native governors would be brought to light, and contact with civilization could scarcely fail to do something towards mending matters. Compare the prison at Tangier with those of Fez, and it will be seen that the presence of Europeans is not unattended by practical results. Means would no doubt be found to repress the slave-trade, as in Egypt and other countries where Christian influences have penetrated. Protection could be limited, and the fraudulent claims and other abuses connected with the authority wielded by Europeans curtailed. Clear out, in fine, the unclean brood of thieving and tyrannical kaids, check the malpractices of scheming Jews and Christians, and this would be something. Commerce would be developed, and the Sultan, probably to his surprise, would find himself a richer man than in the days of his uncontrolled sovereignty.

It has been urged that we have no claim on the good offices of the Sultan that would justify us in demanding him to effect internal reforms. Such an argument, however, is unlikely to carry much weight in these days, when European

Powers show small scruple or delicacy in intervening in the affairs of semi-barbarous States when it suits their purpose to do so. From a moral standpoint, the evils of Moorish rule would afford ample justification. As, however, self-interest is apt to be a more potent plea than principle, I prefer to rest my case rather on the advantages which would accrue to England from opening up the country, and the fact that her position would be materially strengthened thereby. Nor is it probable that any strong opposition from the people, apart from the ruling class, would be encountered. From what I gathered in conversations with natives (and it could hardly be otherwise), they are sick to death of the tyranny and extortion of their present rulers, and foreign intervention would be welcomed by thousands of the oppressed inhabitants. Their fanaticism is not so deep-seated but that it yields to intercourse, fair treatment, and the prospect of gain. The rapid increase in the population of the coast towns, where Christians alone are to be found, and the diminution of those in the interior, do not point to any rooted antipathy to the company of Europeans, nor does their anxiety to become subjects of Christian Powers look as though they altogether appreciated the blessings of Moslem rule.

Every consideration points to the desirability of an early settlement of the question. The agents of France are maturing their schemes for annexing the country, and are only awaiting a favourable opportunity. The acquisition of Marocco would be a great step towards the realization of the pet project of many French statesmen—the creation of a great North African Empire, which, extending from Suez to Cape Spartel, would rob England of whatever naval supremacy is left to her in the Mediterranean, and convert that sea into a French lake. Better far for Marocco herself that her regeneration, if it is to be effected at all, should be brought about by the collective action of Europe, than by that of a single Power whose former colonizing efforts have been notoriously unsuccessful.

Is it too much to hope that diplomatic jealousies —which have hitherto proved at once the bulwarks of Moorish misrule and the ruin of the country and people—may at length yield to the demands which civilization makes upon European States in their dealings with barbarism, and that some settlement may be arrived at, which, while safe-guarding the legitimate interests of each individual Power, shall let the light of modern ideas into this most benighted region of the Dark Continent? No pains are spared to open up the distant, unhealthy, and comparatively barren regions of Equatorial Africa, yet not a finger is stirred to do the like for what is, after all, the cream of the Continent—its North-West corner.

In conclusion, I trust I have shown that the present state of the country is as bad as can be, and that its marvellous isolation, standing as it does at the very threshold of civilization, has been productive of nothing but evil. Five centuries of uninterrupted decay have reduced a people, once the most enlightened as well as the most formidable in the world, to a state of degradation from which of themselves they can never recover. All ideas of reforming the corrupt and effete Moorish administration by any means short of pressure from without may be cast aside. The fruits of their rule are apparent in the waste lands and ruined towns and houses, the misery of the scanty and poverty-stricken population, the like of which is not to be seen in any other country of corresponding wealth and natural resources. At present, Marocco is a monstrous anachronism, and the condition of her people a disgrace to humanity. As has been well said, "God made it a garden, Man made it a wilderness," and the time has come for the hand of civilized man to be called in, and, by utilizing the gifts Nature has bestowed upon it with so lavish a hand, to render it a garden once more.

THE END.

INDEX.

A.

ABDA, 287.
Abdallah, Sultan, 255, 273.
Abd el Kader, the Algerian patriot, 112.
Abd el Malek, 44.
Abder Rhaman, Sultan, 126.
——————— Khalif of Cordova, 20.
Ablutions, Mohammedan, 154, 181.
Absalam, Kaid el Hadj, 40, 184, 193, 306.
Abu Hanifa, 153.
Adool, 85, 208.
Agriculture, Moorish, 10, 43, 312.
Aissa, Mohammed Ben, 36.
Aissauias, the, 36, 123, 164.
Akhbar el Hamra, 11, 40.
Akermout, Plain of, 281.
Alcala, 238.
Alcazar, 44—48.
——— filth of, 45.
Allah, Mohammedan conception of, 150.
Almansor, Sultan, 45, 189, 246.
Almsgiving, 156.

Andalusia, traveller in Marocco should visit, 33.
Andjrâ, 9, 118.
Anfa, 195.
Antæus, the giant, 13.
Aqueducts, Roman, 5, 185.
Argan-tree, 271, 272.
Army of Marocco, 249—252.
Asceticism, 164.
Askar, 242, 250.
Atavism, 115.
Atlas mountains, 218, 232—234.
Averroes, 91, 247.
Awara, 7.
Ayerna root, 62, 182.
Azamoor, 291.
Azrael, the Angel of Death, 30.

B.

BAB-ES-SINSSLA, 89.
Baghala, 290.
Barb horse, the, 287.
Barbary apes, 12.
Barracks at Fez, 79.
Barghash, Sidi Mohammed, 215, 260.
Bascha, a foreign word, 77.

Bascha of Tangier, 3.
— of Fez, 72, 102.
— of Wazan, 59.
Beni Hassen, mountains of, 6, 22, 42, 51.
Beni Hassen tribe, 179, 180.
Beni Miskeen, 222.
Ben rajit, 198.
Berbers, origin of, 108—122.
— legends concerning, 111.
Berbers, language of, 117.
— religion and social system of, 119, 166.
Blake, Mr., 189, 294.
Blood-tax, 173, 321.
Boabdil, 29.
Boar-hunting, 7—9, 16, 303.
— perils of, 9, 16, 305.
Boccanum, 247.
Bœtica, province of, 20.
Bokhari, 251.
Boo el Kheir, 17, 300.
Boo-siri, 219.
Boo Z'neka, 193, 294.
Bread, Moorish, 99.
Bustard, 221, 293.

C.

CARPETS, Moorish, 187.
Casablanca, 194, 292.
Cemetery, Arab, 21, 188.
Ceuta v. Gibraltar, 327.
Chinese Bible, the, 28.
Christian Church in North Africa, 166, 315.
Claims, fraudulent, 75, 205—210.
Coins of Marocco, 18, 225.
Colvile, Captain, 77, 104.
Compliments, Moorish, 58, 103, 173.

Courts of Justice, 3, 85.
Cruelty to animals, 104, 146.
Curiosity of natives, 27, 48, 51.
Curse, belief in efficacy of, 41.

D

DAR EL BAIDA, 194.
Daumas, General, 112.
Day of Judgment, 30, 160.
Decadence of the Moors, 31, 46, 90, 167—170.
Djebel Glaoui, 233.
— Hadid, 281.
— Kebir, 5, 6.
— Moossa, 6.
— Sarsar, 48.
— Ssala, 70, 77.
Djemma el Kairauin, 89.
— Moulai Abdallah Shereef at Wazan, 51.
Djemma Moulai Idrees, 89.
Dogs, Moorish, 42, 173.
Donatists, the, 315.
Druidical remains, 109.
Duars, 67.
Dukala, province of, 288.

E.

ENO, 130, 132.
Ethnology of Marocco, 109.
Eunuchs, 264.
Examination of corpse in grave, 160.

F.

FAMINES, 62, 198, 239.
— the result of misgovernment, 66, 237.

Fanaticism, 18, 67, 98, 163, 248.
Fatalism of the Moors, 10, 80, 160.
Fernau, Mr., 194, 293.
Ferry, native, 186.
Festival of Sidi Mohammed, 32.
Fez, 71—101.
—— history of, 76.
—— population, 78.
—— trade-guilds in, 80.
Flowers, beauty of, 178, 288.
Fondak, on road to Tetuan, 21.
Fondaks, at Fez, 83.
Food-supply of England, 329.
Forests, absence of, in Marocco, 11, 298.
Frost, 203.
Frost, Mr., 189, 295.
Funeral, Arab, 4.

G.

GAETULIANS, the, 113, 114, 314.
Gate, magnificent, at Mequinez, 135.
Gerouan, 172.
Gharb, El, province, 42, 174, 298.
Giralda, the, 191, 245.
Government of Marocco, 320.
Granada, surrender of, 29.
Guards, our, 48, 75, 268.
Gun, Moorish, 183.
—— manufacture of, 24.

H.

HADJ, the, 155.
Haha, province of, 272, 275.

Hamites, 110, 118, 121.
Hanbal, 153.
Hanno, Periplus of, 12, 295.
Haraoun el Raschid, 76.
Hassen tower, 184, 187, 191, 245.
Hay, Sir J. D., 7, 75, 216, 331—335.
Haymaking, 231.
Hell, the Mohammedan, 161.
Hercules, 13, 113.
—— caves of, 6.
Hesperides, Gardens of, 13.
Hhadd el Gharbia, 11, 40.
Hharrah, El, 255.
Hoare, Mr. Sidney, 32, 220, 297.
Hooker, Sir J., 233, 269.
Horse-stealing, 180.
Hospitality, trials of native, 39, 204.
Houris, supplanted by English girls in Moorish Paradise, 162.
House, our, at Wazan, 52.
———— at Fez, 73.
———— at Marocco, 243.

I.

IDRHES, 76.
Indemnity, war, 23.
Intemperance, increase of, among Moors, 157.
Isly, battle of, 319.

J.

JACKSON'S Marocco, 78, 192.
Jellab, 2, 67.
Jews, ill-treatment of, 96.
—— their malpractices, 136—139, 206, 213.

Jews, independent, in Wadnoon, 277.
Jewesses, beauty of, 142.
Joof, El, 280.
Joshua, 111.
Jugurtha, 113.

K.

KABYLES, the, 30, 108, 119.
Kantra, El, battle of, 44, 318.
Kasr el Faraoun, 144, 146.
Kessaria, 93.
Khemis, El, 11, 300.
Kif, 303.
Koos-koossoo, 26, 65.
Koran, the, 28, 104, 153.
Kteeb, 29.
Kubbah, 32, 126, 149, 290.
Kutubia, tower and mosque of, 191, 241, 245.

L.

AB EL BAROUD, 34, 146.
Land-system, 196, 321.
Language, the Moorish, 24, 61.
Larache, 13, 300.
Leo Africanus, 46.
Leprosy, 255.
Library of Fez, 90.
Lixus, the, 12.
Lunatics, 83, 278.
Lys, Punic town of, 13.

M.

MACLEAN, KAID, 243, 256.
Madrid Conference, 196, 211, 215.

Maghreb, El, Arabic name for Marocco, 310.
Maghreb, El, evening call to prayer, 265.
Maghrebbin dialect, the, 24, 61.
Mahdi, the, 63, 160.
Malek, sect of, 68, 153, 154.
Mameluke, the, 44.
Mamora forest, 296.
Manuel Correa, 40, 276.
Maps of Marocco, inaccuracy of, 61, 148.
Marin dynasty, 78, 190, 246.
Marocco, general description of, 310.
Marocco, history of, 314.
——— English interests in, 325.
Marocco City, 242—267.
Matamors, 66.
Mauri, 108, 113.
Mauritania, 21, 147, 314.
"Mecca of Marocco," Wazan the, 50.
Mehediah, 297, 311.
Mellah, or Jewry, 23, 95, 314.
Mendacity, Moorish, 41, 172, 297.
Men la Ouli, 60.
Mequinez, 123—136.
Minerals, 313.
Mirage, 178.
Mogador, 272—275.
Mohammed, the Prophet, 138, 159, 263.
Mokaddem, 38, 63.
Moloya river, 314, 324.
Mona, 41, 65, 172, 200.
——— ambassadors', 229.
Money, Moorish, 18, 221.
Moolsaa, 63, 160.
"Moors," true meaning of word, 108.
Mosques, 23, 89, 245.

Moulai Abdallah Shereef, 51, 57.
Moulai Idrees, 33, 76, 148.
——— Ismael, 14, 126, 146.
——— S'liman, 129.
——— Yezeed, 72.
Mueddin, the, 157, 265.
Murders at Tangier, 35.

N.

NUMIDIANS, 111, 113.
N'zalla, 193.

O.

OATHS, Arab, 8, 59.
O'Donnell, Marshal, 22.
Onkh el Jimmel, 269.
Ophthalmia, 253.
Ornithology of Marocco, 221.
Ouadaiah, Kasbah, 268.
Ouber Mohammed, 64.
Oujda, 103.
Ouled Boo Sba, 272.

P.

PARTRIDGE, Barbary, 12.
Phœnicians, the, 13, 110, 119, 314.
Pig-sticking, 7, 39.
Pirates, Barbary, 29, 185.
Pliny, 13, 113, 234.
Prayers, Mohammedan, 67, 157.
Prisons, 3, 83.
Procession, religious, 25, 33.
Prophecies, Moorish, 63.
Protection, 97, 141, 210—217.
Ptolemy's Geography, 174, 247.
Punishments, 86—88.

R.

RABAT, 187—192, 294.
Ramadan, 154, 156.
Ras ed Daura, 298.
Religion, the Mohammedan, 138, 149—170.
Religion, its practical side, 154.
——— its doctrinal side, 159.
Religion, parallelism with popular Catholicism, 150, 163—165.
Renan, M. Ernest, 109, 114, 168.
Riff country, 29.
Riffians, the, 29, 34, 108, 111, 119.
Roads, absence of, 5.
Rohlfs, Dr. G., 51, 61, 75, 91, 115.
Rosary, Mohammedan, 68, 165.
Ruined towns, 283, 288.
Ruins at Mequinez, 125, 128—133.

S.

SABAB, 48.
Sacrifice, ceremony of, 33.
Saddlery, Moorish, 145.
Saffi, 283.
Sahara, the, 277, 279.
——— flooding the, 280.
Saint-worship, 105, 149—151.
Sala Colonia, 185, 190.
Sallee, 185.
Sallust, 113.
Salutation, Moorish, 59, 64, 238.
Salvation Army, the Aissauias the, of Marocco, 36.
Saraoun, 146.

School, Arab, 68.
Sebastian, Don, 44.
Seraghna, 228, 269.
Shaffei, El, 153.
Shaouia, province of, 220.
Sharf el Akab, 7.
Shellah, 185, 190 (and see "Shlohs").
Shereef of Wazan, 53—59, 83.
——————— now a French subject, 55, 212, 323.
Shiedma, 270.
Shiites, 153.
Shlohs, 30, 107, 275.
Shraa, the, 196, 321.
Sidi Hassen mountains, 70, 103.
Sidi Kassim, 174.
Sidi Mohammed, Sultan, 84, 248, 289.
Sidi Moktar, 270.
Slavery, 26, 278.
S'min, 220, 228.
Snipe-shooting, 7, 23.
Sodom, 111.
Soil, fertility of, 43, 201.
Soko at Tangier, 2, 5, 33.
Sonnites, 63, 153, 285.
Sparrows, tame, 254.
Sport in Marocco, 7, 18, 221.
Sultan, the, 258—263.
Sunset in Marocco City, 264.
Superstition, native, 101, 142, 162.
Sus, 275, 280.

T.

Tabbia, 72.
Tadla, 225.
Tafilet, 82, 126, 262, 317.
Tamashek language, the, 117.
Tamilelt, 241.

Tangier, 1, 32.
Tarik, 108, 316.
Tarudant, 247.
Taxation, 321.
Temsna, province of, 220.
Tetuan, 21—32.
——— battle of, 22.
Thaleb, 69, 90, 270.
Theology, Moorish, 154.
Timbuktoo, 277.
Tocolosida, 174.
Touaricks, 108, 117.
Trade of Marocco, 195, 322.
Troglodytes, 295.
Tunnel at Mequinez, 131.
Tyranny, official, 88, 174—178, 184.

V.

Vandals, the, in N. Africa, 23, 30, 109, 115, 315.
Vaults at Mequinez, 125.
Vendetta, the, in Marocco, 34.
Vizir, the Grand, 86, 259, 320.
Volubilis, 144, 147, 174.

W.

Wad el Abid, 238.
——— Akdour, 238.
——— Ayascha, 21.
——— Boo Ragrag, 187, 295.
——— Fas, 74, 77.
——— Kharrub, 11.
——— Koos, 13, 43, 50, 300.
——— Ma Hassen, 43, 318.
——— N'fitikh, 194.
——— N'fys, 268.
——— Oom R'bea, 220, 227, 291.
——— Oumaourour, 43.

Wad el Seboo, 66, 183, 298.
—— Tensift, 242, 282.
—— Tessoot, 238.
—— Wergha, 61.
Wadnoon, 276.
Walili, 147.
Wall, immense, 134.
Warfare, native, 172, 222.
"Warriors," our, 51, 107.
Wazan, 50—57, 123.
Wedding, ceremonies at native, 4.
White, Mr. Horace P., 72.
Women, status of, in Marocco, 158, 285.
Women, fatness of, 284.

Women-flogging, 86, 196.

Y.

YAKOOB, 78.
Yussoof Ben Tesfin, 246.

Z.

ZAAB, fair men, 115.
Zair tribe, 295.
Zaouias, 290.
Zemmoor tribe, 179.
Zilis, Roman colony of, 20.
Zoroaster, 153.
Z'ttatt, 202.

LONDON:
PRINTED BY GILBERT AND RIVINGTON, LIMITED,
ST. JOHN'S SQUARE

A Catalogue of American and Foreign Books Published or Imported by MESSRS. SAMPSON LOW & CO. *can be had on application.*

Crown Buildings, 188, *Fleet Street, London,*
October, 1885.

A Selection from the List of Books

PUBLISHED BY

SAMPSON LOW, MARSTON, SEARLE, & RIVINGTON.

ALPHABETICAL LIST.

ABOUT Some Fellows. By an ETON BOY, Author of "A Day of my Life." Cloth limp, square 16mo, 2s. 6d.

Adams (C. K.) Manual of Historical Literature. Cr. 8vo, 12s. 6d.

Alcott (Louisa M.) Jack and Jill. 16mo, 5s.

—————— *Old-Fashioned Thanksgiving Day.* 3s. 6d.

—————— *Proverb Stories.* 16mo, 3s. 6d.

—————— *Spinning-Wheel Stories.* 16mo, 5s.

—————— See also "Rose Library."

Alden (W. L.) Adventures of Jimmy Brown, written by himself. Illustrated. Small crown 8vo, cloth, 2s. 6d.

Aldrich (T. B.) Friar Jerome's Beautiful Book, &c. Very choicely printed on hand-made paper, parchment cover, 3s. 6d.

—————— *Poetical Works. Edition de Luxe.* 8vo, 21s.

Alford (Lady Marian) Needlework as Art. With over 100 Woodcuts, Photogravures, &c. Royal 8vo, 42s.; large paper, 84s.

Amateur Angler's Days in Dove Dale: Three Weeks' Holiday in July and August, 1884. By E. M. Printed by Whittingham, at the Chiswick Press. Cloth gilt, 1s. 6d.; fancy boards, 1s.

American Men of Letters. Thoreau, Irving, Webster. 2s. 6d. each.

Anderson (W.) Pictorial Arts of Japan. With 80 full-page and other Plates, 16 of them in Colours. Large imp. 4to, gilt binding, gilt edges, 8l. 8s.; or in four parts, 2l. 2s. each.

Angler's Strange Experiences (An). By COTSWOLD ISYS. With numerous Illustrations, 4to, 5s. New Edition, 3s. 6d.

Angling. See Amateur, "British Fisheries Directory," "Cutcliffe," "Martin," "Stevens," "Theakston," "Walton," and "Wells."

Arnold (Edwin) Birthday Book. 4s. 6d.

A

Art Education. See "Biographies of Great Artists," "Illustrated Text Books," "Mollett's Dictionary."

Artists at Home. Photographed by J. P. MAYALL, and reproduced in Facsimile. Letterpress by F. G. STEPHENS. Imp. folio, 42s.

Audsley (G. A.) Ornamental Arts of Japan. 90 Plates, 74 in Colours and Gold, with General and Descriptive Text. 2 vols., folio, £15 15s. On the issue of Part III. the price will be further advanced.

—— *The Art of Chromo-Lithography.* Coloured Plates and Text. Folio, 63s.

Auerbach (B.) Brigitta. Illustrated. 2s.

—— *On the Heights.* 3 vols., 6s.

—— *Spinoza.* Translated. 2 vols., 18mo, 4s.

BALDWIN (J.) *Story of Siegfried.* 6s.

—— *Story of Roland.* Crown 8vo, 6s.

Ballin (Ada S., Lecturer to the National Health Society) Science of Dress in Theory and Practice. Illustrated, 6s.

Barlow (Alfred) Weaving by Hand and by Power. With several hundred Illustrations. Third Edition, royal 8vo, 1l. 5s.

Barlow (William) New Theories of Matter and Force. 2 vols., 8vo,

THE BAYARD SERIES.
Edited by the late J. HAIN FRISWELL.

Comprising Pleasure Books of Literature produced in the Choicest Style as Companionable Volumes at Home and Abroad.

"We can hardly imagine better books for boys to read or for men to ponder over."—*Times.*

Price 2s. 6d. each Volume, complete in itself, flexible cloth extra, gilt edges, with silk Headbands and Registers.

The Story of the Chevalier Bayard. By M. De Berville.

De Joinville's St. Louis, King of France.

The Essays of Abraham Cowley, including all his Prose Works.

Abdallah; or, The Four Leaves. By Edouard Laboullaye.

Table-Talk and Opinions of Napoleon Buonaparte.

Vathek: An Oriental Romance. By William Beckford.

Words of Wellington: Maxims and Opinions of the Great Duke.

Dr. Johnson's Rasselas, Prince of Abyssinia. With Notes.

Hazlitt's Round Table. With Biographical Introduction.

The Religio Medici, Hydriotaphia, and the Letter to a Friend. By Sir Thomas Browne, Knt.

Ballad Poetry of the Affections. By Robert Buchanan.

Coleridge's Christabel, and other Imaginative Poems. With Preface by Algernon C. Swinburne.

Lord Chesterfield's Letters, Sentences, and Maxims. With Introduction by the Editor, and

Bayard Series (continued):—

Essay on Chesterfield by M. de Ste.-Beuve, of the French Academy.

The King and the Commons. A Selection of Cavalier and Puritan Songs. Edited by Professor Morley.

Essays in Mosaic. By Thos. Ballantyne.

My Uncle Toby; his Story and his Friends. Edited by P. Fitzgerald.

Reflections; or, Moral Sentences and Maxims of the Duke de la Rochefoucauld.

Socrates: Memoirs for English Readers from Xenophon's Memorabilia. By Edw. Levien.

Prince Albert's Golden Precepts.

A Case containing 12 Volumes, price 31s. 6d.; or the Case separately, price 3s. 6d.

Behnke and Browne. *Child's Voice*. Small 8vo, 3s. 6d.

Bickersteth (Bishop E. H.) *The Clergyman in his Home*. Small post 8vo, 1s.

—— —— *Evangelical Churchmanship and Evangelical Eclecticism*. 8vo, 1s.

—— —— *From Year to Year: Original Poetical Pieces*. Small post 8vo, 3s. 6d.; roan, 6s. and 5s.; calf or morocco, 10s. 6d.

—— —— *Hymnal Companion to the Book of Common Prayer*. May be had in various styles and bindings from 1d. to 31s. 6d. Price List and Prospectus will be forwarded on application.

—— —— *The Master's Home-Call; or, Brief Memorials of Alice Frances Bickersteth*. 20th Thousand. 32mo, cloth gilt, 1s.

—— —— *The Master's Will*. A Funeral Sermon preached on the Death of Mrs. S. Gurney Buxton. Sewn, 6d.; cloth gilt, 1s.

—— —— *The Reef, and other Parables*. Crown 8vo, 2s. 6d.

—— —— *The Shadow of the Rock*. A Selection of Religious Poetry. 18mo, cloth extra, 2s. 6d.

—— —— *The Shadowed Home and the Light Beyond*. New Edition, crown 8vo, cloth extra, 5s.

Biographies of the Great Artists (Illustrated). Crown 8vo, emblematical binding, 3s. 6d. per volume, except where the price is given.

Claude Lorrain.*
Correggio, by M. E. Heaton, 2s. 6d.
Della Robbia and Cellini, 2s. 6d.
Albrecht Dürer, by R. F. Heath.
Figure Painters of Holland.
Fra Angelico, Masaccio, and Botticelli.
Fra Bartolommeo, Albertinelli, and Andrea del Sarto.
Gainsborough and Constable.
Ghiberti and Donatello, 2s. 6d.
Giotto, by Harry Quilter.
Hans Holbein, by Joseph Cundall.
Hogarth, by Austin Dobson.
Landseer, by F. G. Stevens.
Lawrence and Romney, by Lord Ronald Gower, 2s. 6d.

* *Not yet published.*

Biographies of the Great Artists (continued) :—

Leonardo da Vinci.
Little Masters of Germany, by W. B. Scott.
Mantegna and Francia.
Meissonier, by J. W. Mollett, 2s. 6d.
Michelangelo Buonarotti, by Clément.
Murillo, by Ellen E. Minor, 2s. 6d.
Overbeck, by J. B. Atkinson.
Raphael, by N. D'Anvers.
Rembrandt, by J. W. Mollett.
Reynolds, by F. S. Pulling.
Rubens, by C. W. Kett.
Tintoretto, by W. R. Osler.
Titian, by R. F. Heath.
Turner, by Cosmo Monkhouse.
Vandyck and Hals, by P. R. Head.
Velasquez, by E. Stowe.
Vernet and Delaroche, by J. Rees.
Watteau, by J. W. Mollett, 2s. 6d.
Wilkie, by J. W. Mollett.

Bird (F. J.) American Practical Dyer's Companion. 8vo, 42s.

Bird (H. E.) Chess Practice. 8vo, 2s. 6d.

Black (Wm.) Novels. See "Low's Standard Library."

Blackburn (Charles F.) Hints on Catalogue Titles and Index Entries, with a Vocabulary of Terms and Abbreviations, chiefly from Foreign Catalogues. Royal 8vo, 14s.

Blackburn (Henry) Breton Folk. With 171 Illust. by RANDOLPH CALDECOTT. Imperial 8vo, gilt edges, 21s.; plainer binding, 10s. 6d.

——— *Pyrenees (The).* With 100 Illustrations by GUSTAVE DORÉ, corrected to 1881. Crown 8vo, 7s. 6d.

Blackmore (R. D.) Lorna Doone. Edition de luxe. Crowr. 4to, very numerous Illustrations, cloth, gilt edges, 31s. 6d.; parchment, uncut, top gilt, 35s. Cheap Edition, small post 8vo, 6s.

——— *Novels.* See "Low's Standard Library."

Blaikie (William) How to get Strong and how to Stay so. Rational, Physical, Gymnastic, &c., Exercises. Illust., sm. post 8vo, 5s.

——— *Sound Bodies for our Boys and Girls.* 16mo, 2s. 6d.

Bonwich (Jos.) British Colonies and their Resources. 1 vol., cloth, 5s. Sewn—I. Asia, 1s.; II. Africa, 1s.; III. America, 1s.; IV. Australasia, 1s.

Bosanquet (Rev. C.) Blossoms from the King's Garden: Sermons for Children. 2nd Edition, small post 8vo, cloth extra, 6s.

Boussenard (L.) Crusoes of Guiana. Illustrated. 5s.

——— *Gold-seekers, a Sequel.* Illustrated. 16mo, 5s.

Boy's Froissart. King Arthur. Mabinogion. Percy. See LANIER.

Bradshaw (J.) New Zealand as it is. 8vo, 12s. 6d.

Brassey (Lady) Tahiti. With 31 Autotype Illustrations after Photos. by Colonel STUART-WORTLEY. Fcap. 4to, 21s.

Bright (John) Public Letters. Crown 8vo, 7s. 6d.

Brisse (Baron) Ménus (366). A *ménu*, in French and English, for every Day in the Year. Translated by Mrs. MATTHEW CLARKE. 2nd Edition. Crown 8vo, 5*s.*

British Fisheries Directory, 1883-84. Small 8vo, 2*s.* 6*d.*

Brittany. See BLACKBURN.

Brown. Life and Letters of John Brown, Liberator of Kansas, and Martyr of Virginia. By F. B. SANBORN. Illustrated. 8vo, 12*s.* 6*d.*

Browne (G. Lennox) Voice Use and Stimulants. Sm. 8vo, 3*s.* 6*d.*

—— and *Behnke (Emil) Voice, Song, and Speech.* Illustrated, 3rd Edition, medium 8vo, 15*s.*

Bryant (W. C.) and Gay (S. H.) History of the United States. 4 vols., royal 8vo, profusely Illustrated, 60*s.*

Bryce (Rev. Professor) Manitoba. With Illustrations and Maps. Crown 8vo, 7*s.* 6*d.*

Bunyan's Pilgrim's Progress. With 138 original Woodcuts. Small post 8vo, cloth gilt, 3*s.* 6*d.*; gilt edges, 4*s.*

Burnaby (Capt.) On Horseback through Asia Minor. 2 vols., 8vo, 38*s.* Cheaper Edition, 1 vol., crown 8vo, 10*s.* 6*d.*

Burnaby (Mrs. F.) High Alps in Winter; or, Mountaineering in Search of Health. By Mrs. FRED BURNABY. With Portrait of the Authoress, Map, and other Illustrations. Handsome cloth, 14*s.*

Butler (W. F.) The Great Lone Land; an Account of the Red River Expedition, 1869-70. New Edition, cr. 8vo, cloth extra, 7*s.* 6*d.*

—— *Invasion of England, told twenty years after, by an Old* Soldier. Crown 8vo, 2*s.* 6*d.*

—— *Red Cloud; or, the Solitary Sioux.* Imperial 16mo, numerous illustrations, gilt edges, 5*s.*

—— *The Wild North Land; the Story of a Winter Journey* with Dogs across Northern North America. 8vo, 18*s.* Cr. 8vo, 7*s.* 6*d.*

Buxton (H. J. W.) Painting, English and American. Crown 8vo, 5*s.*

CADOGAN *(Lady A.) Illustrated Games of Patience.* Twenty-four Diagrams in Colours, with Text. Fcap. 4to, 12*s.* 6*d.*

California. See "Nordhoff."

Cambridge Staircase (A). By the Author of "A Day of my Life at Eton." Small crown 8vo, cloth, 2*s.* 6*d.*

Cambridge Trifles; from an Undergraduate Pen. By the Author of "A Day of my Life at Eton," &c. 16mo, cloth extra, 2s. 6d.

Carleton (Will) Farm Ballads, Farm Festivals, and Farm Legends. 1 vol., small post 8vo, 3s. 6d.

———— *City Ballads.* With Illustrations. 12s. 6d.

———— See also "Rose Library."

Carnegie (A.) American Four-in-Hand in Britain. Small 4to, Illustrated, 10s. 6d. Popular Edition, 1s.

———— *Round the World.* 8vo, 10s. 6d.

Chairman's Handbook (The). By R. F. D. PALGRAVE, Clerk of the Table of the House of Commons. 5th Edition, 2s.

Changed Cross (The), and other Religious Poems. 16mo, 2s. 6d.

Charities of London. See Low's.

Chattock (R. S.) Practical Notes on Etching. Sec. Ed., 8vo, 7s. 6d.

Chess. See BIRD (H. E.).

Children's Praises. Hymns for Sunday-Schools and Services. Compiled by LOUISA H. H. TRISTRAM. 4d.

Choice Editions of Choice Books. 2s. 6d. each. Illustrated by C. W. COPE, R.A., T. CRESWICK, R.A., E. DUNCAN, BIRKET FOSTER, J. C. HORSLEY, A.R.A., G. HICKS, R. REDGRAVE, R.A., C. STONEHOUSE, F. TAYLER, G. THOMAS, H. J. TOWNSHEND, E. H. WEHNERT, HARRISON WEIR, &c.

Bloomfield's Farmer's Boy.	Milton's L'Allegro.
Campbell's Pleasures of Hope.	Poetry of Nature. Harrison Weir.
Coleridge's Ancient Mariner.	Rogers' (Sam.) Pleasures of Memory.
Goldsmith's Deserted Village.	Shakespeare's Songs and Sonnets.
Goldsmith's Vicar of Wakefield.	Tennyson's May Queen.
Gray's Elegy in a Churchyard.	Elizabethan Poets.
Keat's Eve of St. Agnes.	Wordsworth's Pastoral Poems.

"Such works are a glorious beatification for a poet."—*Athenæum.*

Christ in Song. By PHILIP SCHAFF. New Ed., gilt edges, 6s.

Chromo-Lithography. See "Audsley."

Collingwood (Harry) Under the Meteor Flag. The Log of a Midshipman. Illustrated, small post 8vo, gilt, 6s.; plainer, 5s.

———— *The Voyage of the "Aurora."* Illustrated, small post 8vo, gilt, 6s.; plainer, 5s.

Colvile (H. E.) Accursed Land: Water Way of Edom. 10s. 6d.

Composers. See "Great Musicians."

Confessions of a Frivolous Girl. Cr. 8vo, 6s. Paper boards, 1s.

Cook (Dutton) Book of the Play. New Edition. 1 vol., 3s. 6d.

——— *On the Stage: Studies of Theatrical History and the Actor's Art.* 2 vols., 8vo, cloth, 24s.

Costume. See SMITH (J. MOYR).

Cowen (Jos., M.P.) Life and Speeches. By MAJOR JONES. 8vo, 14s.

Curtis (C. B.) Velazquez and Murillo. With Etchings, &c. Royal 8vo, 31s. 6d.; large paper, 63s.

Custer (E. B.) Boots and Saddles. Life in Dakota with General Custer. Crown 8vo, 8s. 6d.

Cutcliffe (H. C.) Trout Fishing in Rapid Streams. Cr. 8vo, 3s. 6d.

DANVERS (N.) An Elementary History of Art. Crown 8vo, 10s. 6d.

——— *Elementary History of Music.* Crown 8vo, 2s. 6d.

——— *Handbooks of Elementary Art—Architecture; Sculpture; Old Masters; Modern Painting.* Crown 8vo, 3s. 6d. each.

Davis (C. T.) Manufacture of Bricks, Tiles, Terra-Cotta, &c. Illustrated. 8vo, 25s.

——— *Manufacture of Leather.* With many Illustrations. 52s. 6d.

Dawidowsky (F.) Glue, Gelatine, Isinglass, Cements, &c. 8vo, 12s. 6d.

Day of My Life (A); or, Every-Day Experiences at Eton. By an ETON BOY. 16mo, cloth extra, 2s. 6d.

Day's Collacon: an Encyclopædia of Prose Quotations. Imperial 8vo, cloth, 31s. 6d.

Decoration. Vols. II. to IX. New Series, folio, 7s. 6d. each.

Dogs in Disease: their Management and Treatment. By ASHMONT. Crown 8vo, 7s. 6d.

Donnelly (Ignatius) Atlantis; or, the Antediluvian World. 7th Edition, crown 8vo, 12s. 6d.

——— *Ragnarok: The Age of Fire and Gravel.* Illustrated, Crown 8vo, 12s. 6d.

Doré (Gustave) Life and Reminiscences. By BLANCHE ROOSEVELT. With numerous Illustrations from the Artist's previously unpublished Drawings. Medium 8vo, 24s.

Dougall (James Dalziel) Shooting: its Appliances, Practice, and Purpose. New Edition, revised with additions. Crown 8vo, 7s. 6d.
"The book is admirable in every way. . . . We wish it every success."—*Globe.*
"A very complete treatise. . . . Likely to take high rank as an authority on shooting."—*Daily News.*

Drama. See COOK (DUTTON).

Dyeing. See BIRD (F. J.).

EDUCATIONAL Works published in Great Britain. A Classified Catalogue. Second Edition, 8vo, cloth extra, 5s.

Egypt. See "De Leon," "Foreign Countries."

Eight Months on the Gran Ciacco of the Argentine Republic. 8vo, 12s. 6d.

Electricity. See GORDON.

Elliot (Adm. Sir G.) Future Naval Battles, and how to Fight them. Numerous Illustrations. Royal 8vo, 14s.

Emerson (R. W.) Life. By G. W. COOKE. Crown 8vo, 8s. 6d.

English Catalogue of Books. Vol. III., 1872—1880. Royal 8vo, half-morocco, 42s. See also "Index."

English Etchings. A Periodical published Monthly.

English Philosophers. Edited by E. B. IVAN MÜLLER, M.A.

A series intended to give a concise view of the works and lives of English thinkers. Crown 8vo volumes of 180 or 200 pp., price 3s. 6d. each.

Francis Bacon, by Thomas Fowler.
Hamilton, by W. H. S. Monck.
Hartley and James Mill, by G. S. Bower.
*John Stuart Mill, by Miss Helen Taylor.
Shaftesbury and Hutcheson, by Professor Fowler.
Adam Smith, by J. A. Farrer.

* *Not yet published.*

Esmarch (Dr. Friedrich) Treatment of the Wounded in War. Numerous Coloured Plates and Illust., 8vo, strongly bound, 1l. 8s.

Etching. See CHATTOCK, and ENGLISH ETCHINGS.

Etchings (Modern) of Celebrated Paintings. 4to, 31s. 6d.

FARM Ballads, Festivals, and Legends. See "Rose Library."

Fauriel (Claude) Last Days of the Consulate. Cr. 8vo, 10s. 6d.

Fawcett (Edgar) A Gentleman of Leisure. 1s.

Feilden (H. St. C.) Some Public Schools, their Cost and Scholarships. Crown 8vo, 2s. 6d.

Fenn (G. Manville) Off to the Wilds: A Story for Boys. Profusely Illustrated. Crown 8vo, 7s. 6d.; also 5s.

—————— *The Silver Cañon: a Tale of the Western Plains.* Illustrated, small post 8vo, gilt, 6s.; plainer, 5s.

Fennell (Greville) Book of the Roach. New Edition, 12mo, 2s.

Ferns. See HEATH.

Fields (J. T.) Yesterdays with Authors. New Ed., 8vo, 10s. 6d.

Fleming (Sandford) England and Canada: a Summer Tour. Crown 8vo, 6s.

Florence. See "Yriarte."

Folkard (R., Jun.) Plant Lore, Legends, and Lyrics. Illustrated, 8vo, 16s.

Forbes (H. O.) Naturalist's Wanderings in the Eastern Archi- pelago. Illustrated, 8vo, 21s.

Foreign Countries and British Colonies. A series of Descriptive Handbooks. Crown 8vo, 3s. 6d. each.

Australia, by J. F. Vesey Fitzgerald.
Austria, by D. Kay, F.R.G.S.
*Canada, by W. Fraser Rae.
Denmark and Iceland, by E. C. Otté.
Egypt, by S. Lane Poole, B.A.
France, by Miss M. Roberts.
Germany, by S. Baring-Gould.
Greece, by L. Sergeant, B.A.
*Holland, by R. L. Poole.
Japan, by S. Mossman.
*New Zealand.
*Persia, by Major-Gen. Sir F. Goldsmid.
Peru, by Clements R. Markham, C.B.
Russia, by W. R. Morfill, M.A.
Spain, by Rev. Wentworth Webster.
Sweden and Norway, by F. H. Woods.
*Switzerland, by W. A. P. Coolidge, M.A.
*Turkey-in-Asia, by J. C. McCoan, M.P.
West Indies, by C. H. Eden, F.R.G.S.

* *Not ready yet.*

Frampton (Mary) Journal, Letters, and Anecdotes, 1799— 1846. 8vo, 14s.

Franc (Maud Jeanne). The following form one Series, small post 8vo, in uniform cloth bindings, with gilt edges :—

Emily's Choice. 5s.	Vermont Vale. 5s.
Hall's Vineyard. 4s.	Minnie's Mission. 4s.
John's Wife: A Story of Life in South Australia. 4s.	Little Mercy. 4s.
	Beatrice Melton's Discipline. 4s.
Marian; or, The Light of Some One's Home. 5s.	No Longer a Child. 4s.
	Golden Gifts. 4s.
Silken Cords and Iron Fetters. 4s.	Two Sides to Every Question. 4s.
Into the Light. 4s.	Master of Ralston, 4s.

Francis (Frances) Elric and Ethel: a Fairy Tale. Illustrated. Crown 8vo, 3s. 6d.

French. See "Julien."

Froissart. See "Lanier."

GALE (F.; the Old Buffer) Modern English Sports: their Use and Abuse. Crown 8vo, 6s.; a few large paper copies, 10s. 6d.

Garth (Philip) Ballads and Poems from the Pacific. Small post 8vo, 6s.

Gentle Life (Queen Edition). 2 vols. in 1, small 4to, 6s.

THE GENTLE LIFE SERIES.

Price 6s. each; or in calf extra, price 10s. 6d.; Smaller Edition, cloth extra, 2s. 6d., except where price is named.

The Gentle Life. Essays in aid of the Formation of Character of Gentlemen and Gentlewomen.

About in the World. Essays by Author of "The Gentle Life."

Like unto Christ. A New Translation of Thomas à Kempis' "De Imitatione Christi."

Familiar Words. An Index Verborum, or Quotation Handbook. 6s.

Essays by Montaigne. Edited and Annotated by the Author of "The Gentle Life."

The Gentle Life. 2nd Series.

The Silent Hour: Essays, Original and Selected. By the Author of "The Gentle Life."

Half-Length Portraits. Short Studies of Notable Persons. By J. HAIN FRISWELL.

Essays on English Writers, for the Self-improvement of Students in English Literature.

Other People's Windows. By J. HAIN FRISWELL. 6s.

A Man's Thoughts. By J. HAIN FRISWELL.

The Countess of Pembroke's Arcadia. By Sir PHILIP SIDNEY. New Edition, 6s.

George Eliot: a Critical Study of her Life. By G. W. COOKE. Crown 8vo, 10s. 6d.

Germany. By S. BARING-GOULD. Crown 8vo, 3s. 6d.

Gilder (W. H.) Ice-Pack and Tundra. An Account of the Search for the "Jeannette." 8vo, 18s.

——— *Schwatka's Search.* Sledging in quest of the Franklin Records. Illustrated, 8vo, 12s. 6d.

Gilpin's Forest Scenery. Edited by F. G. HEATH. Post 8vo, 7s. 6d.

Gisborne (W.) New Zealand Rulers and Statesmen. With Portraits. Crown 8vo,

Gordon (General) Private Diary in China. Edited by S. MOSSMAN. Crown 8vo, 7s. 6d.

Gordon (J. E. H., B.A. Cantab.) Four Lectures on Electric Induction at the Royal Institution, 1878-9. Illust., square 16mo, 3s.

——— *Electric Lighting.* Illustrated, 8vo, 18s.

——— *Physical Treatise on Electricity and Magnetism.* 2nd Edition, enlarged, with coloured, full-page, &c., Illust. 2 vols., 8vo, 42s.

——— *Electricity for Schools.* Illustrated. Crown 8vo, 5s.

Gouffé (Jules) Royal Cookery Book. Translated and adapted for English use by ALPHONSE GOUFFÉ, Head Pastrycook to the Queen. New Edition, with plates in colours, Woodcuts, &c., 8vo, gilt edges, 42s.

——— Domestic Edition, half-bound, 10s. 6d.

Grant (General, U.S.) Personal Memoirs. With numerous Illustrations, Maps, &c. 2 vols., 8vo, 28s.

Great Artists. See "Biographies."

Great Musicians. Edited by F. HUEFFER. A Series of Biographies, crown 8vo, 3*s.* each :—

Bach.	Handel.	Purcell.
*Beethoven.	Haydn.	Rossini.
*Berlioz.	*Marcello.	Schubert.
English Church Composers. By BARETT.	Mendelssohn.	Schumann.
	Mozart.	Richard Wagner.
*Glück.	*Palestrina.	Weber.

* *In preparation.*

Groves (J. Percy) Charmouth Grange: a Tale of the Seventeenth Century. Illustrated, small post 8vo, gilt, 6*s.*; plainer, 5*s.*

Guizot's History of France. Translated by ROBERT BLACK. Super-royal 8vo, very numerous Full-page and other Illustrations. In 8 vols., cloth extra, gilt, each 24*s.* This work is re-issued in cheaper binding, 8 vols., at 10*s.* 6*d.* each.

"It supplies a want which has long been felt, and ought to be in the hands of all students of history."—*Times.*

—————————— *Masson's School Edition.* Abridged from the Translation by Robert Black, with Chronological Index, Historical and Genealogical Tables, &c. By Professor GUSTAVE MASSON, B.A. With 24 full-page Portraits, and other Illustrations. 1 vol., 8vo, 600 pp., 10*s.* 6*d.*

Guizot's History of England. In 3 vols. of about 500 pp. each, containing 60 to 70 full-page and other Illustrations, cloth extra, gilt, 24*s.* each ; re-issue in cheaper binding, 10*s.* 6*d.* each.

"For luxury of typography, plainness of print, and beauty of illustration, these volumes, of which but one has as yet appeared in English, will hold their own against any production of an age so luxurious as our own in everything, typography not excepted."—*Times.*

Guyon (Mde.) Life. By UPHAM. 6th Edition, crown 8vo, 6*s.*

HALFORD *(F. M.) Floating Flies, and how to Dress them.* Coloured plates. 8vo, 15*s.*; large paper, 30*s.*

Hall (W. W.) How to Live Long; or, 1408 *Health Maxims,* Physical, Mental, and Moral. 2nd Edition, small post 8vo, 2*s.*

Hamilton (E.) Recollections of Fly-fishing for Salmon, Trout, and Grayling. With their Habits, Haunts, and History. Illustrated, small post 8vo, 6*s.*; large paper (100 numbered copies), 10*s.* 6*d.*

Hands (T.) Numerical Exercises in Chemistry. Cr. 8vo, 2*s.* 6*d.* and 2*s.*; Answers separately, 6*d.*

Hardy (Thomas). See LOW'S STANDARD NOVELS.

Hargreaves (Capt.) Voyage round Great Britain. Illustrated. Crown 8vo, 5s.

Harland (Marian) Home Kitchen: a Collection of Practical and Inexpensive Receipts. Crown 8vo, 5s.

Harper's Monthly Magazine. Published Monthly. 160 pages, fully Illustrated. 1s.
    Vol. I. December, 1880, to May, 1881.
    ,, II. June to November, 1881.
    ,, III. December, 1881, to May, 1882.
    ,, IV. June to November, 1882.
    ,, V. December, 1882, to May, 1883.
    ,, VI. June to November, 1883.
    ,, VII. December, 1883, to May, 1884.
    ,, VIII. June to November, 1884.
    ,, IX. December, 1884, to May, 1885.
    ,, X. June to November, 1885.
Super-royal 8vo, 8s. 6d. each.

"'Harper's Magazine' is so thickly sown with excellent illustrations that to count them would be a work of time; not that it is a picture magazine, for the engravings illustrate the text after the manner seen in some of our choicest *éditions de luxe*."—*St. James's Gazette.*

"It is so pretty, so big, and so cheap.... An extraordinary shillingsworth—160 large octavo pages, with over a score of articles, and more than three times as many illustrations."—*Edinburgh Daily Review.*

"An amazing shillingsworth ... combining choice literature of both nations."—*Nonconformist.*

Harper's Young People. Vol. I., profusely Illustrated with woodcuts and 12 coloured plates. Royal 4to, extra binding, 7s. 6d.; gilt edges, 8s. Published Weekly, in wrapper, 1d. 12mo. Annual Subscription, post free, 6s. 6d.; Monthly, in wrapper, with coloured plate, 6d.; Annual Subscription, post free, 7s. 6d.

Harrison (Mary) Skilful Cook: a Practical Manual of Modern Experience. Crown 8vo, 5s.

Hatton (F.) North Borneo. With Biographical Sketch by Jos. HATTON. Illustrated from Original Drawings, Map, &c. 8vo, 18s.

Hatton (Joseph) Journalistic London: with Engravings and Portraits of Distinguished Writers of the Day. Fcap. 4to, 12s. 6d.

——— *Three Recruits, and the Girls they left behind them.* Small post 8vo, 6s.
    "It hurries us along in unflagging excitement."—*Times.*

Heath (Francis George) Autumnal Leaves. New Edition, with Coloured Plates in Facsimile from Nature. Crown 8vo, 14s.

——— *Fern Paradise.* New Edition, with Plates and Photos., crown 8vo, 12s. 6d.

Heath (Francis George) Fern World. With Nature-printed Coloured Plates. Crown 8vo, gilt edges, 12s. 6d. Cheap Edition, 6s.

—————— *Gilpin's Forest Scenery.* Illustrated, 8vo, 12s. 6d.; New Edition, 7s. 6d.

—————— *Our Woodland Trees.* With Coloured Plates and Engravings. Small 8vo, 12s. 6d.

—————— *Peasant Life in the West of England.* New Edition, crown 8vo, 10s. 6d.

—————— *Sylvan Spring.* With Coloured, &c., Illustrations. 12s. 6d.

—————— *Trees and Ferns.* Illustrated, crown 8vo, 3s. 6d.

Heldmann (Bernard) Mutiny on Board the Ship "Leander." Small post 8vo, gilt edges, numerous Illustrations, 5s.

Henty (G. A.) Winning his Spurs. Illustrations. Cr. 8vo, 5s.

—————— *Cornet of Horse: A Story for Boys.* Illust., cr. 8vo, 5s.

—————— *Jack Archer: Tale of the Crimea.* Illust., crown 8vo, 5s.

Herrick (Robert) Poetry. Preface by AUSTIN DOBSON. With numerous Illustrations by E. A. ABBEY. 4to, gilt edges, 42s.

Hill (Staveley, Q.C., M.P.) From Home to Home: Two Long Vacations at the Foot of the Rocky Mountains. With Wood Engravings and Photogravures. 8vo, 21s.

Hitchman, Public Life of the Right Hon. Benjamin Disraeli, Earl of Beaconsfield. 3rd Edition, with Portrait. Crown 8vo, 3s. 6d.

Holmes (O. Wendell) Poetical Works. 2 vols., 18mo, exquisitely printed, and chastely bound in limp cloth, gilt tops, 10s. 6d.

Homer. Iliad, done into English Verse. By A. S. WAY. 5s.

Hudson (W. H.) The Purple Land that England Lost. Travels and Adventures in the Banda-Oriental, South America. 2 vols, crown 8vo, 21s.

Hundred Greatest Men (The). 8 portfolios, 21s. each, or 4 vols., half-morocco, gilt edges, 10 guineas. New Ed., 1 vol., royal 8vo, 21s.

Hygiene and Public Health. Edited by A. H. BUCK, M.D. Illustrated. 2 vols., royal 8vo, 42s.

Hymnal Companion of Common Prayer. See BICKERSTETH.

ILLUSTRATED Text-Books of Art-Education. Edited by EDWARD J. POYNTER; R.A. Each Volume contains numerous Illustrations, and is strongly bound for Students, price 5s. Now ready:—

PAINTING.

Classic and Italian. By PERCY R. HEAD.
German, Flemish, and Dutch.
French and Spanish.
English and American.

ARCHITECTURE.

Classic and Early Christian.
Gothic and Renaissance. By T. ROGER SMITH.

SCULPTURE.

Antique: Egyptian and Greek.

Index to the English Catalogue, Jan., 1874, *to Dec.*, 1880. Royal 8vo, half-morocco, 18s.

Indian Garden Series. See ROBINSON (PHIL.).

Irving (Henry) Impressions of America. By J. HATTON. 2 vols., 21s.; New Edition, 1 vol., 6s.

Irving (Washington). Complete Library Edition of his Works in 27 Vols., Copyright, Unabridged, and with the Author's Latest Revisions, called the "Geoffrey Crayon" Edition, handsomely printed in large square 8vo, on superfine laid paper. Each volume, of about 500 pages, fully Illustrated. 12s. 6d. per vol. *See also* "Little Britain."

——————— ("American Men of Letters.") 2s. 6d.

JAMES (C.) Curiosities of Law and Lawyers. 8vo, 7s. 6d

Japan. See AUDSLEY.

Jerdon (Gertrude) Key-hole Country. Illustrated. Crown 8vo, cloth, 5s.

Johnston (H. H.) River Congo, from its Mouth to Bolobo. New Edition, 8vo, 21s.

Jones (Major) The Emigrants' Friend. A Complete Guide to the United States. New Edition. 2s. 6d.

Joyful-Lays. Sunday School Song Book. By LOWRY and DOANE. Boards, 2s.

Julien (F.) English Student's French Examiner. 16mo, 2s.

—————— *First Lessons in Conversational French Grammar.* Crown 8vo, 1s.

Julien (F.) French at Home and at School. Book I., Accidence, &c. Square crown 8vo, 2s.

——— *Conversational French Reader.* 16mo, cloth, 2s. 6d.

——— *Petites Leçons de Conversation et de Grammaire.* New Edition, 3s.

——— *Phrases of Daily Use.* Limp cloth, 6d.

KELSEY (*C. B.*) *Diseases of the Rectum and Anus.* Illustrated. 8vo, 18s.

Kempis (Thomas à) Daily Text-Book. Square 16mo, 2s. 6d.; interleaved as a Birthday Book, 3s. 6d.

Kershaw (S. W.) Protestants from France in their English Home. Crown 8vo, 6s.

Kielland. Skipper Worsé. By the Earl of Ducie. Cr. 8vo, 10s. 6d.

Kingston (W. H. G.) Dick Cheveley. Illustrated, 16mo, gilt edges, 7s. 6d.; plainer binding, plain edges, 5s.

——— *Heir of Kilfinnan.* Uniform, 7s. 6d.; also 5s.

——— *Snow-Shoes and Canoes.* Uniform, 7s. 6d.; also 5s.

——— *Two Supercargoes.* Uniform, 7s. 6d.; also 5s.

——— *With Axe and Rifle.* Uniform, 7s. 6d.; also 5s.

Knight (E. F.) Albania and Montenegro. Illust. 8vo, 12s. 6d.

Knight (E. J.) Cruise of the "Falcon." A Voyage round the World in a 30-Ton Yacht. Illust. New Ed. 2 vols., crown 8vo, 24s.

LANIER (*Sidney*) *Boy's Froissart.* Illustrated, crown 8vo, gilt edges, 7s. 6d.

——— *Boy's King Arthur.* Uniform, 7s. 6d.

——— *Boy's Mabinogion; Original Welsh Legends of King* Arthur. Uniform, 7s. 6d.

——— *Boy's Percy: Ballads of Love and Adventure,* selected from the "Reliques." Uniform, 7s. 6d.

Lansdell (H.) Through Siberia. 2 vols., 8vo, 30s.; 1 vol., 10s. 6d.

—— *Russia in Central Asia.* Illustrated. 2 vols, 42s.

Larden (W.) School Course on Heat. Second Edition, Illustrated, crown 8vo, 5s.

Lenormant (F.) Beginnings of History. Crown 8vo, 12s. 6d.

Leonardo da Vinci's Literary Works. Edited by Dr. JEAN PAUL RICHTER. Containing his Writings on Painting, Sculpture, and Architecture, his Philosophical Maxims, Humorous Writings, and Miscellaneous Notes on Personal Events, on his Contemporaries, on Literature, &c.; published from Manuscripts. 2 vols., imperial 8vo, containing about 200 Drawings in Autotype Reproductions, and numerous other Illustrations. Twelve Guineas.

Library of Religious Poetry. Best Poems of all Ages. Edited by SCHAFF and GILMAN. Royal 8vo, 21s.; re-issue in cheaper binding, 10s. 6d.

Lindsay (W. S.) History of Merchant Shipping. Over 150 Illustrations, Maps, and Charts. In 4 vols., demy 8vo, cloth extra. Vols. 1 and 2, 11s. each; vols. 3 and 4, 14s. each. 4 vols., 50s.

Little Britain, The Spectre Bridegroom, and *Legend of Sleeepy Hollow.* By WASHINGTON IRVING. An entirely New *Edition de luxe.* Illustrated by 120 very fine Engravings on Wood, by Mr. J. D. COOPER. Designed by Mr. CHARLES O. MURRAY. Re-issue, square crown 8vo, cloth, 6s.

Long (Mrs.) Peace and War in the Transvaal. 12mo, 3s. 6d.

Lowell (J. R.) Life of Nathaniel Hawthorn.

Low (Sampson, Jun.) Sanitary Suggestions. Illustrated, crown 8vo, 2s. 6d.

Low's Standard Library of Travel and Adventure. Crown 8vo, uniform in cloth extra, 7s. 6d., except where price is given.
1. The Great Lone Land. By Major W. F. BUTLER, C.B.
2. The Wild North Land. By Major W. F. BUTLER, C.B.
3. How I found Livingstone. By H. M. STANLEY.
4. Through the Dark Continent. By H. M. STANLEY. 12s. 6d.
5. The Threshold of the Unknown Region. By C. R. MARKHAM. (4th Edition, with Additional Chapters, 10s. 6d.)
6. Cruise of the Challenger. By W. J. J. SPRY, R.N.
7. Burnaby's On Horseback through Asia Minor. 10s. 6d.
8. Schweinfurth's Heart of Africa. 2 vols., 15s.
9. Marshall's Through America.
10. Lansdell's Through Siberia. Illustrated and unabridged 10s. 6d.

Low's Standard Novels. Small post 8vo, cloth extra, 6s. each, unless otherwise stated.

A Daughter of Heth. By W. BLACK.
In Silk Attire. By W. BLACK.
Kilmeny. A Novel. By W. BLACK.
Lady Silverdale's Sweetheart. By W. BLACK.
Sunrise. By W. BLACK.
Three Feathers. By WILLIAM BLACK.
Alice Lorraine. By R. D. BLACKMORE.
Christowell, a Dartmoor Tale. By R. D. BLACKMORE.
Clara Vaughan. By R. D. BLACKMORE.
Cradock Nowell. By R. D. BLACKMORE.
Cripps the Carrier. By R. D. BLACKMORE.
Erema; or, My Father's Sin. By R. D. BLACKMORE.
Lorna Doone. By R. D. BLACKMORE.
Mary Anerley. By R. D. BLACKMORE.
Tommy Upmore. By R. D. BLACKMORE.
An English Squire. By Miss COLERIDGE.
A Story of the Dragonnades; or, Asylum Christi. By the Rev. E. GILLIAT, M.A.
A Laodicean. By THOMAS HARDY.
Far from the Madding Crowd. By THOMAS HARDY.
Pair of Blue Eyes. By THOMAS HARDY.
Return of the Native. By THOMAS HARDY.
The Hand of Ethelberta. By THOMAS HARDY.
The Trumpet Major. By THOMAS HARDY.
Two on a Tower. By THOMAS HARDY.
Three Recruits. By JOSEPH HATTON.
A Golden Sorrow. By Mrs. CASHEL HOEY. New Edition.
Out of Court. By Mrs. CASHEL HOEY.
Adela Cathcart. By GEORGE MAC DONALD.
Guild Court. By GEORGE MAC DONALD.
Mary Marston. By GEORGE MAC DONALD.
Stephen Archer. New Ed. of "Gifts." By GEORGE MAC DONALD.
The Vicar's Daughter. By GEORGE MAC DONALD.
Weighed and Wanting. By GEORGE MAC DONALD.
Diane. By Mrs. MACQUOID.
Elinor Dryden. By Mrs. MACQUOID.
My Lady Greensleeves. By HELEN MATHERS.
Alaric Spenceley. By Mrs. J. H. RIDDELL.
Daisies and Buttercups. By Mrs. J. H. RIDDELL.
The Senior Partner. By Mrs. J. H. RIDDELL.
A Struggle for Fame. By Mrs. J. H. RIDDELL.
Jack's Courtship. By W. CLARK RUSSELL.
John Holdsworth. By W. CLARK RUSSELL.
A Sailor's Sweetheart. By W. CLARK RUSSELL.
Sea Queen. By W. CLARK RUSSELL.
Watch Below. By W. CLARK RUSSELL.
Wreck of the Grosvenor. By W. CLARK RUSSELL.

Low's Standard Novels—continued.
  The Lady Maud. By W. CLARK RUSSELL.
  Little Loo. By W. CLARK RUSSELL.
  My Wife and I. By Mrs. BEECHER STOWE.
  Poganuc People, their Loves and Lives. By Mrs. B. STOWE.
  Ben Hur: a Tale of the Christ. By LEW. WALLACE.
  Anne. By CONSTANCE FENIMORE WOOLSON.
  For the Major. By CONSTANCE FENIMORE WOOLSON. 5s.
  French Heiress in her own Chateau.

Low's Handbook to the Charities of London. Edited and revised to date by C. MACKESON, F.S.S., Editor of "A Guide to the Churches of London and its Suburbs," &c. Yearly, 1s. 6d.; Paper, 1s.

Lyne (Charles) New Guinea. Illustrated, crown 8vo, 10s. 6d.
  An Account of the Establishment of the British Protectorate over the Southern Shores of New Guinea.

McCORMICK (R.). Voyages of Discovery in the Arctic and Antarctic Seas in the "Erebus" and "Terror," in Search of Sir John Franklin, &c., with Autobiographical Notice by the Author, who was Medical Officer to each Expedition. With Maps and Lithographic, &c., Illustrations. 2 vols., royal 8vo, 52s. 6d.

MacDonald (G.) Orts. Small post 8vo, 6s.

——— See also "Low's Standard Novels."

Macgregor (John) "Rob Roy" on the Baltic. 3rd Edition, small post 8vo, 2s. 6d.; cloth, gilt edges, 3s. 6d.

——— *A Thousand Miles in the "Rob Roy" Canoe.* 11th Edition, small post 8vo, 2s. 6d.; cloth, gilt edges, 3s. 6d.

——— *Voyage Alone in the Yawl "Rob Roy."* New Edition, with additions, small post 8vo, 5s.; 3s. 6d. and 2s. 6d.

Macquoid (Mrs.). See LOW'S STANDARD NOVELS.

Magazine. See DECORATION, ENGLISH ETCHINGS, HARPER.

Maginn (W.) Miscellanies. Prose and Verse. With Memoir. 2 vols., crown 8vo, 24s.

Manitoba. See BRYCE.

Manning (E. F.) Delightful Thames. Illustrated. 4to, fancy boards, 5s.

Markham (C. R.) The Threshold of the Unknown Region. Crown 8vo, with Four Maps. 4th Edition. Cloth extra, 10s. 6d.

―――― *War between Peru and Chili,* 1879-1881. Third Ed. Crown 8vo, with Maps, 10s. 6d.

―――― See also "Foreign Countries."

Marshall (W. G.) Through America. New Ed., cr. 8vo, 7s. 6d.

Martin (J. W.) Float Fishing and Spinning in the Nottingham Style. New Edition. Crown 8vo, 2s. 6d.

Maury (Commander) Physical Geography of the Sea, and its Meteorology. New Edition, with Charts and Diagrams, cr. 8vo, 6s.

Men of Mark: a Gallery of Contemporary Portraits of the most Eminent Men of the Day, specially taken from Life. Complete in Seven Vols., 4to, handsomely bound, cloth, gilt edges, 25s. each.

Mendelssohn Family (The), 1729—1847. From Letters and Journals. Translated. New Edition, 2 vols., 8vo, 30s.

Mendelssohn. See also "Great Musicians."

Merrifield's Nautical Astronomy. Crown 8vo, 7s. 6d.

Millard (H. B.) Bright's Disease of the Kidneys. Illustrated. 8vo, 12s. 6d.

Mitchell (D. G.; Ik. Marvel) Works. Uniform Edition, small 8vo, 5s. each.

Bound together.	Reveries of a Bachelor.
Doctor Johns.	Seven Stories, Basement and Attic.
Dream Life.	Wet Days at Edgewood.
Out-of-Town Places.	

Mitford (Mary Russell) Our Village. With 12 full-pape and 157 smaller Cuts. Cr. 4to, cloth, gilt edges, 21s.; cheaper binding, 10s. 6d.

Mollett (J. W.) Illustrated Dictionary of Words used in Art and Archæology. Terms in Architecture, Arms, Bronzes, Christian Art, Colour, Costume, Decoration, Devices, Emblems, Heraldry, Lace, Personal Ornaments, Pottery, Painting, Sculpture, &c. Small 4to, 15s.

Morley (H.) English Literature in the Reign of Victoria. 2000th volume of the Tauchnitz Collection of Authors. 18mo, 2s. 6d.

Morwood (V. S.) Our Gipsies in City, Tent, and Van. 8vo, 18s.

Muller (E.) Noble Words and Noble Deeds. By PHILIPPOTEAUX. Square imperial 16mo, cloth extra, 7s. 6d.; plainer binding, 5s.

Music. See "Great Musicians."

NEW Zealand. See BRADSHAW.

New Zealand Rulers and Statesmen. See GISBORNE.

Newbiggin's Sketches and Tales. 18mo, 4s.

Nicholls (J. H. Kerry) The King Country: Explorations in New Zealand. Many Illustrations and Map. New Edition, 8vo, 21s.

Nicholson (C.) Work and Workers of the British Association. 12mo, 1s.

Nixon (J.) Complete Story of the Transvaal. 8vo, 12s. 6d.

Nordhoff (C.) California, for Health, Pleasure, and Residence. New Edition, 8vo, with Maps and Illustrations, 12s. 6d.

Northbrook Gallery. Edited by Lord Ronald Gower. 36 Permanent Photographs. Imperial 4to, 63s.; large paper, 105s.

Nursery Playmates (Prince of). 217 Coloured Pictures for Children by eminent Artists. Folio, in coloured boards, 6s.

O'BRIEN (R. B.) Fifty Years of Concessions to Ireland. With a Portrait of T. Drummond. Vol. I., 16s.; II., 16s.

Orvis (C. F.) Fishing with the Fly. Illustrated. 8vo, 12s. 6d.

Our Little Ones in Heaven. Edited by the Rev. H. ROBBINS. With Frontispiece after Sir JOSHUA REYNOLDS. New Edition, 5s.

Owen (Douglas) Marine Insurance Notes and Clauses. New Edition, 14s.

PALLISER (Mrs.) A History of Lace. New Edition, with additional cuts and text. 8vo, 21s.

—— *The China Collector's Pocket Companion.* With upwards of 1000 Illustrations of Marks and Monograms. Small 8vo, 5s.

Pascoe (C. E.) London of To-Day. Illust., crown 8vo, 3s. 6d.

Pharmacopœia of the United States of America. 8vo, 21s.

Philpot (H. J.) Diabetes Mellitus. Crown 8vo, 5s.

—— *Diet System.* Three Tables, in cases, 1s. each.

Pinto (Major Serpa) How I Crossed Africa. With 24 full-page and 118 half-page and smaller Illustrations, 13 small Maps, and 1 large one. 2 vols., 8vo, 42*s.*

Plunkett (Major G. F.) Primer of Orthographic Projection. Elementary Practical Solid Geometry clearly explained. With Problems and Exercises. Specially adapted for Science and Art Classes, and for Students who have not the aid of a Teacher.

Poe (E. A.) The Raven. Illustr. by DORÉ. Imperial folio, 63*s.*

Poems of the Inner Life. Chiefly from Modern Authors. Small 8vo, 5*s.*

Polar Expeditions. See GILDER, MARKHAM, MCCORMICK.

Porter (Noah) Elements of Moral Science. 10*s.* 6*d.*

Powell (W.) Wanderings in a Wild Country; or, Three Years among the Cannibals of New Britain. Illustr., 8vo, 18*s.*; cr. 8vo, 5*s.*

Power (Frank) Letters from Khartoum during the Siege. Fcap. 8vo, boards, 1*s.*

Poynter (Edward J., R.A.). See "Illustrated Text-books."

Publishers' Circular (The), and General Record of British and Foreign Literature. Published on the 1st and 15th of every Month, 3*d.*

REBER (F.) History of Ancient Art. 8vo, 18*s.*

Redford (G.) Ancient Sculpture. Crown 8vo, 5*s.*

Richter (Dr. Jean Paul) Italian Art in the National Gallery. 4to. Illustrated. Cloth gilt, 2*l.* 2*s.*; half-morocco, uncut, 2*l.* 12*s.* 6*d.*

—— See also LEONARDO DA VINCI.

Riddell (Mrs. J. H.) See LOW'S STANDARD NOVELS.

Robin Hood; Merry Adventures of. Written and illustrated by HOWARD PYLE. Imperial 8vo, 15*s.*

Robinson (Phil.) In my Indian Garden. Crown 8vo, limp cloth, 3*s.* 6*d.*

Robinson (Phil.) Indian Garden Series. 1s. 6d.; boards, 1s. each.
 I. Chasing a Fortune, &c.: Stories. II. Tigers at Large.

—— *Noah's Ark. A Contribution to the Study of Unnatural*
 History. Small post 8vo, 12s. 6d.

—— *Sinners and Saints: a Tour across the United States of*
 America, and Round them. Crown 8vo, 10s. 6d.

—— *Under the Punkah.* Crown 8vo, limp cloth, 5s.

Rockstro (W. S.) History of Music.

Rodrigues (J. C.) The Panama Canal. Crown 8vo, cloth
 extra, 5s.
> "A series of remarkable articles . . . a mine of valuable data for editors and diplomatists."—*New York Nation.*

Roland; the Story of. Crown 8vo, illustrated, 6s.

Rose (J.) Complete Practical Machinist. New Ed., 12mo, 12s. 6d.

—— *Mechanical Drawing.* Illustrated, small 4to, 16s.

Rose Library (The). Popular Literature of all Countries. Each
 volume, 1s.; cloth, 2s. 6d. Many of the Volumes are Illustrated—
 Little Women. By LOUISA M. ALCOTT.
 Little Women Wedded. Forming a Sequel to "Little Women."
 Little Women and Little Women Wedded. 1 vol., cloth gilt, 3s. 6d.
 Little Men. By L. M. ALCOTT. 2s.; cloth gilt, 3s. 6d.
 An Old-Fashioned Girl. By LOUISA M. ALCOTT. 2s.; cloth,
  3s. 6d.
 Work. A Story of Experience. By L. M. ALCOTT. 3s. 6d.; 2 vols.
  1s. each.
 Stowe (Mrs. H. B.) The Pearl of Orr's Island.
 —— The Minister's Wooing.
 —— We and our Neighbours. 2s.; cloth gilt, 6s.
 —— My Wife and I. 2s.; cloth gilt, 6s.
 Hans Brinker; or, the Silver Skates. By Mrs. DODGE.
 My Study Windows. By J. R. LOWELL.
 The Guardian Angel. By OLIVER WENDELL HOLMES.
 My Summer in a Garden. By C. D. WARNER.
 Dred. By Mrs. BEECHER STOWE. 2s.; cloth gilt, 3s. 6d.
 Farm Ballads. By WILL CARLETON.
 Farm Festivals. By WILL CARLETON.

Rose Library (The)—continued.

 Farm Legends. By WILL CARLETON.
 The Clients of Dr. Bernagius. 3*s.* 6*d.* ; 2 parts, 1*s.* each.
 The Undiscovered Country. By W. D. HOWELLS. 3*s.* 6*d.* and 1*s.*
 Baby Rue. By C. M. CLAY. 3*s.* 6*d.* and 1*s.*
 The Rose in Bloom. By L. M. ALCOTT. 2*s.*; cloth gilt, 3*s.* 6*d.*
 Eight Cousins. By L. M. ALCOTT. 2*s.*; cloth gilt, 3*s.* 6*d.*
 Under the Lilacs. By L. M. ALCOTT. 2*s.*; also 3*s.* 6*d.*
 Silver Pitchers. By LOUISA M. ALCOTT. 3*s.* 6*d.* and 1*s.*
 Jimmy's Cruise in the "Pinafore," and other Tales. By LOUISA M. ALCOTT. 2*s.*; cloth gilt, 3*s.* 6*d.*
 Jack and Jill. By LOUISA M. ALCOTT. 5*s.*; 2*s.*
 Hitherto. By the Author of the "Gayworthys." 2 vols., 1*s.* each; 1 vol., cloth gilt, 3*s.* 6*d.*
 Friends: a Duet. By E. STUART PHELPS. 3*s.* 6*d.*
 A Gentleman of Leisure. A Novel. By EDGAR FAWCETT. 3*s.* 6*d.*; 1*s.*
 The Story of Helen Troy. 3*s.* 6*d.*; also 1*s.*

Ross (Mars; and Stonehewer Cooper) Highlands of Cantabria; or, Three Days from England. Illustrations and Map, 8vo, 21*s.*

Round the Yule Log: Norwegian Folk and Fairy Tales. Translated from the Norwegian of P. CHR. ASBJÖRNSEN. With 100 Illustrations after drawings by Norwegian Artists, and an Introduction by E. W. Gosse. Impl. 16mo, cloth extra, gilt edges, 7*s.* 6*d.* and 5*s.*

Rousselet (Louis) Son of the Constable of France. Small post 8vo, numerous Illustrations, 5*s.*

—— *King of the Tigers: a Story of Central India.* Illustrated. Small post 8vo, gilt, 6*s.*; plainer, 5*s.*

—— *Drummer Boy.* Illustrated. Small post 8vo, 5*s.*

Rowbotham (F.) Trip to Prairie Land. The Shady Side of Emigration. 5*s.*

Russell (W. Clark) English Channel Ports and the Estate of the East and West India Dock Company. Crown 8vo, 1*s.*

—— *Jack's Courtship.* 3 vols., 31*s.* 6*d.*; 1 vol., 6*s.*

Russell (*W. Clark*) *The Lady Maud.* 3 vols., 31*s*. 6*d*.; 1 vol., 6*s*.

——— *Little Loo.* New Edition, small post 8vo, 6*s*.

——— *My Watch Below; or, Yarns Spun when off Duty.* Small post 8vo, 6*s*.

——— *Sailor's Language.* Illustrated. Crown 8vo, 3*s*. 6*d*.

——— *Sea Queen.* 3 vols., 31*s*. 6*d*.; 1 vol., 6*s*.

——— *Strange Voyage.* Nautical Novel. 3 vols., crown 8vo, 31*s*. 6*d*.

——— *Wreck of the Grosvenor.* 4to, sewed, 6*d*.

——— See also Low's STANDARD NOVELS.

SAINTS *and their Symbols: A Companion in the Churches* and Picture Galleries of Europe. Illustrated. Royal 16mo, 3*s*. 6*d*.

Salisbury (Lord) Life and Speeches. By F. S. Pulling, M.A. With Photogravure Portrait of Lord Salisbury. 2 vols., crown 8vo, 21*s*.

Saunders (A.) Our Domestic Birds: Poultry in England and New Zealand. Crown 8vo, 6*s*.

Scherr (Prof. J.) History of English Literature. Cr. 8vo, 8*s*. 6*d*.

Schley. Rescue of Greely. Maps and Illustrations, 8vo, 12*s*. 6*d*.

Schuyler (Eugène). The Life of Peter the Great. By EUGÈNE SCHUYLER, Author of "Turkestan." 2 vols., 8vo, 32*s*.

Schweinfurth (Georg) Heart of Africa. Three Years' Travels and Adventures in the Unexplored Regions of Central Africa, from 1868 to 1871. Illustrations and large Map. 2 vols., crown 8vo, 15*s*.

Scott (Leader) Renaissance of Art in Italy. 4to, 31*s*. 6*d*.

Sea, River, and Creek. By GARBOARD STREYKE. *The Eastern* Coast. 12mo, 1*s*.

Senior (W.) Waterside Sketches. Imp. 32mo, 1*s*.6*d*., boards, 1*s*.

Shadbolt and Mackinnon's South African Campaign, 1879. Containing a portrait and biography of every officer who lost his life. 4to, handsomely bound, 2*l*. 10*s*.

Shadbolt (S. H.) Afghan Campaigns of 1878—1880. By SYDNEY SHADBOLT. 2 vols., royal quarto, cloth extra, 3*l.*

Shakespeare. Edited by R. GRANT WHITE. 3 vols., crown 8vo, gilt top, 36*s.*; *Édition de luxe*, 6 vols., 8vo, cloth extra, 63*s.*

Shakespeare. See also WHITE (R. GRANT).

"*Shooting Niagara;" or, The Last Days of Caucusia.* By the Author of "The New Democracy." Small post 8vo, boards, 1*s.*

Sidney (Sir Philip) Arcadia. New Edition, 6*s.*

Siegfried: The Story of. Illustrated, crown 8vo, cloth, 6*s.*

Sinclair (Mrs.) Indigenous Flowers of the Hawaiian Islands. 44 Plates in Colour. Imp. folio, extra binding, gilt edges, 31*s.* 6*d.*

Sir Roger de Coverley. Re-imprinted from the "Spectator." With 125 Woodcuts and special steel Frontispiece. Small fcap. 4to, 6*s.*

Smith (G.) Assyrian Explorations and Discoveries. Illustrated by Photographs and Woodcuts. New Edition, demy 8vo, 18*s.*

—— *The Chaldean Account of Genesis.* With many Illustrations. 16*s.* New Edition, revised and re-written by PROFESSOR SAYCE, Queen's College, Oxford. 8vo, 18*s.*

Smith (J. Moyr) Ancient Greek Female Costume. 112 full-page Plates and other Illustrations. Crown 8vo, 7*s.* 6*d.*

—— *Hades of Ardenne: a Visit to the Caves of Han.* Crown 8vo, Illustrated, 5*s.*

—— *Legendary Studies, and other Sketches for Decorative* Figure Panels. 7*s.* 6*d.*

—— *Wooing of Æthra.* Illustrated. 32mo, 1*s.*

Smith (Sydney) Life and Times. By STUART J. REID. Illustrated. 8vo, 21*s.*

Smith (T. Roger) Architecture, Gothic and Renaissance. Illustrated, crown 8vo, 5*s.*

—————————— *Classic and Early Christian.* Illustrated. Crown 8vo, 5*s.*

Smith (W. R.) Laws concerning Public Health. 8vo, 31*s.* 6*d.*

Somerset (Lady H.) Our Village Life. Words and Illustrations. Thirty Coloured Plates, royal 4to, fancy covers, 5s.

Spanish and French Artists. By GERARD SMITH. (Poynter's Art Text-books.) 5s.

Spiers' French Dictionary. 29th Edition, remodelled. 2 vols., 8vo, 18s.; half bound, 21s.

Spry (W. J. J., R.N.) Cruise of H.M.S. "Challenger." With many Illustrations. 6th Edition, 8vo, cloth, 18s. Cheap Edition, crown 8vo, 7s. 6d.

Spyri (Joh.) Heidi's Early Experiences: a Story for Children and those who love Children. Illustrated, small post 8vo, 4s. 6d.

—— *Heidi's Further Experiences.* Illust., sm. post 8vo, 4s. 6d.

Stanley (H. M.) Congo, and Founding its Free State. Illustrated, 2 vols., 8vo, 42s.

—— *How I Found Livingstone.* 8vo, 10s. 6d.; cr. 8vo, 7s. 6d.

—— *Through the Dark Continent.* Crown 8vo, 12s. 6d.

Stenhouse (Mrs.) An Englishwoman in Utah. Crown 8vo, 2s. 6d.

Stevens (E. W.) Fly-Fishing in Maine Lakes. 8s. 6d.

Stockton (Frank R.) The Story of Viteau. With 16 page Illustrations. Crown 8vo, 5s.

Stoker (Bram) Under the Sunset. Crown 8vo, 6s.

Stowe (Mrs. Beecher) Dred. Cloth, gilt edges, 3s. 6d.; boards, 2s.

—— *Little Foxes.* Cheap Ed., 1s.; Library Edition, 4s. 6d.

—— *My Wife and I.* Small post 8vo, 6s.

—— *Old Town Folk.* 6s.; Cheap Edition, 3s.

—— *Old Town Fireside Stories.* Cloth extra, 3s. 6d.

—— *We and our Neighbours.* Small post 8vo, 6s.

—— *Poganuc People: their Loves and Lives.* Crown 8vo, 6s.

—— *Chimney Corner.* 1s.; cloth, 1s. 6d.

—— See also ROSE LIBRARY.

Sullivan (A. M.) Nutshell History of Ireland. Paper boards, 6*d.*

Sutton (A. K.) A B C Digest of the Bankruptcy Law. 8vo, 3*s.* and 2*s.* 6*d.*

TAINE (H. A.) "Les Origines de la France Contemporaine." Translated by JOHN DURAND.

    I. **The Ancient Regime.** Demy 8vo, cloth, 16*s.*
    II. **The French Revolution.** Vol. 1. do.
    III.   **Do.**   do.   Vol. 2. do.
    IV.   **Do.**   do.   Vol. 3. do.

Talbot (Hon. E.) A Letter on Emigration. 1*s.*

Tauchnitz's English Editions of German Authors. Each volume, cloth flexible, 2*s.*; or sewed, 1*s.* 6*d.* (Catalogues post free.)

Tauchnitz (B.) German and English Dictionary. 2*s.*; paper, 1*s.* 6*d.*; roan, 2*s.* 6*d.*

—— *French and English Dictionary.* 2*s.*; paper, 1*s.* 6*d.*; roan, 2*s.* 6*d.*

—— *Italian and English Dictionary.* 2*s.*; paper, 1*s.* 6*d.*; roan, 2*s.* 6*d.*

—— *Spanish and English.* 2*s.*; paper, 1*s.* 6*d.*; roan, 2*s.* 6*d.*

Taylor (W. M.) Paul the Missionary. Crown 8vo, 7*s.* 6*d.*

Thausing (Prof.) Malt and the Fabrication of Beer. 8vo, 45*s.*

Theakston (M.) British Angling Flies. Illustrated. Cr. 8vo, 5*s.*

Thomson (W.) Algebra for Colleges and Schools. With numerous Examples. 8vo, 5*s.*, Key, 1*s.* 6*d.*

Thomson (Jos.) Through Masai Land. Illustrations and Maps. 21*s.*

Thoreau. American Men of Letters. Crown 8vo, 2*s.* 6*d.*

Tolhausen (Alexandre) Grand Supplément du Dictionnaire Technologique. 3*s.* 6*d.*

Tristram (Rev. Canon) Pathways of Palestine: A Descriptive Tour through the Holy Land. First Series. Illustrated by 44 Permanent Photographs. 2 vols., folio, cloth extra, gilt edges, 31*s.* 6*d.* each.

Trollope (Anthony) Thompson Hall. 1s.

Tromholt (S.) Under the Rays of the Aurora Borealis. By C. SIEWERS. Photographs and Portraits. 2 vols., 8vo, 30s.

Tunis. See REID.

Turner (Edward) Studies in Russian Literature. Cr. 8vo, 8s. 6d.

UNION Jack (The). Every Boy's Paper. Edited by G. A. HENTY. Profusely Illustrated with Coloured and other Plates. Vol. I., 6s. Vols. II., III., IV., 7s. 6d. each.

VASILI (Count) Berlin Society. Translated. Cown 8vo, 6s.

——— *World of London (La Société de Londres).* Translated. Crown 8vo, 6s.

Velazquez and Murillo. By C. B. CURTIS. With Original Etchings. Royal 8vo, 31s. 6d.; large paper, 63s.

Victoria (Queen) Life of. By GRACE GREENWOOD. With numerous Illustrations. Small post 8vo, 6s.

Vincent (Mrs. Howard) Forty Thousand Miles over Land and Water. With Illustrations engraved under the direction of Mr. H. BLACKBURN. 2 vols, crown 8vo, 21s.

Viollet-le-Duc (E.) Lectures on Architecture. Translated by BENJAMIN BUCKNALL, Architect. With 33 Steel Plates and 200 Wood Engravings. Super-royal 8vo, leather back, gilt top, 2 vols., 3l. 3s.

Vivian (A. P.) Wanderings in the Western Land. 3rd Ed., 10s. 6d.

BOOKS BY JULES VERNE.

LARGE CROWN 8vo. WORKS.	Containing 350 to 600 pp. and from 50 to 100 full-page illustrations.		Containing the whole of the text with some illustrations.	
	In very handsome cloth binding, gilt edges.	In plainer binding, plain edges.	In cloth binding, gilt edges, smaller type.	Coloured boards.
	s. d.	s. d.	s. d.	
20,000 Leagues under the Sea. Parts I. and II.	10 6	5 0	3 6	2 vols., 1s. each.
Hector Servadac	10 6	5 0	3 6	2 vols., 1s. each.
The Fur Country	10 6	5 0	3 6	2 vols., 1s. each.
The Earth to the Moon and a Trip round it	10 6	5 0	2 vols., 2s. ea.	2 vols., 1s. each.
Michael Strogoff	10 6	5 0	3 6	2 vols., 1s. each.
Dick Sands, the Boy Captain	10 6	5 0	3 6	2 vols., 1s. each.
Five Weeks in a Balloon	7 6	3 6	2 0	1s. 0d.
Adventures of Three Englishmen and Three Russians	7 6	3 6	2 0	1 0
Round the World in Eighty Days	7 6	3 6	2 0	1 0
A Floating City	7 6	3 6	2 0	1 0
The Blockade Runners			2 0	1 0
Dr. Ox's Experiment	—	—	2 0	1 0
A Winter amid the Ice	—	—	2 0	1 0
Survivors of the "Chancellor"	7 6	3 6	2 0	2 vols., 1s. each.
Martin Paz			2 0	1s. 0d.
The Mysterious Island, 3 vols.:—	22 6	10 6	6 0	3 0
I. Dropped from the Clouds	7 6	3 6	2 0	1 0
II. Abandoned	7 6	3 6	2 0	1 0
III. Secret of the Island	7 6	3 6	2 0	1 0
The Child of the Cavern	7 6	3 6	2 0	1 0
The Begum's Fortune	7 6	3 6	2 0	1 0
The Tribulations of a Chinaman	7 6	3 6	2 0	1 0
The Steam House, 2 vols.:—				
I. Demon of Cawnpore	7 6	3 6	2 0	1 0
II. Tigers and Traitors	7 6	3 6	2 0	1 0
The Giant Raft, 2 vols.:—				
I. 800 Leagues on the Amazon	7 6	3 6	2 0	1 0
II. The Cryptogram	7 6	3 6	2 0	1 0
The Green Ray	6 0	5 0	—	1 0
Godfrey Morgan	7 6	3 6	2 0	1 0
Kéraban the Inflexible:—				
I. Captain of the "Guidara"	7 6			
II. Scarpante the Spy	7 6			
The Archipelago on Fire	7 6			
The Vanished Diamond	7 6			

CELEBRATED TRAVELS AND TRAVELLERS. 3 vols. 8vo, 600 pp., 100 full-page illustrations, 12s. 6d.; gilt edges, 14s. each:—(1) THE EXPLORATION OF THE WORLD. (2) THE GREAT NAVIGATORS OF THE EIGHTEENTH CENTURY. (3) THE GREAT EXPLORERS OF THE NINETEENTH CENTURY.

WAHL (W. H.) *Galvanoplastic Manipulation for the Electro-Plater.* 8vo, 35s.

Wallace (L.) *Ben Hur: A Tale of the Christ.* Crown 8vo, 6s.

Waller (Rev. C. H.) *The Names on the Gates of Pearl,* and other Studies. New Edition. Crown 8vo, cloth extra, 3s. 6d.

—— *A Grammar and Analytical Vocabulary of the Words in the Greek Testament.* Compiled from Brüder's Concordance. For the use of, Divinity Students and Greek Testament Classes. Part I. Grammar. Small post 8vo, cloth, 2s. 6d. Part II. Vocabulary, 2s. 6d.

—— *Adoption and the Covenant.* Some Thoughts on Confirmation. Super-royal 16mo, cloth limp, 2s. 6d.

—— *Silver Sockets; and other Shadows of Redemption.* Sermons at Christ Church, Hampstead. Small post 8vo, 6s.

Walton (Iz.) *Wallet Book,* CIƆIƆLXXXV. 21s.; l. p. 42s.

Walton (T. H.) *Coal Mining.* With Illustrations. 4to, 25s.

Warder (G. W.) *Utopian Dreams and Lotus Leaves.* Crown 8vo, 6s.

Warner (C. D.) *My Summer in a Garden.* Boards, 1s.; leatherette, 1s. 6d.; cloth, 2s.

Warren (W. F.) *Paradise Found; the North Pole the Cradle of the Human Race.* Illustrated. Crown 8vo, 12s. 6d.

Washington Irving's Little Britain. Square crown 8vo, 6s.

Watson (P. B.) *Marcus Aurelius Antoninus.* Portr. 8vo, 15s

Webster. (American Men of Letters.) 18mo, 2s. 6d.

Weir (Harrison) *Animal Stories, Old and New, told in Pictures and Prose.* Coloured, &c., Illustrations. 56 pp., 4to, 5s.

Wells (H. P.) *Fly Rods and Fly Tackle.* Illustrated. 10s. 6d.

Wheatley (H. B.) and Delamotte (P. H.) *Art Work in Porcelain.* Large 8vo, 2s. 6d.

—— *Art Work in Gold and Silver.* Modern. Large 8vo, 2s. 6d.

—— *Handbook of Decorative Art.* 10s. 6d.

Whisperings. Poems. Small post 8vo, cloth extra, gilt edges, 3s. 6d.

White (R. Grant) *England Without and Within.* Crown 8vo, 10s. 6d.

—— *Every-day English.* Crown 8vo, 10s. 6d.

—— *Studies in Shakespeare.* Crown 8vo, 10s. 6d.

White.(R. Grant) Fate of Mansfield Humphreys, the Episode of Mr. Washington Adams in England, an Apology, &c. Crown 8vo, 6s.

———— *Words and their uses.* New Edit., crown 8vo, 10s. 6d.

Whittier (J. G.) The King's Missive, and later Poems. 18mo, choice parchment cover, 3s. 6d.

———— *The Whittier Birthday Book.* Extracts from the Author's writings, with Portrait and Illustrations. Uniform with the "Emerson Birthday Book." Square 16mo, very choice binding, 3s. 6d.

———— *Life of.* By R. A. UNDERWOOD. Cr. 8vo, cloth, 10s. 6d.

Williams (C. F.) Tariff Laws of the United States. 8vo, 10s. 6d.

Williams (H. W.) Diseases of the Eye. 8vo, 21s.

Wills, A Few Hints on Proving, without Professional Assistance. By a PROBATE COURT OFFICIAL. 8th Edition, revised, with Forms of Wills, Residuary Accounts, &c. Fcap. 8vo, cloth limp, 1s.

Wimbledon (Viscount) Life and Times, 1628-38. By C. DALTON. 2 vols., 8vo, 30s.

Witthaus (R. A.) Medical Student's Chemistry. 8vo, 16s.

Woodbury, History of Wood Engraving. Illustrated. 8vo, 18s.

Woolsey (C. D., LL.D.) Introduction to the Study of International Law. 5th Edition, demy 8vo, 18s.

Woolson (Constance F.) See "Low's Standard Novels."

Wright (H.) Friendship of God. Portrait, &c. Crown 8vo, 6s.

Written to Order; the Journeyings of an Irresponsible Egotist. Crown 8vo, 6s.

YRIARTE (Charles) Florence: its History. Translated by C. B. PITMAN. Illustrated with 500 Engravings. Large imperial 4to, extra binding, gilt edges, 63s.; or 12 Parts, 5s. each.

History; the Medici; the Humanists; letters; arts; the Renaissance; illustrious Florentines; Etruscan art; monuments; sculpture; painting.

London:
SAMPSON LOW, MARSTON, SEARLE, & RIVINGTON,
CROWN BUILDINGS, 188, FLEET STREET, E.C.

www.ingramcontent.com/pod-product-compliance
Lightning Source LLC
Chambersburg PA
CBHW060551170426
43201CB00009B/744